The Multiple Presidencies Thesis

Matthew Caverly

The Multiple Presidencies Thesis

Presidential-Congressional Foreign Policy Relations Across Issues Areas and Political Time

VDM Verlag Dr. Müller

Impressum/Imprint (nur für Deutschland/ only for Germany)
Bibliografische Information der Deutschen Nationalbibliothek: Die Deutsche Nationalbibliothek
verzeichnet diese Publikation in der Deutschen Nationalbibliografie; detaillierte bibliografische
Daten sind im Internet über http://dnb.d-nb.de abrufbar.
Alle in diesem Buch genannten Marken und Produktnamen unterliegen warenzeichen-, marken-
oder patentrechtlichem Schutz bzw. sind Warenzeichen oder eingetragene Warenzeichen der
jeweiligen Inhaber. Die Wiedergabe von Marken, Produktnamen, Gebrauchsnamen,
Handelsnamen, Warenbezeichnungen u.s.w. in diesem Werk berechtigt auch ohne besondere
Kennzeichnung nicht zu der Annahme, dass solche Namen im Sinne der Warenzeichen- und
Markenschutzgesetzgebung als frei zu betrachten wären und daher von jedermann benutzt
werden dürften.

Coverbild: www.purestockx.com

Verlag: VDM Verlag Dr. Müller Aktiengesellschaft & Co. KG
Dudweiler Landstr. 99, 66123 Saarbrücken, Deutschland
Telefon +49 681 9100-698, Telefax +49 681 9100-988, Email: info@vdm-verlag.de
Zugl.: Gainesville, University of Florida, Diss., 2008

Herstellung in Deutschland:
Schaltungsdienst Lange o.H.G., Berlin
Books on Demand GmbH, Norderstedt
Reha GmbH, Saarbrücken
Amazon Distribution GmbH, Leipzig
ISBN: 978-3-639-09456-5

Imprint (only for USA, GB)
Bibliographic information published by the Deutsche Nationalbibliothek: The Deutsche
Nationalbibliothek lists this publication in the Deutsche Nationalbibliografie; detailed
bibliographic data are available in the Internet at http://dnb.d-nb.de.
Any brand names and product names mentioned in this book are subject to trademark, brand or
patent protection and are trademarks or registered trademarks of their respective holders. The use
of brand names, product names, common names, trade names, product descriptions etc. even
without a particular marking in this works is in no way to be construed to mean that such names
may be regarded as unrestricted in respect of trademark and brand protection legislation and
could thus be used by anyone.

Cover image: www.purestockx.com

Publisher:
VDM Verlag Dr. Müller Aktiengesellschaft & Co. KG
Dudweiler Landstr. 99, 66123 Saarbrücken, Germany
Phone +49 681 9100-698, Fax +49 681 9100-988, Email: info@vdm-publishing.com
Copyright © 2008 VDM Verlag Dr. Müller Aktiengesellschaft & Co. KG and licensors
All rights reserved. Saarbrücken 2008

Printed in the U.S.A.
Printed in the U.K. by (see last page)
ISBN: 978-3-639-09456-5

DEDICATION

To Sharon Ann Matthews Caverly and Estelle Vivian Delp Matthews, mother and grandmother who encouraged and loved along the way. And, to Amy Lynn Hager who was a friend to me when I needed one the most!

ACKNOWLEDGEMENTS

I would like to thank the good people at VDM publishing for giving me this opportunity. There thoughtful project of bringing entry level scholarship to a broader audience provides an excellent opportunity for those of us at the beginning of our careers. Additionally, I would like to thank the students, staff, faculty, and administration of the University of Florida, where I received the majority of my education. Finally, I would like to thank the administration, faculty, staff, and students of the University of North Florida for teaching me more than I could ever teach them.

TABLE OF CONTENTS

LIST OF TABLES

10

LIST OF FIGURES

CHAPTER 1
INTRODUCTION: THE MULTIPLE PRESIDENCIES THESIS AND ISSUE AREAS
ANALYSIS

"There is one president but in the office of a single president there are two presidencies,
one for defense and foreign policy and the other for domestic policy."

— Aaron Wildavsky, "The Two Presidencies Thesis," *Trans-Action* (4) (December 1966)

Introduction

With that line, Aaron Wildavsky drew a map of executive-legislative relations bordered on
its edges by the political society writ large and composed in the interior by two policy making
continents. One such continent was exclusive to foreign affairs where the president rules as an
absolutist monarch protecting the interests of all by ensuring the rule of the one. However, on the
other continent existing for the domestic sphere the Congress reigned supreme as a democratic-
polity standing virtuous in its representative ensemble ensuring the rule of the many or at least
the few.[1] Nothing short of a "cottage industry" of scholarship emanated out of Wildavsky's
thesis wherein attempts to measure explain and refute the phenomenon competed against one
another for over a forty plus year period.[2] However, in all that time very little real empirical
results have been found which either fully corroborate or effectively refute the basic thesis that
presidents dominate the construction of policy in foreign affairs but are impeded in those efforts
in the domestic sphere by a recalcitrant Congress which has carved out its own place of
institutional power (from Wildavsky 1966).

As an empirical theory, the findings of this study contrary to some of the extant literature
produced in recent years regarding the two presidencies is that it is a real depiction of the actual
executive-legislative policy making relationship. The vast majority of the studies on the two
presidencies in some fashion or form find evidence for differential policy success rates for
presidents in their relationship with the Congress. Presidents do significantly better in foreign
policy construction relative to the Congress than they do in such attempts within the domestic
sphere. However, the explanation for such success rates is not clear as to whether it is an
institutional, partisan or cultural phenomenon but some patterns are existent. The classical

---

[1] Taken from Aristotle's *The Politics* (Ernst Barker edition 1958).

[2] See Shull 1991 for the most comprehensive review of the two presidencies literature though a number of studies
have been added to the canon already in place in the decade and a half since Shull's edited volume was published.

version of the thesis (the institutional) is most associated with support for the two presidencies while the cultural version is most associated with rejecting it. The partisan two presidencies may be overstated as to its actual role in explaining the executive-legislative divide but this point is still very much in contention.

Furthermore, most of the research on the two presidencies has actually had discordant findings, with one study or another supporting the thesis and yet others refuting it. However, all of them have been consistent in that they have been leveled on the notion of presidential strength in foreign policy versus its lack thereof in domestic policy. This facet is the primary reason I believe for the lack of consistency within the empirical findings themselves. Thus, the fate of the two presidencies lies not on its findings or lack thereof but rather on its assumptions. What is needed is a new analytical and methodological approach to understanding and studying executive-legislative relations in foreign policy which captures the inherent nuances of the relationship yet also identifies a theoretically consistent pattern to those relations.

This project moves away from the canonical analytical and methodological treatments of the past which portrayed foreign policy as "this one thing." I have opened the door to a new way of conceptualizing the politics of foreign affairs which will allow for the development of a more encompassing theory of executive-legislative Post-War (since the end of the Korean War in 1953) foreign policy relations. Also, the empirical shortcomings of the two presidencies thesis' central claim that presidents dominate the construction of policy in the foreign relations sphere needs to be addressed. On the surface it seems almost endemic that presidents are so empowered in foreign policy making. However, the systematic tests of this thesis have not provided any conclusive findings as to the duration or even the existence of the two presidencies as an accurate and predictable theory of executive-legislative relations (Shull 1991).

The Multiple Presidencies Thesis

Theoretically, I claim that there are in fact multiple issue area presidencies within the office of a single foreign policy president. Wherein a security dominant and dependent president squares off against a domestically oriented and hence intermestic driven Congress. Intermestic policies are those which exist amidst *issue areas of foreign affairs* being composed of a *co-mixture* of *domestic and foreign policies*. At one end of the spectrum, exist those foreign issue areas with the *least* domestic component (hence, least intermestic)—the high politics arena issue areas of national security, domestic security and diplomacy. At the other end are those foreign

14

issue areas with the *most* domestic composition (hence, most intermestic)—the low politics arena issue areas of trade, foreign aid and immigration. Patterns of executive-legislative conflict and corroboration appear across up to six distinct as well as mixed policy issue areas within the realm of foreign affairs. These issue areas can be arranged along a dimension which groups them into first high politics arenas (security, domestic security and diplomacy)—essentially those issue areas of foreign policy which deal with the politics of war and peace.

Secondly, another set of issue areas can be categorized as being roughly consistent with the notions of low politics (trade, foreign aid and immigration)—essentially those issue areas which are most prone to have domestic aspects (the politics of everything else). Thus, *the multiple presidencies thesis claims that foreign policy is best seen as a series of up to six issue areas arranged in high and low politics arenas.* Furthermore, trade, foreign aid and immigration can be thought of as being fully *intermestic* in nature (a co-mixture of international with national politics) (Manning 1977). As Manning (1977) has shown, foreign policy is actually a polyglot of potential issue areas based around the degree of interpenetration between foreign and domestic politics. What Manning did not contend and what is vital to my theoretical reasoning is that such interpenetration exists along a continuum from being almost completely absent as in national security affairs to being interlinked as in trade. Finally, in the area of immigration the foreign-domestic divide is virtually completely absent. Each issue area or mixed issue area has its own set of presidential-congressional relations which display some interdependence with one another but are in fact distinct enough to be treated as separate cases of inter-institutional interaction. Therefore, *the multiple presidencies thesis tells us that there are multiple "sets" of presidential-congressional foreign issue area relations and key to understanding that relationship is the role or relative absence of intermestic (co-mixture of foreign and domestic policy attributes) aspects within each issue area.*

Presidential power in foreign policy diffused across these disparate yet related issue areas is a function of the ability of president's to "securitize" the issue at hand and at times even entire issue areas. Securitization is the notion that issues and issue areas of foreign policy are prone to being presented and argued within the light of a "war and peace" discourse of high over low politics. When this happens and is successful, the institution most suited to take advantage in the policy making process is the one most historically, philosophically and institutionally strengthened in the conduction of high politics. That institution is now and has always been the

15

executive branch. Likewise, congressional power across the same issue areas can be seen as a product of the ability of the Congress to "domesticize" the issue or even the whole issue area. These two arenas of power (securitization v. domestication) within executive-legislative foreign policy making are then the fundamental bases from which the empirical patterns derive. In sum, *the multiple presidencies thesis suggests that executive-legislative foreign policy relations are best summarized as "a securitizing president versus a domesticating Congress."* Therefore, *the multiple presidencies thesis further contends that there is an "opportunity structure of power" in security which allows the high politics arena of foreign issue areas to be largely set by presidentialized conditions for policy making.* Also, *the low politics arena is subject to congressionalization of policy construction conditions due to its component foreign issue areas as being more intermestic in orientation (higher degree of interpenetration between foreign and domestic aspects within the foreign issue areas themselves).*

Presidentialization of foreign issue areas' policies is akin to the notion of securitization meaning that the *president dominates the process of policy construction relative to the Congress.* The president can do this because the presidency itself as an institution is in a better position vis-à-vis the Congress regarding agenda control. In other words, we can say that the "conditions governing presidential-congressional policy making in the high politics arena take on a presidency-centered aspect." Hence, the presidency as an institution is largely setting the terms of debate by invoking its historical-institutional prerogatives as an "opportunity structure" of power in the high politics of war and peace (Figure 2-2). Congressionalization of foreign issue areas' policies is the same thing as domestication meaning that the *Congress dominates the process of policy construction relative to the presidency.* The Congress can do this because of its historical-institutional prerogatives in the sphere of domestic policy construction. Therefore, as issues within foreign affairs take on a more domestic cast, in other words as they become more intermestic and hence less securitized then it is the Congress that increasingly sets the parameters of policy making debate. Additionally, there are two forces which exert influence on the presidential-congressional foreign policy/issue area relationship which operate at two distinct levels of analysis (Figure 2-2).

At the unit level of the two competing/cooperating institutions themselves (the presidency and the Congress), presidential securitizing plays out most effectively in its institutional locus of power within and proximate to the security issue area itself. In other words, the high politics issue areas are arrayed in order of proximity to the opportunity structure of securitized power as national security policy, domestic security policy and diplomatic policy. Similarly, congressional domestication is most pronounced among those issue areas that are the more naturally intermestic in orientation within foreign policy. In other words, the low politics issue areas of foreign policy can be arrayed along a spectrum of *least* to *most* domestic in the foreign-domestic admixture including trade policy, foreign aid policy and immigration policy.

The unit level of analysis is an important operating principle for this study because it locates the conduct of inquiry directly at the "major politics producing forces" involved (Mannheim and Rich 1995). Units are collections of aggregates. The most common employed in international relations research has been the state (Waltz 1956). In this study, I have broken the black box of the state wide open, by locating my research at two of its most prominent parts at least as regards foreign policy production, the presidency and the Congress. By viewing the presidency and the Congress as institutional aggregates, I hold constant the impacts of much of the individual agency which other previous research privileges. Besides offering a new theoretical twist to a long examined research tradition, I provide a fully developed institutional account that transcends the limitations of single personality based studies of individual administration's foreign policy relationship with the Congress. Other research on this topic often does treat the Congress as a unit (read collection of aggregates) but treats the presidency as an institution of one rather than what it is: an institution which privileges the rule of the one but is composed of the many (i.e. the White House Staff, The Executive Office of the President and the Cabinet).

In fact, among the high politics issue arena of foreign policy there is some bureaucratic dispersal that plays out along its component issue area lines. Some such differentiation includes but is certainly not limited to the Department of Defense and the National Security Council for national security, the Department of Homeland Security for domestic security and the State Department for diplomacy. Also, amidst the low politics issue arena we find the US Office of Trade Representative, Departments of Treasury and Commerce as well as Labor for trade policy. Foreign aid policy has been subject to administration and policy from entities such as USAID, the Department of Energy as well as all other departments previously discussed and of course the myriad of organizations under the Directorate of Central Intelligence. Lastly, immigration administration and policy development has been looked over by the US Border Patrol, Drug

17

Enforcement Administration as well as others. In sum, a *unit* level of analysis treats the presidency and Congress as what they in fact are, institutions which have and continue to influence foreign policy development *across time* regardless of their individual actor compositions by treating them as compositions of aggregates.

Operating at the structural level of analysis (also called the systemic), macro-oriented political, economic and historical forces exert an exogenous influence over presidential-congressional relations. The structural or in other words systemic level of analysis focuses attention on the environmental effects conditioning the behavior of the sub-ordinate actors (in this case the executive and legislative branches) themselves (Mannheim and Rich 1995 and Waltz 1956). The employment of this level of analysis is important for two reasons, one because it provides the "widest empirical scope possible" while retaining a high degree of parsimony. Second, this level provides researchers of US foreign policy the ability to place the American case in its international contexts. Additionally, the structural level serves as a facilitating device for cross-time inquiry by capturing the political ebb and flow of time itself as an exogenous variable. Specific to this study the above impacts move the multiple sets of foreign policy issue area relationships between the national executive and legislature. They do this across time itself pushing and pulling those relationships into periods of stasis punctuated with dynamic reconstitutions in the nature of the inter-relationships themselves. The above theory may be termed the *multiple presidencies thesis* and I believe that it serves as a strong analytical alternative to the two presidencies thesis. However, it is only the first objective of this research project. For in order to understand the nuances and complexities of executive-legislative foreign issue area relations we must examine them by employing as wide an analytical lens as possible and that is what I now turn to. I do this by offering a methodological-theoretical approach which by its design captures the inherent nuances of foreign policy's component issue areas.

Issue Areas Analysis

Issue area analysis is critical to understanding the multiple presidencies framework because it opens up the executive-legislative foreign policy divide with its emphasis on the *component issue areas themselves*. We must first turn our attention to the conceptualization of foreign policy issue areas, as prior attempts to theorize about executive power in the constitutional order have either exaggerated or otherwise over limited such conditions relative to foreign policy construction.

18

In previous research into the fundamental question of power's location in foreign policy construction, two competing streams of research have been proffered. One such endeavor has been articulated by Realists who call for a "statist" approach which suggests that the best way to view foreign policy making is an outcome of a unified, centralized and elite dominated "core foreign policy executive" or the even more self-selected "national security state" (from Krasner 1978, Kennan 1979 and Rothkopf 2005). Another such method called the "domestic variables approach" suggests that foreign policy is in fact the result of a confluence of actors that engage in a pluralist interaction when constructing policy in foreign affairs (from Rogowski 1987, Wittkopf and McCormick 1999 as well as Gourevitch 1996). Therefore, statist approaches tend to down play internal factors by treating foreign policy as the outcome of the *few*. Likewise, the domestic variables approach tends to get a bit unwieldy by including an ever expanding number of external factors in the production of foreign policy as the result of the *many*. Thus, *the employment of issue areas analysis in this sense calls for the co-integration of state-centered and domestic variable approaches by viewing foreign policy as the product of presidency-centered versus Congress-centered conditions.* More specifically, presidency-centered conditions for US foreign affairs policy making follow the *assumptions of a state-centered approach*. Meanwhile, those foreign policy making conditions which are said to privilege the Congress follow the *assumptions of the domestic variables method of analysis*. Combining the issue areas approach with the multiple presidencies thesis leads to the conclusion that *the high politics issue arena issue areas (national security, domestic security and diplomacy) are given more to being defined in terms of presidency-centered conditions* regarding executive-legislative foreign policy making. Likewise, *low politics arena issue areas (trade, foreign aid and immigration) are more prone to be seen as following the prescriptions of Congress-centered conditions* regarding presidential-congressional foreign policy relations.

The statist/state-centrist method of foreign policy analysis certainly privileges the president as the leader of the national security state. And, for that matter the president serves as the very embodiment of the core foreign policy executive, which is fruitful for a presidency-focused analysis. Unfortunately, as a tool to guide the conduct of inquiry for executive-legislative relations state-centrism fails to account for congressional behavior and influence, if any, on the processes of foreign policy development. Statist scholars' preoccupation with parsimony (as it is most persuasively witnessed in formal modeling scenarios of the foreign policy process like

Alison's (1971) "rational actor model") in practice limits its own utility as a methodological endeavor because it limits the conduct of inquiry by making strict assumptions on the scope of analysis. These studies do this through biasing the selection of the unit of analysis in a presidency-focused direction at the expense of other actors in the foreign policy process like the Congress.

What hurts the statist approach helps the domestic variables method by opening up the door of model inclusion to external as well as increasing numbers of internal variables. This development allows for a process of model specification that is more prone to reducing variance and increasing robustness regarding inferential capacities and explanatory forces. However, this process also leads to over-specification where the land of parsimony has been sacrificed to a bewildering sea of context and interpretation. The simple truth is that domestic forces have a more variable impact on the foreign policy process; therefore they are both more tenuous and tertiary in their overall and even specific influences relative to the occupants of the executive branch and its head in particular. For the purposes of this study, what is most helpful about the domestic variables system for foreign affairs study is its allowance for ongoing congressional agency within the foreign policy structure itself. What is needed is a methodological approach that keeps the best of parsimony from the state-centered perspective and compliments it with the best of context as offered by the domestic variables framework.

As a methodological-theoretical frame, the issue areas analysis of foreign policy serves as something of a synthesis between the two extremes of state-centrism and domestic variables. It does this by assuming the potential for co-existent differential sets of relationships within foreign policy. In application to this present study that means the simultaneous existence of a series of relationships between the president and the Congress within the issue areas of foreign policy which captures the context dimension. Furthermore, that means that those relationships are governed by both static and dynamic forces (including history itself) but are given to a certain pattern predicated on the notions of institutional power—for the president the high politics security arena and for the Congress the low politics domestication arena. The final area of inquiry which needs to be attended to in a more in-depth manner is the role which political time itself plays in this analysis of executive-legislative foreign issue area relations.

Political Time

The idea of "political time" emanates out of the study of American political development which privileges the role of politics as a fundamental force in the development of historical phenomenon of interest (Orren and Skowronek 2004). Taking this notion one step further we find that the two analytical operating principles—the unit and structural level of analyses are the principle structuring entities "conditioning" and being "conditioned" by foreign issue area policy behavior *across time*. Hence, time itself is subject to and in this case is a fully *politicized* construct that can be examined as such. It is one of the purposes of this project to do just that by operationalizing an ongoing test of presidential success in institutional foreign issue area policy relationships. Another purpose is to theorize about the *exact inter-institutional foreign affairs relationship shared between the president and the Congress across history itself during the Post-War Era (1953-2004)*. Political time serves as a vehicle for both of those projects by setting the *scope of inquiry* for the analysis and privileging the *specifically political roles* of the presidency and the Congress in the *conduct of inquiry*.

Furthermore, the multiple presidencies of the issue areas of foreign policy can be identified and then tracked in order to develop *periods* of dominant and sub-ordinate presidential-congressional relations during the Post War Era. Of course, such privileging and identification is easier said than done and a more precise statement of methods is needed in order to "flesh out" the finer details of this examination of Post-War executive-legislative foreign policy developments across its component issue areas.

Methods

As previously stated the overarching methodological-theoretical approach which guides all methods prescriptions in this project is the employment of an issue areas analysis. However, the specific methods themselves are posited in order to test the strength of presidential success vis-à-vis the Congress across the Post War Era (1953-2004). They do this by measuring the success rate of presidencies (Eisenhower-W. Bush) on the *population* of foreign policy roll call votes taken between 1953 and 2004 sub-categorized by myself according to their component issue area. The actual presidential success rate itself in foreign policy and in the various issue areas and even mixed issue areas is *annualized* as a measure for both convenience and ease of comparison with similar roll call based studies. Therefore, the ongoing *primary and secondary*

21

dependent variables of interest (what is to be explained) are the *aggregate annual presidential success rates on foreign, issue area and mixed issue area roll call votes in the Congress during the Post War Era (1953-2004).* These variables provide a solid *proxy measure* of the executive-legislative foreign and issue area relationship at specific points in time. But, these variables' real contribution is their ability to approximate a *direct measure* of such a relationship *systematically* as well as *across (political) time.*

The independent variables were selected according to their ability to serve as measures of macro-level historical, economic and political impacts on extant presidential-congressional foreign, issue and even mixed issue area annual presidential roll call success rates. The historical and economic forces are measured at the structural (systemic) level of analysis as these conditions are best seen as being impact-full from this perspective. The reason for this is that they are condition setting forces which are either products of history itself like the relative size of the armed forces, the presence of war/peace and size of the defense budget, etc... Likewise, additional condition setting forces can be discerned from prevailing and ever changing economic conditions. These conditions include such things as a measure of overall national economic performance Real GDP growth (or decline) or the degree of unit level (for the presidency or Congress) opportunity/constraint conditions provided by the size of the budget surplus (or deficit).

The models utilized to capture the across political time executive-legislative foreign, issue and mixed issue area relationship take on a longitudinal format as *first order autoregressive time series*. These models track the primary and secondary dependent variables as a series of auto-regressions moving backward in time from point *Yo* at *To*. What this means is that the annual presidential success rates in foreign, issue and mixed issue areas in 2004 serve as the *base end points* and are tracked along a trend line of auto-regressions back to the *base origination point* of 1953. The results of these longitudinal models as well as their implications for executive-legislative foreign issue area interactions are gone over in chapter 4. In sum, I will examine the above conditions through the lenses provided by the basic notions of the *multiple presidencies thesis* and employing an *issue areas analysis.*

Models that were specified in order to capture the *within political time* presidential-congressional foreign issue area relationship took the form of *cross-sectional* un-standardized ordinary least squares regression (OLS). In these, all variables (both dependent and independent) were operationalized according to *distinct time frames* that were bounded by a periodization scheme. This scheme divided US executive-legislative foreign policy relations into *four distinct systemic (environmental) orders of inter-institutional interactions* including: the War Power Order (1953-1972), the Confrontational Politics Order (1973-1989), the Imperial Presidency Politicized Order (1990-2000) and the Extra-Systemic Dilemma Order (2001-2004). These orders represent prevailing conditions under which the presidency and the Congress (the unit level actors) debated, conflicted and either collaborated or deadlocked over the specific issues of foreign policy. The results and implications of these cross-sectional models for extant presidential-congressional foreign issue area relations are discussed in chapters 5-8. Lastly, I take all of the above and examine it in a fashion consistent with a hypothesis testing process that emanates out of the *multiple presidencies thesis*. This procedure is done by using an *issue areas analysis* based around fundamental notions of *presidency versus Congress-centered conditions* as to the direction of the inter-institutional relationships involved.

Contextual Development

Keeping with the historical nature of this enterprise, I engage in a series of context-setting qualitative narratives relevant to both the across and within political time analyses. While, these should *not* be viewed as systematized historical study they do serve as empirical "jumping off points" for future fully developed qualitative study. First, I set the broad contours of *event-based* executive-legislative history in foreign affairs in chapter 4. Then, in chapters 5-8 I overview some of the *legislative histories* drawn from my archival research in the *Congressional Quarterly Almanacs* that speak to the level of collaboration or confrontation between the president and the Congress in international affairs policy making. In both of the above efforts, I carry forth with my "issue area analysis" by attending to relevant issue areas' role within and across political time throughout. Finally, I tie everything together by stating the findings and implications in terms of the *multiple presidencies thesis itself*.

Having laid out the basic purpose, argument, method and context for articulating and ultimately defending the multiple presidencies thesis, I will now turn to more prosaic matters by engaging the reader with a discussion of the plan for this research project.

Project Plan

The remainder of this introduction is given over to laying out the general plan of action for this research project. Chapter 2 details the premises and provides the basics for an answer to the guiding research question, *"What is the inter-institutional policy making relationship between the president and Congress in foreign affairs?"* The theorized answer is the multiple presidencies thesis *wherein a securitizing president faces a domesticating Congress across the six issue areas of foreign policy*. Furthermore, this relationship is subject to both periods of stasis as well as dynamism over the ebb and flow of political time.

Chapter 3 details the methodologies employed to test relevant hypotheses emanating out of the multiple presidencies thesis by employing an issue areas analysis. Synthesizing the parsimony of the statist method of interpretation with the contextually rich domestic variables approach will allow for a truer picture of American foreign policy to be taken and framed. Hypothesis generation and testing will use presidency-centered versus Congress-centered conditions as its operating principle. This technique is done to showcase the "places of institutional power" via foreign policy issue areas regarding presidential dominance, collaboration or even acquiescence relative to the Congress. Furthermore, once these "loci of power" are identified they can be "tracked across political time" for observations of stasis or dynamism in the foreign issue area executive-legislative relationship.

Chapter 4 presents the longitudinal findings, mapping out executive-legislative relations across the last half century. Chapter 5 takes a look at the early Cold War (1953-1972) wherein *securitization* by the president was predominant in foreign affairs. During this time period, issue areas of foreign policy were presented by the executive branch to the legislative branch from a high politics perspective. The presidency set the legislative agenda in foreign policy by arguing that *all foreign policy was essentially security in orientation*. Furthermore, the presidency largely controlled the outcomes of legislative deliberations by routinely emphasizing the national security aspect of foreign policy in an intensified Cold War political environment. The success of this strategy, whether intentional or implied, was that the Congress routinely acquiesced to presidential prerogatives in foreign affairs. Hence, we can conclude that foreign policy itself was completely given over to a process of regularized securitization. This period of American foreign policy history saw a de-politicization in executive-legislative international relations. This process was engendered by the presence of a bi-partisan conservative Congress relative to Cold War policy making in the so called Cold War Consensus regarding a "hawkish" stance toward the Soviet Union and its satellites. This stance existed regardless of whether the Congress was controlled by Democrats (as it normally was during this time) or Republicans. Likewise, the maintenance of presidential securitized prerogatives in the realm of foreign policy promoted an atmosphere where foreign affairs issues and issue areas were presented in a discourse of high over low politics with a corresponding expectation of congressional acquiescence to the presidency. Specifically, the combination of the Conservative Coalition on defense issues and the Liberal Coalition on foreign aid and immigration issues allowed presidents of both parties to govern in a relatively harmonious manner during the height of the individualized committee dominated Textbook Congress (Davidson and Oleszek 2005).[3] I call this period of political time the War Power Order (1953-1972) because of the privileged role of securitization and hence presidential dominance over the Congress in foreign policy relations.

Chapter 6 will deal with another cross-sectional set of findings that indicate the rise of a resurgent partisan and liberal Congress anxious to establish and in some cases re-establish its institutional prerogatives in international policy making. In the aftermath of the Vietnam War and the start of détente, a confrontational Congress began to domesticate the issue areas of foreign policy and continued to do so until the end of the Cold War (1973-1989). During this time there was an emerging view of an imperial presidency that had abused power in Vietnam. The Congress, partially in response to these events, engaged in a series of institutional changes in order to displace the Southern Democratic conservative committee barony with a sub-committee government system of liberal Northern Democrats known as the Post-Reform Congress. This Congress would prove to be a thorn in subsequent presidencies' sides as it became a place of alternative institutional power that would effectively permeate *all issue areas of foreign policy* by the end of the Confrontation Politics Order. Additionally, as high politics declined in importance due to the Nixon Doctrine, SALT I & II, the development of the "Vietnam Syndrome" in defense affairs, and most importantly détente with the Soviet Union and Communist China *soft power* began to overtake *hard power* as a guiding dogma in foreign policy construction within *the Congress and even certain presidencies like Jimmy Carter's* (Nye 2000).

---

[3] I am synthesizing notions derived from James MacGreogor Burns' (1963) ideas about regional coalitional voting and presidential support known as "four-party politics" with Roger Davidson's (1996 in Thurber 1996) notions about "the presidency in congressional time."

Additionally, there was an emergence of a more defined role for low politics due to increasing economic interdependence (made real to the average American by the oil shocks and their corresponding recessions) allowed for the steady "domestication" of foreign policy across its component issue areas (Keohane and Nye 1977). Deference by the Congress previously given to presidents in traditionally non-security issue areas such as trade, foreign aid and immigration was no longer as quickly given as congressmen and women as well as senators found that much of foreign policy had in fact become intermestic in nature (Manning 1977). Indeed, the employment of politics by the Congress during this time often utilized the low politics issue areas as starting points for encroaching upon the high politics realm of presidential foreign policy making. I refer to this category of political time as the Confrontation Politics Order (1973-1989) because of its central characteristic of congressional domesticating opposition to an exclusively presidentialized (and hence securitized) foreign policy.

In chapter 7, the aftereffects of the end of the Cold War take pre-eminence and new structural opportunities as well as constraints contribute to the evolution of the presidential-congressional relationship in foreign affairs. These changes include but are certainly not limited to the outgrowth of economic interdependence into the disparate socio-cultural forces of integration and fragmentation that comprise what is collectively referred to as globalization (see Dierks 2001). The Post Cold War promise of its "peace dividend," coinciding with the emergence of "new security dilemmas" led to executive-legislative conflict/cooperation over such issues as base force restructuring and arms procurements emanating out of the "revolution in military affairs." Additionally, the two institutions battled over domesticated struggles like the "war on drugs" or the renewed saliency of international terrorism. In sum, presidential-congressional foreign policy relations had developed into a new status quo with a rough parity held between the two branches across all issue areas but continued loci of power in their traditional arenas as especially seen in the first Bush's Persian Gulf War in 1991. I term this period of political time The Imperial Presidency Politicized Order (1990-2000) because of the intermittent expansion and subsequent debilitation of presidential power in foreign affairs due to ideological party government in the Congress.[4]

---

[4] See Schlesinger (1989) for a discussion of the theoretical concept her refers to as "the imperial presidency."

Following the completion of the substantive chapters, I conclude in chapter 8 with some summary commentary and a discussion of the potential opportunities as well as constraints of the Post-9/11 world in which we now live regarding executive-legislative relations in foreign policy. The promises of an extra systemic international environment driven by extra-state actors like multinational corporations (MNC's) and non-governmental organizations (NGO's) under both legal and illegal conditions leads one to the conclusion that extant presidential-congressional foreign policy relations will increasingly reflect a Post-Systemic character. *Presidential-congressional relations in foreign policy will be more completely merged with domestic politics as "all policy becomes intermestic" during the 21st century.* This means that the historic institutional centers of power that have governed the unit level interactions may no longer be as prescient since the line between security and domesticated politics is fading. Perhaps of even greater significance, is the potential merging of high and low politics at the structural level as new security supplants old security and soft power overtakes hard power. Foreign policy orders of political time in the future may no longer be subject to a patterned understanding as nuanced context may indeed overtake parsimony in theory and methods. The heart of the problem for future executive-legislative foreign issue area relations is found in the term I have coined for our current state of political time—the Extra-Systemic Dilemma Order (2001-2004).

Prior to delving into the substance of this project, I would like to bring the reader's attention to the theoretical and methodological background of this effort. I will do this by reviewing the extant body of relevant literature that collectively informs *both* the multiple presidencies thesis and its component issue areas analysis. This review is *off-set* into an un-numbered chapter all its own in order to emphasize its contributions to the larger work but also to allow for its simultaneous separation so that readers already familiar with this body of literature can skip over the discussions and move directly into the argument itself (see chapter 2).

Literature Review

Whither the Two Presidencies?

This critical literature review of the two presidencies thesis is done in order to answer a very basic question, "Whither the two presidencies?" This question emanates naturally out of Wildavsky's (1966) formulation that no less than two presidencies existed within the office of a single president. One presidency was defined by broad executive prerogatives in the realm of foreign policy construction while another was defined by a recalcitrant Congress which forced the president to "share" if not acquiesce in domestic policy construction (Wildavsky 1966). The extant body of literature produced over the last four decades has led some scholars to support (62.5%) and others to reject (38.5%)[5] the tenets of the two presidencies thesis (see Shull 1991 for an excellent review). With this in mind, I will conduct a literature review of the major published scholarly works done on the two presidencies thesis (N=24). I critically review the literature in a systematic fashion searching for points of commonality and dissimilarity between the works. I then "map out" the two presidencies thesis theoretically, empirically, methodologically and normatively in order to expose both its contributions as well as its deficiencies. Finally, I call for the theory's displacement at least as regards its position as a device for understanding extant Post-War executive-legislative relations in international affairs policy making.

I find ample evidence, in concert with previous studies, to support the two presidencies thesis. But this study offers a far more subtle approach to understanding the phenomenon. I also find that the two presidencies exist in one of three main versions including: a classic institutional one (Wildavsky 1966), an alternative partisan version (Edwards 1986) and a cultural version used principally to "reject" the two presidencies as an empirical theory (or at least an institutional one) (Peppers 1975). Further, I find that relationships exist between the type of methodology employed and the version of the theory supported. For instance, the strongest supported version of the two presidencies is the institutional one as an aggregate level phenomenon. The review also reveals that the partisan version of the two presidencies is perhaps overstated as there is no direct link between support and opposition to the thesis itself. Finally, the perceived role played by the individual level of analysis within the partisan two presidencies (see Conley 1997) while supportable has limits in its generalizability.[6] Therefore, the basic methodological design employed by the individual researcher when examining the two presidencies may in fact be privileging certain outcomes as to whether or not the thesis is

---

[5] Data drawn from a previous study by the author entitled, "The Two Presidencies an unfinished Project: A Theoretical, Methodological, Empirical and Normative Meta-Analysis" paper presented at the Southwest Social Science Association's Annual Conference at San Antonio, Texas April 2006.

[6] See Caverly (2006) "The Two Presidencies an Unfinished Project: A Theoretical, Methodological, Empirical and Normative Meta-Analysis," paper presented at the Southwestern Social Science Association 2006 Annual Meeting at San Antonio, TX April 11-15, 2006.

supported. Also, such design formulations may be dictating what form the two presidencies thesis ultimately takes as an institutional, partisan or cultural phenomenon.

Additionally, there is an utter lack of normative inquiry into the thesis itself as well as any reflexive discussion that researchers' biases (ideological, paradigmatic, philosophical, etc…) may have on the conclusions regarding the two presidencies. However, I do find that there does not seem to be a *periodized*, in other words, a time-bounding character to the two presidencies literature in that time is not related to support or refutation of the thesis itself. There is no "Golden Age" of the two presidencies when it was a near-universally accepted theory of executive-legislative policy construction, in fact it has always been challenged. Likewise, there is no evidence to suggest that in a later period of time, the two presidencies thesis was regularly rejected as having little or no utility as a theoretical device. This theory has always had a certain level of acceptance among presidential-congressional relations scholars.

Lastly, I believe that this review calls for a re-theorization of executive-legislative policy making relations. Perhaps, there has been an over reliance upon "dualism" in the attempt to produce the most "parsimonious theory possible" probably due to the over whelming empirical quality of the two presidencies thesis itself. A more nuanced examination of the domains themselves will inevitably lead to a multiplication of executive-legislative relations across multiple issue areas. Also, the theory needs to be moved beyond the empirical and into the realm of normative political science in order to revitalize it for a world of "internationalized domestic politics"—i.e. globalization's co-mixture of foreign and domestic politics within *intermestic policies* (see Manning 1977, Keohane and Nye 1977) and *domesticated foreign policies*—i.e. the War on Terror (Dodd in Conley 2003).

Critical Literature Review of the Two Presidencies Thesis:

The two presidencies thesis is premised by the assertion that policy is best examined from a domain-specific orientation (from Spitzer 1983). Furthermore, that domain structure to policy making is best seen in a bifurcated manner with the intent of the policies being differentiated along their teleological "goals" as fundamentally endogenous (domestic) or exogenous (foreign) in nature (from Snow and Brown 1999). Additionally, the more proactive policy initiators are viewed as the most appropriate "units of analysis," those being the president and the Congress at the national level of inquiry (from Shull and Shaw 1999). Finally, the choice of our national executive and legislative branches of government is in keeping with a long held view that "institutions do matter" as foci of inquiry for social scientific and specifically politically based research (from Weaver and Rockman 1993). With these thoughts in mind let us turn to the two presidencies thesis itself.

Simply stated, the two presidencies thesis suggests that at least two "presidencies" exist within the confines of the office occupied by a single "president" (Wildavsky 1966). Aaron Wildavsky (1966) was the progenitor of this idea claiming that executive-legislative policy making relations was in fact "governed" by a bi-presidencies notion; wherein an unrestrained foreign policy president co-existed with a congressionally restrained domestic policy president. This idea was suggested to be an institutional phenomenon that held across time regardless of the composition of the Congress, the occupant of the White House, the condition of the economy, or even the presence of war or peace (1966). Wildavsky explained this condition by positing that the president is constitutionally and institutionally set up to be the dominant actor in foreign policy construction because of his greater control over informational and general policy construction/implementation resources in this policy arena (1966). Regarding the second presidency, the president is constrained by a more proactive Congress in the realm of domestic initiative production (1966). In domestic affairs, the Congress is seen by Wildavsky to have the same level of informational as well as general policy production/implementation resources as the president (1966).

Analytically, this theory exists in a broader context of presidential-congressional policy making theories that emphasize the role of the president at the expense of the Congress as the primary focus of inquiry and device for explanation/prediction (e.g., Rossiter 1956, Neustadt 1960, Robinson 1967, Huntington 1961 and Edwards 1980). Methodologically, this theory employed roll call analysis placing it into a larger school of thought which suggests that quantitative "vote studies" can reveal empirical support for theoretical contentions regarding political behavior (e.g., Niemi and Weisberg 2001 for general American voting behavior, Key 1949 and 1955 for early regional application, Black and Black (2002) for later regional application, Stewart 2001 for application in the Congress, Cameron (2000) for application to the presidency, and Conley (2002) for application to American executive-legislative relations). Finally, the two presidencies can be seen to be in a larger paradigmatic context as an "institutional" theory; whereby it is the institution(s) that has the most theoretical power in discerning the nature of political conditions as well as relationships (e.g., Weaver and Rockman

1993 for a general application of institutionalism in comparative contexts, Pierson and Skocpol 2002 for an application of new institutionalism in American politics, Skowronek 1997 for an application of the phenomenon in the American presidency, and Wilson 1885 for an early application of the "old institutionalism" to the American Congress).

Regarding Wildavsky's (1966) study, he tested his theory by analyzing congressional roll call votes from the New Deal Era forward (to 1965) that were listed in the congressional roll call record as "congressional box scores." These scores were derived from those roll call votes on presidential initiatives in both Houses of Congress during the period under analysis, 1933-1965 (1966). The results indicated support for a two presidencies phenomenon regardless of the exogenous or endogenous conditions existent during the time frame of the research (1966). As an example of this, Wildavsky reported that in an examination of congressional responses to presidential legislative initiatives from 1948 to 1964 the president prevailed about 70% of the time in foreign and defense policies and only about 40% of the time in domestic policies (1966). Admittedly, the explanatory and predictive power of these findings is a bit questionable due to the limited time frame but it does cross presidencies and congresses under both divided and unified government, in war and peace, and through economic recession and recovery (from Shull and Leloup 1979, ch. 16 in Shull and Leloup 1979). Nevertheless, it is a point from which to begin.[7]

There are three general points of criticism that are leveled at the two presidencies theory, which can also be utilized as heuristics for the purpose of organizing the methodological, empirical and most importantly the theoretical development of the two presidencies literature through time. Of course, this portion of the analysis reveals the most apparent though understated "gap" in the two presidencies literature itself, that being the pronounced lack of a normative account of the two presidencies both as a research agenda and its implications for real world application.

The Methodological Critique: The "Construction" of the Two Presidencies

The first such criticism aimed at Wildavsky's thesis is found in the argument made that the theory was methodologically flawed in its initial testing phase, thus leading to conclusions

---

[7] I will engage in a stronger critique and discussion of the two presidencies literature in the future, for the purposes of this paper I will keep my commentary to a minimum.

that were possibly misinterpreted if not completely open to accusation as being nothing more than a tautology. For instance, Sigelman's (1979) study of the two presidencies contends that the usage of congressional box scores as the dependent variable for indicating presidential success/failure rates on congressional roll calls was an insufficient operationalization of presidential "success/failure" vis-à-vis the Congress. Sigelman (1979) made this claim based on the fact that the congressional box scores only included presidential legislative initiatives and not those congressional initiatives that the president took a position on. Unfortunately, after making this statement, Sigelman did not actually re-operationalize the dependent variable in his own analysis (Sigelman 1979). Instead, he re-worked the congressional box scores to reflect presidential success on "key votes." These votes were roll calls wherein support or rejection of the proposed presidential legislative initiative was garnered at or below an 80% threshold (Sigelman 1979). These votes are called by the recorders of them (the Congressional Record) "contentious" as opposed to "consensual" votes with the so named consensual votes being characterized as those roll calls that have an 80% or above threshold of support or rejection (*Congressional Almanacs*, published annually). Sigelman was the first scholar to conclude based on his own independent study of the two presidencies that the phenomenon was non-existent and to him was the result of nothing more than "measurement error" on Wildavsky's part (Sigelman 1979). Sigelman's usage of key votes as the independent variables and usage of the same dependent variable congressional box scores during the time frame of 1957 and 1978 provides some cross-over with its cotemporaneous study (Leloup and Shull 1979) as well as Wildavsky's (1966) analysis but the difference in operationalizations on the independent variables prevents a one-to-one comparison of the findings.

Another point of methodological criticism given in Wildavsky's direction is found in the initial study's lack of replicability, especially for the purposes of updating because of the abandonment of recording presidential legislative initiatives by the editorial staff of *Congressional Quarterly* in 1975 (Leloup and Shull 1979 and "forward" to *Congressional Almanac 1975*). This prevented scholars from recreating the "congressional box scores" for time frames beyond the mid-1970s. For their own part, Leloup and Shull (1979) updated Wildavsky's data set through 1974 and found support for a two presidencies phenomenon though they found that the gap between success rates for the president in the relevant policy domains had narrowed significantly over the previous decade.

Beginning in 1975, *Congressional Quarterly* began recording a new measure of presidential-congressional policy making relations with "presidential box scores" (now more routinely referred to as "presidential position support scores") which record the aggregate percentage totals of presidential success/failure relative to aggregate congressional vote support/opposition to legislative initiatives that the president takes a stated "position" on regardless of the origin of the initiative ("forward" to the *Congressional Almanac 1975*). Since that time, scholars using roll call analysis to test for the two presidencies have relied on this measure for their operationalizations on both dependent (the aggregate scores themselves) and independent variables (the disaggregated votes themselves) (Shull 1991 "Introduction" to Shull 1991). Most contend that the new variables are adequate proxies to the previous measures, however, this is an assumption therefore we should be wary of attempts to "compare" one study with another because they are "different" at their methodological origination.

Terry Sullivan (1991) introduced an alternative to Sigelman's key votes by conducting congressional "headcounts" in order to get a sense of the "ebb and flow" of congressional responses to presidential "positioning." Sullivan (1991) refuted the institutional basis for the two presidencies finding that it was the result of partisanship.[8] [9] This finding was consistent with George C. Edwards (1986a, 1986b and 1989) works where he suggested that presidential position scores had to be disaggregated in order to get at the true nature of the relationship between the president and the Congress which was an "individually not an aggregate based one." The result of Edwards' research was that the two presidencies was at its heart a partisan not an institutional phenomenon but what was perhaps most telling was that Edwards was the first to employ an individual level of analysis to the two presidencies (Edwards 1989). Unfortunately, Edwards' research has been criticized for not being able to discern whether the president "wins" more on foreign policy votes relative to domestic policy votes because of the effect of the disaggregating process (Bond and Fleisher 1990).

Despite this, there has been at least one attempt to develop a proxy measure that has utility for longitudinal analyses. Jeffrey Cohen (1982) utilized presidential proposal enactments by the Congress as a measure for assessing domain specific policy making relations between the

---

6 There is a whole school of thought regarding a partisan rather than an institutional basis for the two presidenicies or lack thereof.

president and the Congress from the Lincoln to the early Nixon administrations. To this day, this is the longest time frame ever analyzed by two presidencies researchers and interestingly, in contrast to some later accusations about the two presidencies being a "time and culture" bound phenomenon, Cohen found a two presidencies playing out across over 100 years of American political history (Cohen 1982). The question arises, is individual presidential proposal enactment success or individual presidential position success equate-able to aggregate presidential initiative or aggregate presidential position success? They all very well could be, however, a single measure at a given level of analysis is needed in order to provide results that can actually be compared both cross-sectionally and longitudinally. This is especially true given the differential findings regarding the inclusion versus the exclusion of contentious versus consensus voting and whether or not presidential initiation of policy is actually important regarding presidential-congressional policy making relations as well as whether or not you can safely compare varying "levels and even units of analysis."

Other recent scholarly attempts to test the two presidencies phenomenon have moved beyond the confines of roll call analysis because it has been felt by these scholars that mere "presidential success/failure" rates on one measure—legislation is inadequate for use as a sole set of independent variables and/or the dependent variable regarding the executive-legislative policy making relationship (Lindsay and Steger 1993, Lewis 1997, Page and Jordan 1992). Methodologically, these social scientists emphasize alternatives to roll call analysis like content analysis of presidential addresses (Lewis 1997). Also, these social researchers call for the employment of new independent variables indicative of presidential policy making discretion like executive orders and executive agreements. They also advocate the re-operationalization of the dependent variable in terms of agenda setting (Lindsay and Steger 1993). Finally, non-institutionally oriented studies employing behavioral tools like public opinion surveys have been used recently to get a broader sense of the executive-legislative policy relationship (Page and Jordan 1992).

Lindsay and Steger's (1993) study is not an independent analysis but functions more as a "call to research." Basically, theses scholars suggest alternative measures to roll call analysis for American executive-legislative policy making relations. These measures include looking at procedural reforms as explanatory devices in order to get at a perceived "ebb and flow" to the executive-legislative policy making divide (1993). Another proposal is measuring the degree of

34

oversight engaged in by the Congress relative to administration "activities" with a hypothesis that differential "levels" of oversight" will be found in separate policy domains of administration activity (1993). Along similar lines, Lindsay and Steger (1993) call for the study of "legislative escape clauses" premised by the idea that legislation in different policy domains will allow different "levels of executive discretion in policy action." The problem with these scholars' suggestions is just that, they are only suggestions and no one in the discipline has undertaken their "call to analytical and methodological arms."

Lewis (1997) does seem to follow at least the "letter of Lindsay and Steger's intent" by conducting a content analysis of presidential public discretionary addresses between 1947 and 1991. He concludes that there exists a "rhetorical two presidencies" regarding foreign and economic policies. Wherein, presidents' addresses in economic policy areas tend to take on an advertising modus operandi; the president engages in a "going public" strategy using calls for "public support," "congressional legislative actions" and "citizen mobilization for grassroots lobbying of the Congress" (1997).[10] Meanwhile, in the realm of foreign affairs the president engages the public in a completely different manner; where the president assumes a singular leadership role and conveys that image to the country by shaping his public addresses in such a way as to imply this power (Lewis 1997). While Lewis' work is empirically sound it perhaps overstates the role presidential public discretionary addresses have in the actual policy construction process, especially as an executive-legislative relations phenomenon. Also, Lewis tests foreign versus economic policy making which does not portray the actual tenets of the two presidencies thesis because economic policies are not analogous to domestic policies. In fact, economic policies may be either domestic or foreign in origin, therefore, they are actually portions of both the general categories established in the two presidencies literature. However, Lewis' greatest contribution may be that he expands the two presidencies as a test of more than just domestic and foreign affairs influence, by introducing a new category—economic affairs— to the presidential-congressional policy influence divide.

Page and Jordan (1992), utilizing public opinion research with surveys and content analyses of administration policy advertisements, find that the two presidencies thesis is not supported since the policy impact on the electorate is essentially the same regardless of the

---

7 See Kernell's (1997) *Going Public: New strategies of Presidential Leadership*

domain involved. In other words, the shaping of public opinion relative to international relations is not substantially different from that used by presidents in constructing domestic initiative support (1992). While this research is important for political behavioralists, however, it does not address the institutional relationship between the executive and the legislative branches of government.

The Empirical Critique: The "Real" vs. the "Imagined" Two Presidencies

The second general area of criticism leveled at Wildavsky's perspective involves the correctness or existence of the theory in the "real world." What this entails is the question as to whether the two presidencies ever actually existed, and if it did, does it still govern American national executive-legislative policy making relations? In other words, many of Wildavsky's critics and he himself later in life came to believe that the two presidencies was a "time and culture bound phenomenon," a product of a now non-existent Cold War consensus (Peppers 1975; Oldfield and Wildavsky 1989). According to this view, the Cold War placed a certain "structure" over the relations between the executive and legislative branches (Peppers 1975; Oldfield and Wildavsky 1989). This structure governed relations between the two institutions in such a manner that the executive was continually deferred to in matters of foreign policy due to the "imminent threat" posed by the Cold War (Peppers 1975; Oldfield and Wildvasky 1989). However, when the structure changed (as the Cold War was cooled by détente and eventually ended with the tearing down of the Berlin Wall followed by the subsequent "implosion" of the USSR) the relations between the two branches of government also changed (from Peppers 1975; Oldfield and Wildavsky 1989).

Table 1-1 tells a "story" that the president and the Congress live in two different policy making "worlds." However, to those researchers that label the two presidencies nothing more than a character of historical space and time these "structures" are merely fluid variables altering through "political time" in response to both internal and external circumstances. In the first major criticism of the two presidencies thesis, Peppers (1975) suggested that the policy context which encapsulated executive-legislative relations had fundamentally been altered by a series of systemic changes. These changes included; the lessening of congressional acquiescence to presidential military adventurism because of the debacle in Southeast Asia, lack of faith in executive secrecy due to the excesses of the Nixon White House regarding Watergate, the relative economic decline of the American macro and micro economies due to the advance of world industrialism in the years since the end of the Second World War, and the rise of "intermestic affairs" with both strong domestic and foreign policy aspects to them in an era of détente and economic interdependence (1975). These developments led Peppers (1975) to conclude that the "free hand" once given to the president in the conduct of foreign affairs was merely a product of a Cold War consensus on presidential deference in that realm that would no longer be observed.

Similar to Peppers' (1975) assertions Oldfield and Wildavsky (1989) in a follow-up analysis to the original thesis likewise concluded that the "systemic structure" which had allowed for a two presidencies was no longer valid. In fact, these scholars found that with the end of the Cold War there was no basis whatsoever for a dual presidencies phenomenon governing American executive-legislative policy making relations (Oldfield and Wildavsky 1989). Oldfield and Wildavsky concluded and even popularized the phrase that the two presidencies was nothing more than a "time and culture bound phenomenon" (Oldfield and Wildavsky 1989). Tables 1-2 and 1-3 highlight this "systemic change" by comparing Wildavsky's (1966) original "institutional policy context" with those dissimilar settings as portrayed by Peppers (1975) as well as Oldfield and Wildavsky (1989). The second table (Table 1-3) has also been updated by the author with some additional information from relatively recent events in the late 1980s and early 1990s.

While the "space and time" argument for the two presidencies or more appropriately the lack of it is in itself compelling, such a thesis raises more questions than it does answers. For example, studies have shown the presence of differential policy success rates for the president vis-à-vis the Congress regardless of a Cold War timeline. As we have already seen Cohen (1982) found a two presidencies phenomenon dating back to the Lincoln administration, some twenty years before the US began its rise as a great economic power and at least thirty-five to fifty years before American rise as a world political power (from Kennan 1979, Kissinger 1994, and Zakaria 1999). Also, as we will see in the upcoming critique of the "partisan two presidencies" some of these studies extend beyond the confines of the Cold War and at times do find differential levels of success or invalidate the two presidencies regardless of time or location (those that favor or somewhat favor i.e., Fleisher, Bond, Krutz, and Hanna 2000; those that mostly do not support i.e., Malbin and Brookshire 2000). On a positive finishing note, the contextually oriented studies are a bit revolutionary in that they suggest the strong utility for qualitative analysis regarding executive-legislative policy making relations. More than anything else these studies, few as they are, indicate that there is a need to look "below the numbers" to get at the true nature of this inter-institutional relationship.

Theoretical Critique: The Institutional vs. the Partisan Two Presidencies

The final area of criticism garnered from a literature review of the two presidencies is found in the notion that the real policy making relationship exhibited between the president and the Congress is characterized not as an "institutional" one but is in fact a "partisan" based process. George Edwards (1986a, 1986b and 1989) was the first such scholar to find evidence for a "partisan two presidencies." Edwards (1989) found that the two presidencies was the result of differential levels of policy support given to presidents by *opposition party members* in the Congress. Hence, the two presidencies is a *by-product* of opposition support for presidential positions in foreign policy which less frequently appears in domestic policy affairs. Furthermore, with the increase in periods of divided government this scholar found that there was a precipitous decline in the power of the two presidencies (Edwards 1989). This is fascinating because it suggests that institutional conceptions of the two presidencies have actually attributed the causal mechanism for differential policy making outcomes to the wrong source—institutional power; when in fact, it has been and continues to be nothing more than "Republicans versus Democrats." The fact that these partisans are in different institutions becomes virtually a moot point (from Edwards 1989).

Bond and Fleisher (1988 and 1990) also find a partisan basis for the two presidencies by updating Sigelman's (1979) data into the 1980s covering the Reagan and some of the Bush administrations. These scholars find a more nuanced version of the "partisan two presidencies" than that one found by Edwards (1989), in that, it seems to only hold for Republican presidents. In fact, the causal force for this relationship is found by these two researchers to be in the discovery of a "Conservative Coalition" of Southern Democrats and Republicans relative to issues of foreign policy (Bond and Fleisher 1988 and 1990). Additionally, such a coalition is lacking in domestic policy and there is no such coalition among moderate Republicans and Democratic presidents regardless of policy domain (Bond and Fleisher 1988 and 1990). Interestingly, this research may actually suggest for an "ideological two presidencies" except that it does not seem to find a moderate/liberal Republican to liberal Democratic coalition on foreign

38

policy between the presidency and the Congress even though there may be one within the Congress itself regarding domestic policy.[11]

Sullivan (1991) further "fine tuned" the notions of a partisan two presidencies. Like Bond and Fleisher (1988 and 1990), it was only applicable for Republican presidents. However, unlike his predecessors, Sullivan (1991) discovered that the two presidencies may indeed be more nuanced. He found the Republican president needed to have partisan control in at least one of the two houses of Congress in order to acquire a higher level of foreign policy success. While this is an interesting finding, we seem to be getting very parochial in our understanding of this phenomenon but that may be the decisive method needed to understand executive-legislative policy making relations.[12]

Unlike previous and some current studies, only two analyses are in the extant literature regarding the two presidencies that deal with the phenomenon in administration specific circumstances (e.g., Renka and Jones 1991; Conley 1997). Both of these present the two presidencies from partisan rather than strictly institutional perspectives and find evidence for the presence/refutation of a two presidencies. Renka and Jones (1991) find support in their analysis of the Reagan administration in a year-by-year study of presidential success rates on congressional roll call votes regarding "controversial issues." Of course, this leads to the same problem as Sigelman's (1979) "key votes" wherein certain non-controversial issues which may say a lot about congressional deference or the lack thereof are not kept in the study.

Unlike Renka and Jones (1991) and similar to Sigelman (1979), Conley (1997) generally rejects the two presidencies in his study of the first two years of the Clinton presidency under unified government. Specifically, Conley (1997) tests the partisan two presidencies associated with Republican presidents. As already stated, Conley (1997) finds only weak evidence for differential levels of policy making and largely explains the phenomenon as the result of highly ideological and partisan support/opposition to President Clinton during the 103rd Congress. This study is groundbreaking in that Conley (1997) along with Lewis (1997) are the first and so far only researchers to increase the division of policy areas into more than just two domains. While Conley (1997) tri-furcated policy along domestic, foreign/defense and "intermestic" lines Lewis

---

[11] This is pure conjecture because as Poole and Rosenthal (1997) show conservative Democrats still tend to be to the ideological left of liberal Republicans overall.

[12] More on this in the theory section.

(1997) used the categories of domestic, foreign/defense and economic policies. Even though Conley largely refutes the two presidencies and Lewis basically supports it, they both find some difference in levels of congressional support (for Conley's (1997) study) or how policies are presented to the public (for Lewis' (1997) study). This is consistent with Oldfield and Wildavsky's (1989) review of the new political environment faced by the president in his relations with the Congress. It is also consistent with King and Ragsdale's (1988) call for the possibility of a "multiple policy presidency" impact on "multiple policy domains" with the Congress. Finally, Conley (1997) does find some evidence for an ideological and partisan refutation of the two presidencies thesis overall. However, his conclusions are limited due to the time constraints placed on his study. Most importantly, the general limitation of Conley's (1997) research is that it was located in a period of unified government when the broader confines of recent presidential-congressional historical context have been characterized by *divided* and not unified government. Additionally, Conley's (1997) research is a bit unique and possibly limited in that rather than "looking for the presence of the two presidencies" he is actually "looking for the absence of such a phenomenon."

The final studies that cast the two presidencies in a mostly partisan/institutional light have an expansive scope regarding their time boundary, essentially encompassing the era of the modern presidency. However, these studies have alternative interpretations as to the presence or inexistence of a two presidencies of any kind--partisan, institutional or otherwise. The first is actually an older study but it has had a great deal of influence regarding re-interpreting the "dynamics" of the two presidencies. Harvey Zeidenstein's (1981) expansion of Sigelman's (1979) study using "key votes" finds evidence for a "nuanced two presidencies" being present in the presidential-senatorial relationship only at least since 1973. It could be suggested that this is evidence for a Republican two presidencies as well as a senatorial two presidencies both being based on foreign policy bi-partisanship. Of course, it is difficult to see where the Carter presidency fits into the above formulation under such conditions (from Zeidenstein 1981). One interesting note is that Zeidenstein uses Sigelman's study as his base and finds an alternate conclusion, one where the two presidencies is supported with qualification for institutional and partisan effects (from Zeidenstein 1981 and Sigelman 1979).

In more recent work, Fleisher, Bond, Krutz and Hanna (2000) find weak evidence supporting the two presidencies. They suggest that it is in decline due to the increased levels of party line voting as a result of the ideological and partisan polarization of the Congress in recent years. Finally, Malbin and Brookshire (2000) suggest that the two presidencies was actually an overstatement of executive-legislative policy making relations. These authors do find support for a "Cold War" two presidencies between 1945 and 1972 but only as a strictly presidential-senatorial relations phenomenon (2000). Like the other two final analyses, this study leaves open the question as to how much the two presidencies, if it is there at all, is a partisan or an institutional phenomenon as the results of these studies seem to be able to be interpreted either way. A part of my dissertation and possibly broader research project is to try to answer that very question because if there are differential levels of policy making authority vested in the president relative to the Congress, then it could be attributed to either partisan/ideological or institutional reasons. I believe that it is primarily institutional where partisan/ideological conflict is played out within a broader "opportunity structure" of institutional power between the presidency and the Congress.

The Normative Critique: A Two Presidencies full of Promise but Little Reward

What is striking about the two presidencies literature is its pronounced lack of normative analysis both at the implications of an "imperial foreign policy presidency" and an "imperiled domestic policy presidency" (from Schlesinger 1973, 1989 & Ford 1980). Additionally, and perhaps more profoundly, an intellectual historiography of the topic has never been conducted as to the possible inherent "research biases" regarding normative implications of a presence or lack of a two presidencies phenomenon in the real world of executive-legislative relations. While the methodological debates regarding the proper measuring, variable operationalization and extant time frame of the two presidencies have been engaged ad nauseum, little effort has been made regarding the outcomes of such studies' implications (from Bond et al. 1991 in Shull 1991). In the executive-legislative relations literature writ large, such a debate has been present and is ongoing between those, like James Sundquist (1981) who, see a resurgent Congress "checking" the more abusive executive excesses in the wake of the Vietnam War and Watergate scandals. Another group of scholars, led principally by Louis Fisher (2000 and 2004) in political science and Arthur M. Schlesinger, Jr. (1973, 1989 and 2005) in history, find a presidency still empowered (excessively in their view) particularly in the realm of foreign/defense policy making relative to the Congress and even the totality of the American polity.

The vast majority of the studies contained within the two presidencies literature are behaviorally oriented empirical analyses that emphasize parsimonious theorizing and methodological "rigor." However, they do this at the expense of the possibilities inherent within this topic for normative "value-laden" political science. For instance, even in Wildavsky's (1966) initial analysis there is little time given to the ethical and even moral implications of a "Constitutional Dictator" in the realm of presidential foreign/defense policy construction (from Rossiter 1956). This is particularly interesting given the fact that Wildavsky's study was only four years removed from the Cuban Missile Crisis where presidential decision making would eventually be critiqued as being "too hastily made, with too few options put forward" (Alison and Zelikow 1999).

As Ellsberg (1971) has demonstrated, presidential decision making (in this case regarding US intervention into Southeast Asia) was hampered by pre-set "Cold War" oriented images leading to what Irving Janis would eventually describe as a "groupthink" phenomenon (Janis 1982). Ellsberg's (1971) idea of a "quagmire machine model" to explain such a case specific intervention (Vietnam being that case) could be seen as a normative (and hence subjective) example of Putnam's formal theoretic (and hence objective) "two level games" scenario with one "game" of interactions accounting for domestic policy construction (composed of multiple "sets") and another "game" of interactions (composed of a more finite number of relevant "sets"—Ellsberg's "quagmire machine-model) accounting for foreign policy development (Putnam 1988). A similar application, in theory at least, could exist within the two presidencies framework but a review of the extant literature on the subject does not find one.

Why is it the case that the two presidencies literature lacks such a normative component? I believe the answer rests in two parts, one general and one more specific. First, the behavioral revolution, for good or bad, has left the social sciences with a predilection toward empirical theorizing. While in and of itself this is not an undesirable development, the treatment of the empirical vs. normative "divide" within the social sciences (and in particular political science) as a "zero-sum" phenomenon has left the two groups largely ignorant and even worse dismissive of each others' work. This is disappointing on many levels least of which is that the persistence of differential levels of policy making success between the executive and the legislature has continued even in the wake of executive "excesses" in foreign policy like the Vietnam War and possibly (according to some anyway) the current war(s) (War on Terrorism, War In Afghanistan,

War In Iraq) (from Dodd in Conley 2003). Also, the inability of presidents to govern on the domestic front under both divided and unified government conditions has continued to "feed" the tendency for presidents to emphasize foreign over domestic policy because that is where they "can win regardless" (Shull and Shaw 1999). Finally, periods of governmental domestic success continue to be more tenuous and contingent on short term electoral/public opinion forces relative to presidential foreign policy activism. These last two points cry-out for an interpretive-based examination that brings out the inherent nuances often missed in more positivist based research (from Bond and Fleisher 1990, Conley 2002, Edwards 2000 in Shapiro, Kumar & Jacobs 2000).[13]

More specifically, the attempt by two presidencies researchers to produce the most parsimonious theory possible or to negate it in a similar such fashion has kept the two presidencies relatively undeveloped as a reflexive concept but highly developed as a research program. In other words, the current level of two presidencies research is basically an extended "methodological debate" which emphasizes the measuring (or lack thereof) of the phenomenon disguised as a "theoretical one" looking for the presence or absence of the phenomenon itself. What of course is missing is why such a policy making differential between the presidency and the Congress in the realms of domestic and foreign policy construction is even important. The answer should be obvious that since the Founding over 200 militarized disputes involving the US (many involving some level of combat) have occurred and they have largely been the "exclusive domain" of presidential power (Fisher 2004). Also, that in an age of "polarized politics" the national government is often impeded in domestic action and what action that does occur is often contradictory leading to massive budget deficits, inefficient decision making procedures and often ineffective governance processes (Bond and Fleisher 2000). However, the two presidencies literature not only does not answer these questions. Indeed, in large measure it does not even ask the questions. Given the size of the normative "gap" in the two presidencies literature, and to paraphrase the Democratic response to the 2005 presidential inauguration speech by Virginia Governor Kaine, "There is a better way!" (CNN State of the Union Speech January 20, 2005). While promoting such an alternative is beyond the scope of this paper it should suffice to say

---

[13] Interpretivism as a philosophy of science has not been employed in the study of the two presidencies or in presidential research in general. However, its strengths in identifying "underlying causes" and deeper attention to the role of context in shaping inter-actor behavior would be a first step in improving theorization in this field (see Thiele 2003).

that the normative implications of the two presidencies at a minimum at least need to be addressed in future research and not just ignored as "unscientific."

A final normative area for examination regarding the two presidencies is the need for some type of phenomenological recognition of the researchers' role as analyzers of this phenomenon. A reflexive analysis of the scholars' own contextual biases is needed in order to "see where they are coming from" and provide a "map for the intellectual history" of the two presidencies thesis. Examining the intellectual history of the two presidencies thesis through reflexive lenses indicates that the two presidencies to at least a certain extent are "what the researchers make of it!" This is consistent with some constructivist international relations and post-modern deconstruction political theory analyses that find reified and objectified empirical referents. Furthermore, the conclusions reached through such referents have led to absolutist determinations a la positivistic and even ideologically based interpretations (Oren 2003, Best and Kellner 1991 and Thiele 2003).

For example, researchers have largely looked at the same general "type" of data, presidential position roll calls yet have concluded numerously different findings either supporting, refuting or somehow or another "qualifying" the presence, rise, decline or absence of a "two presidencies" (Wildavsky 1966, 1989, Siglemen 1979, Zeidenstiein 1981, Shull and Shaw 1979, Bond and Fleisher 1988, Fleisher et. al. 2000, Conley 1997, Conley in Conley 2003). Another area of criticism emanating out of the two presidencies as a reflexive approach is that the search for a bi-furcated "answer" to the question of "Whither a two presidencies?" actually limits the number of potential "questions." This is especially true regarding notions of differential policy outcomes as a result of domain specific contexts because it presages any answer by framing it in zero-sum terms (which in itself is a bit ironic given the pronounced lack of rational choice applications in the two presidencies literature). Lastly, those who "go out to find a two presidencies almost inevitably do, while those who go out to "negate" the phenomenon also accomplish their task" The "finders" include Wildavsky (1966) (initially), Zeidenstein (1981), Shull and LeLoup (1979) Shull (1997), Shull and Shaw (1999), Bond and Fleisher (1988) (initially), Edwards (1986) among others.[14] The "negators" of the two presidencies thesis include Wildavsky and Oldfield (1989), Fleisher et al. (2000), Conley (1997),

---

[14] I have subsumed both the institutional and partisan versions of the two presidencies into the same category as "finders" of the two presidencies thesis.

44

(Conley in Conley 2003), Sigelman (1979), Peppers (1975), Malbin and Brookshire (2000), Fleisher et. al (2000) and others despite the fact that for the most part not only the same data have been examined but also the same time frame and no real conclusion has been reached (see Table 1-4 for this and other information).

In keeping with the idea that the "two presidencies is often what scholars make of it," as Table 1-4 indicates the methodological biases of the researchers seem to have a bearing on how they interpret the presence or lack of a two presidencies. Those using an aggregate approach (quantitative or qualitative) regarding the level of analysis employed largely finding support for the two presidencies thesis as either an institutional or partisan executive-legislative policy making relationship. However, those scholars more predisposed to study the phenomenon with an individual level of analysis approach tend to find evidence contrary to a predicted two presidencies domain-specific presidential-congressional policy making relationship.

As previously discussed in the paper, Malbin and Brookshire (2000) and Fleisher et al. (2000) both in some form or another support but also suggest a decline in the two presidencies in some qualified form as a partisan and cultural phenomenon that was built around the Cold War. These studies seem to represent some kind of "middle category" that neither supports nor refutes the two presidencies; therefore I left them out of Table 1-4.

Conclusion

This critical literature review has examined the two presidencies thesis as a body of scholarly work across the last four decades. In this effort I have developed four propositions assessing the quality of the two presidencies thesis as an empirical theory, a methodological debate and most critically as its unfulfilled promise to serve as a normative critique on extant executive-legislative policy making relations. A fourth proposition coming out of the two presidencies scholarship rests with the notion that the research has been "trapped" by its own dualistic nature.

As an empirical theory, the findings of this study contrary to some of the extant literature produced in recent years regarding the two presidencies is that it is a real depiction of the actual executive-legislative policy making relationship. The vast majority of the studies on the two presidencies in some fashion or form find evidence for differential policy success rates for presidents in their relationship with the Congress. Presidents do significantly better in foreign policy construction relative to the Congress than they do in such attempts within the domestic

45

sphere. However, the explanation for such success rates is not clear as to whether it is an institutional, partisan or cultural phenomenon but some patterns are existent. The classical version of the thesis (the institutional) is most associated with support for the two presidencies while the cultural version is most associated with rejecting it. The partisan two presidencies may be overstated as to its actual role in explaining the executive-legislative divide but this point is still very much in contention.

As a methodological debate the two presidencies thesis showed some tendencies toward being "methodologically determined" but a systematic review of the literature reveals that it is not principally a product of methodology despite early critics' contentions (see Sigelman 1979 and Edwards 1986). Left unexamined are the larger paradigmatic roles played by elitist versus pluralist accounts of American politics in the two presidencies analysis, however, I believe that they may prove fruitful for a broader inquiry currently beyond the scope of this study.

Finally, and also somewhat beyond the scope of this current study, the greatest area for future research on the two presidencies must come from its realization as a tool for normative critique. Not a single study I reviewed ever systematically addresses the potential of the two presidencies as a platform for questioning the policy making divide between the president and the Congress. Also, the lack of a reflexive interpretation of the individual authors' own philosophical biases (towards science as well as politics) prevents the two presidencies from being more than just an "empirical phenomenon."

The last conclusion that can be reached regarding the results of this literature review is that the two presidencies must be more than just a mere report on behaviorally based empirics but truly explained according to the hidden nuances within its own framework. Nearly 40% of the researchers who have examined the two presidencies thesis have rejected it as a theory of American politics. Therefore, a closer examination of the tenets of the thesis is needed in order to re-theorize executive-legislative policy making relations so as to produce greater empirical "fit," stronger explanative/predictive "power," as well as begin to establish a normative "critique" of extant presidential-congressional policy making.

State-Centrism versus Domestic Variables Approaches to American Foreign Policy Analysis

Next, I will discuss the statist-domestic variables alternatives as methodological-theoretic approaches to the study of US foreign policy from extant international relations research. This review of the literature, while not comprehensive is presented with an eye for direct relevance to the *issue areas* alternative that I propose in the third chapter. Accordingly, I will first present the basics and some exemplifying canonical *statist/state-centrist* based US foreign policy analyses by showcasing their strengths but more importantly their *weaknesses* as method and theory devices for such exploration. In particular, I plan to present the statist method and theory as a *presidential-centered* device which garners its "strength" from privileging those conditions associated most with a presidentialist perspective on foreign policy.

Then, I follow the same procedure for discussing the *domestic variables* alternative to analyzing American foreign policy. However, in this effort I will propose that the domestic variables approach is essentially a *Congress-centered* mechanism for US foreign policy study because it privileges those conditions associated with a congressionalist take. Finally, I will briefly tell how an *issue areas analysis* is an improvement on this prior research tradition which will serve as a bridging tool for the more developed treatment discussed in the methods chapter (see chapter 3).

State-Centrism/Statism

Under the auspices of the statist/state-centrist approach to the study of US foreign policy, foreign policy construction is seen to be biased in favor of central over adjacent decision makers. What this means in practice is that certain relationships between real and potential "actors" in foreign policy are such that some basic assumptions can be made asserting that (1) the presidency will dominate the Congress, (2) the foreign policy "Establishment" will be more influential than the "non-Establishment" actors and (3) the "core foreign policy executive" will ultimately make its decisions independent of the other executive branch actors. Finally, as a theoretical approach this assumes that outside interests like parties, interest groups, non-foreign policy oriented congressional committees and non-military/foreign policy oriented interests will have little if any impact on the creation of foreign policies. The methodological principle produced from the above theoretical premise is that central/core actors serve as the primary variables of interest for any study of US foreign policy.

The primary reason given for the above conditions is that central decision makers in foreign policy share a common organizational "culture" including similar policy goals, views regarding interventionism, state-to-state relations and the primary control over the definition and hence application of the "national interest" (Kennan 1979). Furthermore, the external policy

47

makers are viewed as too isolated from the formal powers granted to the central decision makers either by constitutional or legislative delegations. This is perhaps most important regarding the assumption of an asymmetrical information flow for foreign policy that empowers the core foreign policy executive (the president and a close coterie of advisors today represented in the National Security Council and some economic equivalents like the Office of the US Trade Representative) at the expense of those "outside the black box of the state" (from Waltz 1979).

In large measure, state-centrist analyses have been the dominant theoretical starting point for most US foreign policy research since the start of the Cold War. Early game theory applications regarding the development of state-to-state strategic interactions and eventually the establishment of deterrence theory both as an academic and practical foreign policy program were in place by the 1950's.[15] In these presentations the "US state" was nothing more than the "people at the top" who all were presumed to "think alike, act alike and in general be alike" while this may seem simplistic it was and is viewed as very parsimonious. For instance, as complex interactions like those that occurred between Kennedy and Khrushchev over the Cuban Missile Crisis can be examined in an empirically valid manner through a mechanism like the "chicken game matrix" (Snyder and Diesing 1977). Or, the rise of an aggressive based American foreign policy doctrine like Containment or even Roll Back as a by-product of the "failure at Munich" leading to the need to provide a "credible threat" in the face of "inevitable attack" (Payne 1970).[16]

The Munich analogy of the ultimate failure of appeasement in dealing with foreign policy crises involving naked aggression is taken one step further by Yuen Foong Khong. Khong (1992) attributes Truman's war decision regarding the Korean War as a direct outcome of the perceived negative results of US isolationism during the interwar years (the 1920's and 1930's). Furthermore, this study claims that the negative outcomes of the 1938 Munich Agreement between Neville Chamberlain and Adolf Hitler over Czechoslovakia served as the direct

---

[15] See Von Neuman 1943, Schelling 1960, Shubick 1964, Snyder and Diesing 1977 for game-theoretic applications both in general and in specific foreign policy "dilemmas" as well as George and Smoke 1974 and Payne 1970 for deterrence theory and its specific application to the US case.

[16] The "failure at Munich" is a common utilized phrase within the foreign policy community to indicate the negative consequences of appeasement of aggressors as a diplomatic initiative and strategy. The specific reference is employed to showcase the risks of appeasement as witnessed by Chamberlain's diplomatic venture with Hitler over Czechoslovakia in 1938 which was seen in retrospect to "give Hitler a *carte blanche*" to carry our further aggression on the European continent.

"guiding principle" in checking communist aggression on the Korean peninsula (Khong 1992). Earnest May's (1973) historical analysis claims that virtually all US foreign policy decisions are based on previous evaluations of those situations that are deemed "similar," however, it is stressed throughout his work that it is only a small number of people that are doing this activity which leads to certain "misuses" of history. Perhaps the greatest single application of a state-centrist model for foreign policy decision making is in the prevalence of the *rational actor model* which posits that state's unitary actors utilize cost vs. benefits analyses in reaching decisions regarding foreign policy situations (see Alison and Zelikow 1999). Bueno de Mesquita's (1981) war trap model based on expected utility maximization is probably the best single employment as well as the most favorable one for the usage of the rational actor model as an exploratory device. One possible reason for this exists in the model's own negation because many American foreign policy researchers have found little applicability for this model beyond Bueno de Mesquita's version of war decision implementation (see Snyder and Diesing 1977 and Anderson 1987 in Hermann, Kegley and Rosenau 1987 for criticisms).

Braybroke and Lindblom (1969 in Rosenau 1969) suggest that *incrementalism* is a better way of examining foreign policy decision making by accounting for Simon's (1959) ideas about *satisficing* due to the lack of review potential regarding all possible policy alternatives. These authors are responding to the long held criticism of the rational actor model as not being empirically possible due to the strictness of its assumptions which while excellent for parsimonious modeling may in fact be detrimental in real world application (see Green and Shapiro 1994 for an extended empirically based criticism). Incrementalism is based on making decisions around evaluations by central decision makers of the previous policy already in place. The result of this model is that policies routinely chosen are in fact "non-optimal," but the authors of this thesis conclude that war decisions lie outside the parameters of "normal foreign policy decision making" and hence cannot be accounted for by this model (Braybroke and Lindbolm 1969 in Rosenau 1969). What is interesting is that the "preferred model" used to explain/predict American foreign policy decision making seems to be dependent on the issue area it is being applied to.

Other applications of the statist model have looked at certain "issue area specific" points in US foreign policy construction like for instance in foreign economic policies. Krasner's (1978) suggests that US foreign economic policy regarding raw material investments reflected the concerns of a small group of central decision makers "leading" rather than being "led" by corporate interests who were quite hostile at the start of these efforts in the late 19th century. This is particularly noted given the fact that most analyses of US foreign economic policies have given the Congress not the executive branch (much less the presidency) the central place in policy formulation during that time period (Lindsay 1994). Lake (1988) claims that US trade policy between 1884 and 1934 actually reflected a "supply side" approach to trade strategy development which supported a state-centered argument rather than the more conventional view of a "demand side" strategic approach that supports a society-centered explanation. Ikenberry et al. (1983) contrast the systemic, state and society oriented analyses regarding the development of US foreign economic policies and find support for the state as an intervening variable between the systemic and domestic forces. However, these researchers also find that the US state is limited in its ability to be that intervening variable due to its persistence as a generally "weak force" in regulating the economy (Ikenberry et al. 1983). Therefore, a relationship seems to exist between the "levels of impact" a state can have depending on the particular issue area of foreign policy. Hence, in the realm of security where central decision makers have the most "impact" the study of them (a statist formulation) is called for but where it is doubtful or even absent (i.e. foreign economic policies) then an alternative conception is called for.

Psychological approaches to foreign policy construction in themselves do not support state-centrism because they operate at a different level of analysis. However, they do offer insights as to the elitist quality of foreign policy construction relative to that found in domestic politics. For instance, in the 1980's Reagan's very personalized views of the Soviet Union as an "Evil Empire" had a profound impact on East-West relations regarding the massive defense buildup undertaken by the US during that time. However, in domestic affairs, Reagan's views regarding the need to "scale back the welfare state" did have some impact regarding a "devolution revolution" in federalism. In fact, the simple truth of the matter is that domestic spending remained largely intact throughout his administration (with 1981 as something of an outlier) leading directly to the deficit crisis of the early 1990's. What this suggests is that in the elite politics of foreign affairs the psychological predisposition of a president has a greater direct policy impact than those same predilections do in the more pluralistic domestic arena.

Khong's (1992) perspective of basing foreign policy decision making on analogy with perceived similar situations from the past is an example of in-direct statist application from the psychological approach literature. Since according to the statist model the number of decision makers is kept "naturally" at a minimum then skewed ideas about extant and previous conditions will appear and guide such decision making. Furthermore, such decision making can lead to the *groupthink* phenomenon as articulated by Irving Janis (1982) where alternative policy proposals "are kept off the table" due to a certain "go along attitude" that emerges among isolated groups as foreign policy decision makers are if the state-centered perspective is the correct one. The Iraq War decision possibly fits this conception since there are reports that right from the start a certain consensus built around the President, Vice-President, Secretary of Defense and National Security Advisor that war with Iraq was necessary and desirable (Phillips 2005). However, it is difficult if not impossible to find an application of groupthink outside of security policy decision making. In sum, then the statist approach has its most profound utility regarding the development and execution of national security policies whether viewed as a product of the rational actor model, incrementalist model or even indirectly in the psychological approaches.

Domestic Variables Approach

The domestic variables approach assumes a more society centered approach to the study of foreign policy design where diverse sets of interests, each with their own group of elites contend for influence under conditions that roughly approximate pluralism and the outcomes produced generally reflect this give and take (from Ikenberry et. al. 1983, as well as Snow and Brown 1999). It is important to note that this approach does not assume that the state is a unitary actor but rather a composite of diverse interests who work through as well as outside the extant institutions of the society in order to come up with aggregate solutions to aggregate problems. The organizational process model formalized but later revised by Graham Allison (1971) views the state as a kind of corporation of loosely allied semi-feudal organizations whose behavior is largely determined by *standard operating procedures* (SOPs). Under this formulation, central decision makers have only an influence and not a determinative impact on the behavior of these organizations because problems are deliberated over and solutions conceived largely independent of one another as the responsibility for such foreign policy construction is "divided up" according to preset operational codes (Allison 1971).

It is interesting to note, Allison rejects this model for explaining his central case study the Cuban Missile Crisis of 1962. However, when utilized in combination with the governmental process model as the *Bureaucratic Politics Model* Alison found that SOPs in conjunction with the independent agency of actors within the structure (in this case the executive branch) was the determining factor in the decisions made during those eventful 13 days in October of 1962 (Allison and Zelikow 1999). While these results certainly question the utility of a statist model for foreign policy crisis resolution they are not necessarily generalizable outside the case Allison analyzed. For instance, US response to the October War by the Nixon administration was almost entirely contained to a few people around President Nixon (principally his then National Security Advisor Henry Kissinger), so it seems that the individual "character" of a president and his National Security Council may be the intervening variable as to how much influence is allowed in foreign policy decision making particularly in "crisis" periods (from Ambrose 1979). Likewise, Anderson's (in Hermann, Kegley and Rosenau 1987) analysis suggests just this by finding no direct relationship between institutional/organizational domain and foreign policy suggestions among the actors in those domains. Shepard (1988) also finds that it is difficult to determine the effect of Secretaries of State and Defense's roles on the positions that they took on issues involving the employment of US force. Both of these studies were cross-case and cross-time in formulation and hence may be seen as superior systematic evidence opposing the bureaucratic politics model and indirectly not supporting the domestic variables approach writ large.

The domestic variables approach seems to have its greatest utility in foreign economic affairs policy making where a number of domestic interests are directly involved including but certainly not limited to political parties, interest groups, the Congress and judiciary, as well as various state and even local governments, corporations and labor unions (Wittkopf & McCormick in Wittkopf & McCormick 1999). Even the well known example used to support elitist perspectives on US policy making in general the "military-industrial complex" made popular with C. Wright Mills (1956) "power elite school" is in fact an agglomeration of said "elites" including relevant interest groups, congressional committees and the Department of Defense. While this may seem elitist with regards to domestic policy making which is said to be governed by "issue networks" rather than "iron triangles of sub-governments" it is still a composition where unitary action (rational or not) cannot be assumed (Loomis and Baumgartner 1994).

In the realm of trade policy in particular a predominant amount of evidence has been suggested to support the thesis that until the Trade Act of 1934 it was the Congress not the president who was the dominant actor in this area. The reason for such preeminence is found in the activities of state and local party organizations and "pressure groups" of various economic interests battling it out over the contours of American trade policy throughout the 18th and 19th centuries as the word "lobbying" came into being in the halls of Congress (Lindsay 1994, Lindsay in Wittkopf and McCormick 1999, Cooper in Dodd and Oppenheimer 2005, and Fisher 2000). Furthermore, in the wake of the Cold War growing economic interdependencies as well as congressional resurgence in such matters has become par for the course rather than the aberration as evidenced in the establishment of an economically oriented rather than a politically/militarily oriented "New China Lobby" on K-Street (Bernstein and Munro in Wittkopf and McCormick 1999).

Lastly, even in the realm of humanitarian activities that involved the employment of US military force like in Somalia, Bosnia and Kosovo the Congress as well as public opinion and trans-national interest groups have been shown to have played a central role in either supporting or opposing these Bush-Clinton foreign policies (Snow and Brown 1999). In particular, the rise of "new security issues" involving basic humanitarian "needs" like water and food security have been seen as places for adjacent actor incursion because the systemic "life and death" issues of Cold War "old security" are to some extend modified if not moved out of prevalence (Mathews 1989).

However, the events of 9/11 have shown us that the old ways are not in fact gone forever, but have just re-emerged under new guises. Whether Huntington's well known thesis about a "Clash of Civilizations" comes to pass may be the determining point as to whether central or adjacent decision makers will be the "Foreign Policy Establishment of the 21st century" (see Huntington 1996)? The real problem with the domestic variables approach is not that it is invalid but that it is only valid in certain areas at certain times. This limitation is similar to the statist approach's own constraints in examining American foreign policy, though of course the areas and times of "validity" are what separate the applicability of the two "competing" approaches. Accordingly, I will attempt a synthesis of the two that keeps what is best and rejects what is worst in order to produce a methodological-theoretical approach to US foreign policy that captures its inherent nuances but yet also retains its unique qualities.

53

Table 1-1. Institutional "Structures" of the President and Congress[17] Policy Characteristics

Foreign	Domestic
President centered	Congress/bureaucracy centered
few participants	many participants
unity	diversity
uncertain, high risk	more certain, low risk
secret, stable	more visible, fluid
few options	many options
intangible	tangible
low information	high information
short decision time	long decision time
bi- or non-partisan	partisan

Table 1-2. Institutional Policy Context circa Cold War Era[18]

(1) Much of the president's power derives from the immediacy of the Cold War.

(2) The president's "formal powers" to commit resources in foreign affairs and defense are vast.

(3) The need for secrecy restricts the ability of others to compete with the president in foreign affairs.

(4) The rise of defense intellectuals has given the president enhanced ability to control defense policy.

(5) Presidents devote a great deal of resources to foreign policy because they are perceived to be both important and irreversible.

---

[17] from Shull and Leloup's (1979) *"Presidential Impact: Foreign versus Domestic Policy" in The Presidency: Studies in Policy Making* Shull and Leloup (1979)

[18] Taken from Wildavsky (1966) and Peppers (1975) also reprinted in Oldfield and Wildasvsky (1989)

(6) Presidents refuse to become prisoners of their advisors and remain in control of their staff.

(7) Reactions against the blatant isolationism of the 1930s has led to a concern with foreign policy that is worldwide in scope.

Table 1-3. Institutional Policy Context Circa late and/or Post-Cold War

(1) The Cold war has lost its sense of urgency as a result of the loss in Vietnam, the start of détente, glastnost, perestroika, and ultimately the fall of the USSR—the end of the Cold War.

(2) The War Powers Act and a resurgent Congress in general has curtailed the president's "formal" powers in military foreign affairs.

(3) The impacts of investigations into the CIA, Watergate, the Pentagon Papers, Iran-Contra, etc… have opened the political environment to make subordinates in the executive branch more willing to "violate" protocol, Congress more willing to use its oversight power relative to the executive, and the public more skeptical regarding "executive discretion."

(4) Negative reactions to Vietnam, the nuclear arms race, Cold War interventions, and military spending deficits has led to the establishment of a group of experts and supporters exogenous to administrations who openly question the president and the Pentagon.

(5) Due to the failure of US policy in Vietnam, sloganeering which previously led to irreversible positions (like in the Cuban Missile Crisis) may not tempt a president as much as it once did since he/she may not want to "risk" the political capital necessary for such sloganeering to be successful.

(6) Foreign policy formulation and execution by presidents has been revealed to be the result of a process characterized by numerous and multiple inputs within his/her own administration.

(7) An emergent neo-isolationism has developed within both political parties, the Congress, the executive branch itself, and even within the electorate which will stifle presidential interventionism in the future.

Table 1-4. The Two Presidencies Scholarship at a Glance

Support 2 Presidencies Thesis	Oppose 2 Presidencies Thesis
Institutional 2 Presidencies	Cultural 2 Presidencies
Wildavsky 1966,** LeLoup and Shull 1979, ** Shull and Leloup 1981, ** Shull 1997, ** Shull and Shaw 1999, ** Cohen 1982 **	Peppers 1975, ** Wildavsky and Oldfield 1989, ** Conley in Conley 2003*
Partisan 2 Presidencies	Methodological 2 Presidencies
Edwards 1986, 1989, * Bond and Fleisher 1988, 1990 * Sullivan 1991, * Zeidenstein 1981, * Renka and Jones 1991 **	Siglemen 1979, * Siglemen 1981, * Page and Jordan 1992, * Conley 1997*

*=individual level of analysis **=aggregate level of analysis (Source=compiled by author)

CHAPTER 2
THE MULTIPLE PRESIDENCIES THESIS: A RE-CONCEPTUALIZATION OF
EXECUTIVE-LEGISLATIVE RELATIONS IN FOREIGN AFFAIRS

Introduction

This chapter proposes an alternative theoretical framework that will attempt to discern the exact inter-institutional policy making relationship which the president shares with the Congress in the realm of foreign affairs. This theory is the multiple presidencies thesis which proposes that multiple foreign policy presidencies occupy the office of a single president in his policy making relationship with the Congress. Additionally, I will promote the employment of a new methodological-theoretical approach to American foreign policy analysis which amounts to a synthesis of previous work. This synthesis is called an issue areas analysis which breaks American foreign policy down into its component issue areas and studies them accordingly. The reason for proposing such an effort is that the extant scholarship on American national executive-legislative foreign policy making relations has "missed the trees for the forest." The idea that foreign policy is somehow different in its formation and execution relative to domestic policy is pervasive throughout both American politics and international relations literature in political science (e.g., Almond 1950 and Huntington 1961 for early examples). However, it is my contention that despite Snow and Brown's (1999) suggestion that foreign relations lies "beyond the water's edge," foreign policy is as nuanced and differentiated among its various "sub-categories" as domestic policy is. Lowi (1964, 1972) posited that domestic policy was best viewed as being composed of a series of "issue domains" that had differential types and levels of policy conflict. In fact, Spitzer (1983) used Lowi's "policy typology thesis" to suggest that the president had different levels of influence in the construction of policy relative to the Congress across these domains. If that was true for Spitzer, why cannot a similar such dynamic be occurring between the president and Congress over the construction of foreign policy across "multiple issue areas" including national security, domestic security, diplomacy, international trade, foreign aid and immigration?

A strong case can be made that such a dynamic is going on and has so possibly through time, particularly in the Post War Era of the Eisenhower to W. Bush administrations (1953-2004). It is the purpose of this chapter to examine the nuances of that dynamic from a new theoretically informed framework. Accordingly, this framework answers the fundamental question: *"What is the inter-institutional relationship between the president and Congress in foreign policy?"* This question stems naturally from previous works' accomplishments and even more importantly from their failures to get at the "heart" of the presidential-congressional foreign affairs relationship. A number of scholars have addressed the issue of executive-legislative relations. According to an excellent recent summary of that work by Shull and Shaw (1999) most if not all of those studies can be broadly categorized as being presidency- or congressional- centered studies. This body of research calls for the emplacement of the "locus" of power within one or the other institution. The difficulty is that this body of work despite being "labeled as executive-legislative analyses" they are in fact single institution centered studies that view one or the other institution as posing/lacking "some causal force" on the institution that actually concerns them. This analysis provides a conceptual model for additional work on the presidential-congressional relationship because it treats both institutions as proactive entities in the process and does not privilege the "role" of one institution over the other.[1]

Accordingly, the central argument of this chapter is that *executive-legislative relations in Post-War foreign affairs are best examined through a "multiple issue areas perspective." Each issue area is characterized by a unique albeit related set of interactions that are themselves contingent on time and context.* Furthermore, the examination of these afore-mentioned relations is guided by a theoretical framework called the *Multiple Presidencies Thesis.* The framework accounts that at least in the realm of foreign affairs the presidential-congressional policy making relationship is contingent on the larger forces of "political time" and exhibits a nuanced pattern across multiple issue areas.

The "causal mechanism" governing the inter-institutional foreign policy process consists in a *two part endeavor* with one part existing at the unit level of institutional interaction between the presidency and the Congress. The other process operates at the structural level of the political environment itself influencing in a systemic manner how the unit level activity takes place. First, the unit level activity between the presidency and the Congress is a function of the executive branch's historical-institutional *opportunity structure of power* within *national security.* Therefore, issue areas within the *high politics arena* (national security, domestic security and

---

[1] Some presidentially based studies include, among others, Rossiter 1956, Neustadt 1960, Robinson 1967, Huntington 1961 and Edwards 1980. Congressionally based analyses include, among others, Chamberlain 1946, Sundquist 1968, Moe & Teel 1970, Fisher 1972, Orfield 1975, Gallagher 1977, Edwards 1989, Bond & Fleisher 1990, Ripley and Lindsay 1994, Peterson 1994 and Brady & Volden 1998.

diplomacy) are subject to higher levels of ongoing "control" by the president vis-à-vis the Congress. Second, as the foreign policy construction process moves outside the national security domain into the other issue areas the component issue areas become more *intermestic in orientation* (the co-mingling of foreign and domestic policies like in the *low politics arena* of trade, foreign aid and immigration). Thus, the Congress's own *opportunity structure of power* within the domestic sphere comes into greater play in influencing foreign policy outcomes in the executive-legislative relationship by empowering the Congress at the expense of the presidency. Third, when *the political environment itself alters the conditions regarding the number of opportunities versus constraints within the presidential-congressional foreign policy relationship* then the executive-legislative relationship is subject to a shift of in the direction of institutional policy making power. This shift in power can either impede or strengthen one institution (the presidency or the Congress) over another regarding the construction of foreign policy. Such a shift can never have a negligible impact on the inter-institutional relationship because power is not a neutral quantity. Therefore, attention to such shifts as well as the recognition of historical conditions of institutional power (like national security for the presidency and domestic qualities of policy for the Congress) is absolutely necessary for understanding the foreign policy dynamic in executive-legislative relations. *In sum, executive-legislative relations in foreign policy are best thought of as "a securitizing presidency versus a domesticating Congress across the issue areas of foreign policy."*

This theoretical notion can be used to *"periodize"* the executive-legislative foreign relations policy making dynamic during the Postwar Era (1953-2004). These are the separate *"orders"* of presidential-congressional relations according to the historical context they are found in. First is a **War Power Order from 1953-1972** characterized by presidential dominance and congressional acquiescence to successfully securitized foreign policy making. Second is a **Confrontation Politics Order from 1973-1989** characterized by an aggressive presidential-congressional foreign policy politics where even the president's power over security affairs is openly questioned. During this time, the Congress asserts its institutional prerogatives in foreign policy and the presidency battles on for a continuance of the old order. Presidential derailment occurs in the wake of Vietnam but some restoration of foreign policy prominence occurs under Reagan. Third is the **Imperial Presidency Politicized Order from 1990-2000** where a re-empowered commander-in-chief grapples with a very partisan Congress over the various issue areas of foreign policy—with deference given to security (but not acquiescence) and open defiance presented in all other domains not successfully *"securitized"* by the president. The promise of the Persian Gulf War victory for a full restoration of presidential power in international affairs is offset by the difficulties over trade and foreign aid policies faced by both the Bush and Clinton administrations. Fourth, there are the possibilities and constraints of an ongoing **Extra-Systemic Dilemma Order (2001-2004)** as the defining characteristic governing the foreign policy relationship between the two national proactive institutions in the Post-9/11 world. However, the reliance of a new securitized opportunity structure of power built around the War on Terror has by its very intermestic nature served as an invitation for continued congressional encroachment.

A subset of the extant literature on executive-legislative relations is of particular interest to this study because it serves as its "starting point." These studies propose the idea that the best way to examine relations between our national executive and legislature is through the mechanism of "institutional policy making authority." These studies tend to either locate institutional policy making authority as either existing within the presidency, the Congress or in one or the other varying across historical and contextual circumstances (within the presidency— Mezey 1989 and Spitzer 1993; within the Congress-- Bond and Fleisher 1990 & Ripley and Lindsay 1993; in *tandem (or equal) institutions* Peterson 1990, Leloup and Shull 1993 and Thurber 1996). It is in this last group of scholars that will ground the multiple presidencies project as a contribution to understanding executive-legislative policy making "authoritative" relations in foreign affairs. However, as Shull and Shaw (1999) suggest, all of these scholars, even themselves, view foreign affairs policy making as a whole. This is what I find to be the "root of the problem" revealed in the inconsistent findings of the *two presidencies thesis* discussed in Part I of the literature review (see Wildavsky 1966).

Theory: The Multiple Presidencies Thesis: An Alternative to the "Two Presidencies"

The multiple presidencies thesis suggests that executive-legislative relations in foreign policy making exist in historically and contextually specific patterns that are based on an "issue areas" perspective wherein the president is most empowered in national security affairs relative to the Congress. Additionally, the Congress exists in a more equal and of-times empowered position relative to the presidency in those issue areas that exist in an arena (low politics issue areas which include trade, foreign aid and immigration) that is more subject to being

61

"domesticated." This last point is especially true when the political environment disallows presidential "securitization" of policies and domains beyond his normal "arena of power (high politics issue areas which include national and domestic security as well as diplomacy)."[2]

Given the criticisms leveled against the two presidencies thesis regarding its theoretical, methodological, empirical and normative shortcomings, what does this have to say about the advantages of a multiple presidencies effect regarding presidential-congressional *foreign affairs policy making* in the Post War Era? First, extant scholarship on the two presidencies establishes the notion that foreign affairs is a unique arena of policy making because of the presidency's perceived or real authoritative role in this activity relative to the Congress. Second, given the inconsistent findings of the two presidencies literature, no one knows the authoritative role, if any, for the presidency in such executive-legislative relations. Third and more specifically, the role of context, partisanship and most importantly institutional relationships have never been adequately "mapped-out." Finally, a comparative, "institutionally based" methodology has not been adequately applied to the subject of "authoritative policy making" in foreign relations. I believe that a multiple presidencies conception will address all of these areas left either not studied or inadequately pursued by the previous work on this topic. I engage each area in turn. However, methods will be discussed in the methodology chapter. Before engaging the nuances of the theory itself, I will set forth the reasons for selecting its placement within the Post War Era (1953-2004).

According to both Louis Fisher (2000) and James Sundquist (1981) the Post War Era (the time after the end of WWII) has been a seminal point in the political history of executive-legislative policy making relations. These scholars disagree as to what has actually happened regarding the power distribution of "authoritative policy making" in foreign policy. To Sundquist (1981) the legislative presidency in foreign affairs first developed into an unchallenged dominant force but then declined in the wake of a resurgent Congress fed up with the "imperial presidencies" of Johnson and Nixon (see also Schlesinger 1973 & 1989). Fisher (2000), on the other hand, sees that Congress failed in its resurgence attempt and the "imperial presidency" in

---

[2] I borrow a number of analytical "tools" from other researcher's to construct the multiple presidencies thesis and will discuss those contributions in this section including notions of transformative analysis, opportunity structures of power, historical-institutionalism as a paradigm and rational choice theory as a paradigm for understanding individual actor actions as well as periodicity for historical analysis of "political time" (Dodd 1986, McAdam 1982, Orren and Skowronek 1994 in Dodd and Jilson 1994, Mayhew 1974, Skowronek 1997 and Conley 2003).

foreign affairs as well as spending policies has actually advanced rather than retreated in the intervening years since the end of Sundquist's (1981) analysis. Both scholars are correct but in their own nuanced ways and the multiple presidencies thesis will be the keystone that links their perspectives together. The reason for this is due to the theory's notion of "executive-legislative orders" at the structural level (the notion of the political environment as a function of political time) and altering "opportunity structures" at the unit level of presidential-congressional issue area-specific policy construction (the idea of a securitizing presidency versus a domesticating Congress).

Regarding the contention that there is something unique about foreign relations where the presidency and Congress are concerned the basic assumptions of the two presidencies thesis are correct on this matter. The problem has lain in the fact that when we are discussing foreign affairs we are actually discussing a very disparate "group of issue areas." These issues/policies include national security, domestic security, diplomacy, trade, foreign aid and immigration. In other words, foreign affairs are virtually as diverse as domestic relations regarding the sheer scope of policies and hence "politics" involved. The two presidencies thesis, in my view, erred right from the beginning because it assumed that international relations were not as diverse and hence easier to be guided by a policy of "national interest" (from Shull and Leloup 1979).

What makes international policy making different from domestic policy construction regarding executive-legislative relations is not the scope of the policies within the issue areas but the "opportunity structures" in place across those areas. In the realm of national security affairs, the president is constitutionally, institutionally, and historically advantaged so as to allow him/her to *dominate* the construction of policies. The Congress is likewise *subordinate* relative to the presidency in this area. In no other issue area of foreign policy does the president have such advantages but the fact that he/she has this advantage in foreign affairs but not the domestic sphere makes all the difference. This is because in the domestic realm no such favorable "opportunity structure" is even possible. In fact the structures in that realm largely *favor the Congress at the expense of the presidency*. That last point will be an area for later research but will not be examined in this project because it is the opportunity structure in national security affairs that allows the executive-legislative process to play-out the way it does. This process ultimately leads to the classification of "orders" for executive-legislative foreign policy relations across "political time."

63

The above comments also speak to the second "gap" in the two presidencies by suggesting how the authority dynamic in executive-legislative foreign policy making relations is distributed. However, the role of the structural level component of history and context is important to note here. While the presidency may lose "institutional authority" over policy construction relative to the Congress when policies move outside the realm of national security and its larger arena of high politics, historical contexts differ over time. In certain "orders" of political time like the War Power Order (1953-1972) the president often successfully "securitized" issues that under different "orders," say the Confrontation Politics Order (1973-1989), were resisted by a recalcitrant Congress.

This notion of "securitizing" issues comes from Mathews' (1989) concept of a new type of "security" which included humanitarian concerns in a way that previous Realist conceptions of "old security" did not recognize because of their predilection toward viewing "material concerns." I expand the notion to include any issue in foreign policy that the president can "sell" successfully to the Congress as a "security issue" thus invoking the "opportunity structure" favoring presidential empowerment and hence congressional acquiescence. In application, as Figure 2-1 shows the probability of presidential success vis-à-vis the Congress on a foreign policy issue is a direct function of the president's ability to "securitize" that issue or even entire issue area.

Regarding the third weakness in the two presidencies literature, the multiple presidencies thesis takes on the issues of partisan versus institutional conceptions of executive-legislative relations by suggesting that both rather than one or the other play a predominant role in the "governing" of this relationship by taking into account the "context" of "political time." The categorization that arises out of an analysis of presidential-congressional foreign policy making relations across issues areas leads to the conclusion that in general national security affairs and to a lesser extent the rest of the high politics arena is less "politicized" and hence less partisan (meaning more institutional in its character of policy construction relations). However, in all other issue areas, especially those found in the low politics arena such a condition is absent and hence less institutional and more "politicized" (meaning more partisan in the character of policy making relations). These issue areas are more subject to being domesticated because they are characterized by an *"intermestic nature" (the confluence of foreign and domestic policies),* therefore, the Congress has an increased probability of successfully challenging presidential prerogatives (Manning 1977, Conley 1997, Lewis 1997). What follows is a brief section dedicated to laying out the contours of the "map" of presidential-congressional relations in foreign policy as revealed through the multiple presidencies thesis.

Political Time in Executive-Legislative Foreign Policy Issue Area Relations

The War Power Order 1953-1972

National security affairs expands into all/most other issue areas of foreign policy establishing the president as a foreign affairs "hegemon" with Congress relegated to a virtually complete acquiescent and peripheral status as a foreign policy actor. The politics that the president and Congress "make" regarding one another is one of master-servant and is institutional, non-partisan and de-politicized.

The Confrontation Politics Order 1973-1989

In the wake of Vietnam and Watergate, a resurgent challenger Congress juxtaposed to a weakly dominant presidency in foreign relations is openly and vigorously questioning presidential prerogatives in the vaunted realm of national security. The power of the president to successfully "securitize" issues outside national security affairs is deterred and quite often the president fails in the effort as intermestic (the co-integration of foreign and domestic policy) affairs become the norm rather than the aberration in foreign policy construction. The politics that the president and the Congress "make" in international relations is characterized as reactionary-revolutionary and is partisan, non-institutional and highly politicized.

The Imperial Presidency Politicized Order 1990-2000

A re-empowered national security affairs presidency that is said to be strongly dominant relative to the Congress in the construction of international relations policies but does not re-attain a hegemonic position due to continued Congressional assertion of institutional and partisan prerogatives. However, a Congress that never fully "backed down" impedes presidential "discretion" with limits placed at the same time that authority is given. While the president has regained the ability to successfully "securitize" issues/policies outside the realm of national security and thus invoke the "powers" of that realm's opportunity structure he/she is held at abeyance from exerting a renewed "hegemonic" presence and is often forced to "compromise" and even to "follow the lead" of the Congress in some non-securitized foreign policy domains.

The relationship between the president and the Congress as well as the "politics" that they "make" in foreign affairs is said to be one of management-labor and is partially partisan based, partially institutionally based as well as being at times de-politicized and at other times highly politicized. Furthermore, this relationship is a function not only of security but also the continued role of intermestic politics left over from the previous order.

The Post-9/11Extra-Systemic Dilemma Order 2001-2004

What time do we find ourselves in now regarding presidential-congressional foreign policy relations? The simple problem is that there is no simple solution. Presidential hegemony over foreign affairs is a thing of the past; however congressional resurgence has also been left incomplete. The line between foreign and domestic affairs is now so porous as to be virtually transparent. Existing research has seemingly been unable to grapple the new empirical reality of a globalized world, what Friedman (2002) refers to as the "world going flat." Finally, at the level of presidential-congressional interaction the ability to discern the perspective "loci" of power under the conditions of an increasingly interdependent and even synergistic foreign policy making process are formidable to say the least. If we integrate more subtle issue areas into the analysis, a multiple presidencies approach has the potential to provide a lasting theoretical framework and methodology due to its adaptability to changing contexts.

Analytically, this is a work of historical-institutionalism which employs quantitative based research to a field that is largely qualitative in nature. This research does import some concepts from rational choice theory, especially regarding the president's role as an individual seeker of policy primacy through his/her "securitization" efforts. However, beyond that application this is a work very much grounded in "institutionalist" conceptions of politics. This is especially true regarding the employment of "opportunity structures" as historical, institutional and constitutional avenues for policy making empowerment (from McAdam 1982). Also, my usage of "political time" for the purposes of "periodizing" the "history" of executive-legislative relations is a by-product of the historical-institutional perspective (Orren and Skowronek 1994 in Dodd and Jilson 1994).

Theoretically, I borrow from American foreign policy research regarding *state-centered versus domestic variables approaches* to understanding policy formation. Emanating out of these notions, the high politics issue arena (national security, domestic security and diplomacy) is understood from the perspective of a "state-centered" approach. Likewise, the low politics arena

66

(trade, foreign aid and immigration) are characterized as responding more to a "domestic-variables" approach (Kissinger 1994 and Gourevitch 1996). Though, in this project these approaches are mostly utilized as the principle foundation for the development of my issue areas methodology (see chapter 3). Additionally, Dodd's (1986) transformative approach is employed to showcase the "ebb and flow" of the president's ability to "securitize" policies as a function of both the unit level endogenous conditions (presidential-congressional relations) among the issue areas and the exogenous structuring forces of historical context (the political environment as determined by political time). Furthermore, in this effort, rational choice assumptions about self-directed behavior in institutions are imported regarding the impetus to "securitize" in the first place (from Mayhew 1974, Fenno 1973 and Dodd 1977).

Finally, the "theoretical" relationship between the "securitization" of issues can be "mapped out" along a continuum of high to low politics arenas which include those that are already "security" (essentially, the politics of war and peace) in nature to those increasingly reflective of "intermestic" (the politics of everything else) policy making. As Figures 2-2—2-5 display, the high politics arenas' issue areas are arrayed in order of proximity to the presidency's opportunity structure in national security. This includes national and domestic security as well as diplomacy where the president is most institutionally empowered to set the agenda and control it. Furthermore, there is an internal hierarchy where the closer the issue area is to the security opportunity structure (i.e., national security) the *most* likely it is to be securitized (see Figures 2-2 and 2-4—2-5).

Meanwhile in the low politics arena which includes the following issue areas trade, foreign aid and immigration are arrayed along a continuum of increasing domestic composition (hence, these issue areas are ever more intermestic in their general orientation). Figure 2-4 shows that the Congress will play a more proactive role in its foreign policy relationship with the presidency the more intermestic the general orientation of the foreign policy issue area (Manning 1977; Conley 1997). Running along that continuum we see that there is a hierarchy like that observed amidst the high politics issue arena though in this sense the more intermestic the issue area (i.e., immigration) the *less* likely the president is able to securitize (see Figure 2-2). Now, we will examine the larger methodological-theoretical approach which complements the multiple presidencies thesis. This approach was initially introduced in part II of the literature review and serves as a synthesis between the state-centered and domestic variables techniques of US foreign policy examination—*issue areas analysis*.

Issue Areas Analysis

The issue areas approach does two things, on a theoretical level it suggests that the Aristotelian "Golden Mean" between statist and domestic variables approaches is found in their *joint applicability as a function of time and space regarding the specific issue areas of foreign policy and the temporal period in question*. Secondly, from a purely methodological perspective this approach produces models that account for the *inherent nuances of foreign policy construction behavior by dealing with them in a disaggregated manner*. Collectively, by breaking foreign policy up into its distinct "issue areas" national security, domestic security, diplomacy, trade, foreign aid and immigration as well as looking at "mixed categories" we can see those inherent nuances of foreign policy making come to empirical light. Furthermore by looking for within category differences according to the traditional "opportunity structures" of power, security orientations for statist formulations and domestic orientations for domestic variables approaches we may be able to ascertain the true "nature" of foreign affairs activities.[3]

As has been shown in the previous literature review, statist approaches seem to have their best applicability in the realm of security politics. The reason for this is three-fold; first, the American separation of powers system with its division of responsibilities for policy construction gives to the president and the Executive Branch more generally a prominent if not pre-eminent role in foreign policy construction (See Hamilton [1787] *Federalist 70* in Rossiter 1965). However, the concept of "checks and balances" led to the establishment of a constitutional system of "separate institutions sharing powers" (see Neustadt [1960] 1990). Since the Senate is constitutionally mandated a role in foreign policy construction and the House of Representatives has the power of initiation for spending bills, the president has in fact never "dominated" all aspects of foreign affairs except one—the war power and to a lesser extent security policies in general. As Vessey (1987) stated, "Congress may have the power to declare war but presidents make war."

---

[3] See the State-Centrism and Domestic Variables sections for evidence supporting this notion of "opportunity structures." For a more detailed account of the utility for opportunity structure analyses see the Comparative and American Political Development literature especially Orren and Skowronek 2002.

Perhaps it is the prevalence of high politics over low politics in mainstream US foreign policy research that developed during the Cold War which led to the conclusion that presidents dominated foreign policy writ large. Therefore, with such a predilection the incorporation of such models as the rational actor, deterrence theory and psychological based leadership decision making became the "standard" for foreign policy research. Or, perhaps it was due to the requirements of positivistic behaviorally and rational choice oriented social science's call for parsimony. Nevertheless, it is not surprising that such theories and methods have had difficulty accounting for "low politics" in foreign policy activities. This is especially true as there has been a rise in the saliency of such issues emanating out of "low politics" among both the lay and the academic communities since the end of the Cold War (and many would say before—Keohane and Nye 1977).

Therefore, with the rise of low politics we also have the commensurate rise of the domestic variables approach as its wider theoretical and methodological lenses have reached out to the various "domestic communities" influencing or being influenced by world politics (Wittkopf and McCormick in Wittkopf & McCormick 1999). In a world that is increasingly interdependent as was displayed in glaring detail by the 1970's era "oil shocks," even superpower security was shown that it could be threatened in a "non-security way" (Keohane and Nye 1977). The stress on adjacent over central decision makers has brought more and more groups and individuals into the foreign policy environment at the expanse of parsimony in methods (and theory for that matter). Unfortunately, at least among some in the foreign policy research community this has led to scholars over looking the very real fact that like it or not high politics still matters.

The strongest utility for an issue areas approach is in its applicability to examine American foreign policy in the widest way possible but still be attendant to the nuances within such policy construction and execution. By assuming that low politics is the purview of the domestic variables approach and high politics the central concern of the statist approach due to historic, political and economic opportunity structures. Then, using these two as methods prescription devices in tandem rather than at paradigmatic "poles" provides the most parsimonious yet encompassing method to analyze US foreign policy from an empirical perspective.

Discussion

This section of the chapter calls the reader's attention to some empirical work that provides at least a glimpse at the complexities of the executive-legislative foreign policy making divide and the possibilities for my theoretical accounting of these empirical referents. Stemming from my current research, I have some empirical referents to report which, while merely suggestive of the utility for a multiple presidencies conception of executive-legislative foreign relations policy making, have some warrant for supporting the continuance of this research project.

First, I have found a significant diversity within presidential position roll call voting in both houses of the Congress, though the Senate seems to be more proactive probably due to its greater constitutional role regarding foreign affairs. For example, in Eisenhower's first year in office (1953) he won all 7 of the foreign policy votes he took a position on in the 83rd Congress' House of Representatives—2 of the votes were security, 2 securitized foreign aid, 1 conventional foreign aid vote and 1 on immigration. In the Senate, Ike took 18 roll call positions in 1953 on foreign policy matters and won 13 of them—7 votes occurred on domestic security issues, 1 on immigration, 2 on diplomacy, 4 on trade, 3 on security proper and 2 on securitized foreign aid. Eisenhower's losses occurred on 4 of the domestic security issues and 1 of the trade votes. Eisenhower's victories in both the House and the Senate reflect a securitizing-domesticating dynamic between the president and the Congress. In the arena where Eisenhower loses the most (domestic security) it is due to Senators being more "hawkish" on Cold War issues than Eisenhower was himself (this is after all the height of McCarthyism) and the trade vote was a Senate resolution to call for the restricting of presidential authority in negotiating executive agreements—hence, an early attempt at senatorial resumption of trade authority long before the "Era of Congressional Resurgence" popularized by James Sundquist (1981).

As a final example, the president receives his lowest support threshold among his first five House position votes on an immigration issue (the Refugee Act) which was "sold" as a "security" issue by Eisenhower surrogates (see debates in CQ Almanac 1953 edition). Even in the height of the Cold War an issue like immigration with its inherent intermestic overtures made its potential for "securitization" an uphill battle to begin with. This is quite telling as an empirical referent for the multiple presidencies.

As a final area for theoretical potential, I have found some anecdotal evidence that supports the possibility of a periodization scheme for executive-legislative "orders." Other research has shown that differential "policy making environments" have appeared and then been summarily displaced across time. For instance, Conley (2003) found that the character of divided government faced by presidents since the time of Reagan has been substantially more partisan in character than previous periods of divided government. The *bipartisan* context of congressional relations in the Eisenhower presidency serves as a counterpoint, or historical anomaly. Similarly, Bond and Fleisher (in Bond and Fleisher 2000) suggest an even more expansive degree of "polarized politics" virtually nullifying the bi-partisan coalitions both within the Congress and between the president and the Congress over the last two decades. This can be seen as evidence for the fall of an era of "consensus politics" and the emergence of an era of "confrontational politics." Finally, some scholarship has shown that there is an ongoing ebb and flow between the president and Congress and it has persisted since the start of the republic (Dodd in Dodd and Oppenheimer 1977).

As for my current research, I have some qualitative evidence garnered from my content analysis of congressional roll calls which shows an increase in congressional challenge of presidential foreign policy making during the late 1960s. Furthermore, review of the legislative histories on a number of these votes in foreign aid, national and domestic security (all dealing directly or indirectly with the Vietnam War) indicates an increasing reluctance by the members of the Congress to trust the initiatives of the Johnson administration. It also is indicative of the responses by congressmen and senators to their constituencies, for this level of activity corresponds to declining poll numbers regarding support for the war and the Johnson administration more broadly.

These accounts can be taken as generally descriptive evidence of a significant change in the nature of the executive-legislative foreign affairs policy making relationship, which suggests support for at least part of my proposed periodization scheme for such inter-institutional relations. Future research will have to deal with this material in a more systematic manner, as my current study is aimed at assessing the foreign affairs relationship between the president and the Congress utilizing roll calls as the primary unit of analysis. From that then the primary dependent variable of interest to this study is the presidential success rate on foreign policy position votes within the Congress.[4]

From a more quantitatively oriented perspective, I have found some additional corroborating evidence. Something decisive occurred in the early 1970's relative to presidential-congressional relations at least as far as those relations is subject to measurement by roll call

---

[4] See Chapter 4 for more on this subject.

analysis. A cursory review of the average foreign policy success rate across individual presidencies (see Table 2-1) indicates that the Eisenhower through Nixon administrations' success rate was a robust 82%. The success rate for the Ford through W. Bush administrations was a significantly reduced 69%. Re-calculating the scores by (1) removing Nixon from the earlier group in order to remove the effects of Watergate and (2) removing W. Bush from the later group to hold constant any 9/11 impacts reveals that presidential success in foreign policy drops to 66%. Finally, adding Nixon to the later group with first W. Bush included and then removed leads to only modest increases in the overall foreign policy success rates for presidents (70.1% in the first case and 67.8% in the second case).

In sum, this suggests that around the time of the start of Nixon's second term (1973) the fundamental relationship between the executive and the legislature altered irrevocably. In fact, there is a drop in the rate of presidential success in foreign affairs that begins from a high of 93% in 1969 to a low of 59% during 1974, when Nixon resigned[5]. Finally, this decline is most present in Nixon's re-election year (1972, success rate=70%) and his second term (1973, success rate=60%). It needs to be stated that this high level of variation occurs entirely under conditions of divided government and Nixon's electoral mandate was actually higher in his second term (60.8% of the popular vote) than in his first term (he only defeated the Democratic nominee Humphrey by .01% of the popular vote) when his foreign policy success rate was at its height.

Previous explanations that discuss cultural alterations to the political environment (Wildavsky and Oldfield 1989 or Peppers 1975) do not specifically address the role of the Congress itself in the decline of presidential foreign affairs success rates. And, those explanations that do assert a role to Congress do so in such a manner as to make the condition of the Congress determinant on presidential success itself (Bond and Fleisher 1988 and 1990). In both cases, some empirical referents are missing and hence any reasonable way to develop an all-encompassing theory of presidential-congressional relations in foreign policy. First, the president himself is missing as an empirical actor with independent agency potential, especially regarding "issue framing" and general agenda setting as the modern legislative president that he is.[6] Second, "context-alteration" is not the same as "context-dependency" and the "cultural two

---

[5] See Nixon Table (Tables 5-28 and 6-13) for individuated foreign policy success scores as well as by issue area.

[6] See Clinton Rossiter (1956) *The Constitutional Dictator* for a classic treatment of the rise and impact of the legislative presidency.

presidencies" school of thought seems to have conflated those. If it was true that the aftermath of Vietnam and Watergate so altered the existing relationship between the president and the Congress in foreign policy we would not find success rate averages that are still far above the 50% threshold. Also, if it were true that it is all about congressional "conditions" like the existence and even type of divided government then we would see greater variance in the foreign policy success rate averages due to the persistence of the divided government condition since the start of our time frame (1953). In fact, the general conditions point to relative stasis in presidential success rates in foreign policy with the exception of the "dynamic drop" in the average starting in the early 1970's and the possibility of even more nuanced changes which I will deal with in later chapters.

Summary

This chapter has offered an alternative theory called the *multiple presidencies thesis* re-interpreting the first of the two presidencies governing executive-legislative foreign policy making. I argue that there are multiplicities of inter-institutional relations within foreign policy's component issue areas of national security, domestic security, diplomacy, trade, foreign aid and immigration. These sets of relationships are also a reflection of the historical context that they are found in referred to as "political time." Furthermore, I suggest that those relations are contingent on the ability of the president to successfully "securitize" issues relative to the Congress. Juxtaposed against this activity of presidential agency, the Congress is engaged in an ongoing process of "domestication," wherein, the members of Congress as individuals and groups attempt to re-orient foreign policy issue areas in such a way as to favor their own unit level "opportunity structure" in domestic affairs. Finally, the arrangement of the issue areas themselves reflect their existence within larger "arenas of politics," wherein high politics issue areas like national and domestic security as well as diplomacy are more given to presidentialization/securitization. Likewise, low politics issue areas like trade, foreign aid and immigration are by their nature closer to domestic politics due to their high level of intermestic character (the mixing of foreign and domestic politics in a single issue). Their increased intermestic nature makes them more subject to the processes of congressionalization/domestication.

This phenomenon is given to a certain "ebb and flow" throughout time and within policy domains, which then allows for a re-working of the executive-legislative foreign policy relationship into a series of overarching orders that has guided those inter-institutional relations since the start of the Post War Era (1953-2004). Also, periods of dynamic change do occur wherein one order of presidential-congressional foreign policy construction falls and is summarily displaced by a new such constituted order. And, now in the next chapter I will detail the corresponding methodology that carries the theoretical nuances of the multiple presidencies into the conduct of inquiry itself. I conduct this effort by offering a methodological synthesis of the statist and domestic variables approaches to understanding US foreign policy making as an *issue areas analysis*. I believe that this synthesis shows the best promise as a tool for finding the "empirically nuanced trees within the American foreign policy forest."

Figure 2-1. Path Diagram of Presidential Policy "Securitization" Relative to Congress

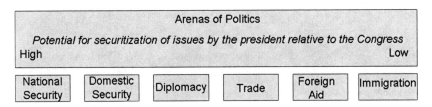

Figure 2-2. The Mapping of "Securitization" Potential for Policies on a Continuum of Foreign
Policy "Issue Areas"

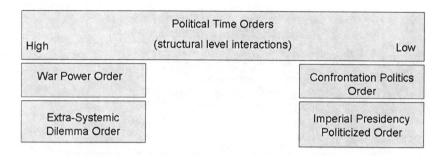

Figure 2-3. Political Time Orders (Structural Level Interactions)

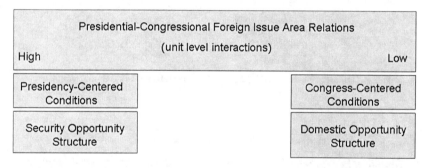

Figure 2-4. Presidential-Congressional Foreign Issue Area Relations (Unit Level Interactions)

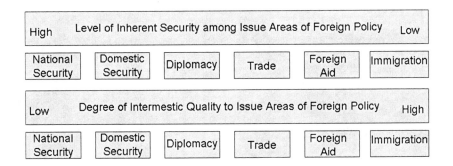

Figure 2-5. Level of Inherent Security and Degree of Intermestic Quality in Issue Areas of
Foreign Policy

Table 2-1. Average Presidential Success Rates by Presidency on Foreign Policy Position Votes

DDE	.80
JFK	.89
LBJ	.82
RMN	.77
GRF	.64
JEC	.79
RWR	.69
GB	.56
WJC	.62
GWB	.84

CHAPTER 3
AN ISSUE AREAS ANALYSIS OF AMERICAN FOREIGN POLICY: A SYNTHESIS OF STATIST AND DOMESTIC VARIBALES "APPROACHES"

Introduction

In this chapter, I map out the contours of an issue areas analysis by placing it within its proper theoretical frame, prescribing the appropriate secondary methodologies which are necessary for testing the properties of the multiple presidencies thesis through longitudinal and cross-sectional means. Then, I will operationalize the dependent and independent variables of interest along two dimensions including presidency-centered and Congress-centered conditions in order to capture as much of the "within case as well as without case" variance as possible. What I mean by this is that the variables will perform a dual function by being able to measure *longitudinal* and *cross-sectional* patterns of presidential-congressional policy making. This will allow for the maintenance of parsimony throughout the empirical tests of the hypotheses emanating out of the multiple presidencies thesis. Finally, we will engage in a discussion about the future potential for this line of methodological inquiry at least as far as the possibilities of the multiple presidencies thesis allow us.

I believe that the issue areas analysis serves as a dynamic alternative to the more static statist and domestic variables approaches by casting a specific light on the inherent nuances of foreign policy construction. By filling this theoretical and empirical gap in the extant literature the issue areas analysis will help bring a rigor and multifaceted characteristic to foreign policy research that has previously been neglected in standard accounts. This form of rigorous analysis already exists in the study of US domestic policy. However such studies' methods are difficult to translate into the foreign policy research agenda because they do not account for foreign policy's "uniqueness" relative to those who study the "politics within as opposed to from without the waters' edge[1]." Specifically, this methodology measures the *central empirical hypotheses* that statist approaches have their greatest applicability in understanding the "high politics" of war and peace. Meanwhile, the domestic variables approach is superior for discerning the "low politics" of economy and society.

---

[1] Taken from Snow and Brown's (1999) *Beyond the Water's Edge: An Introduction to US Foreign Policy* St. Martin's Press: NY, NY.

Given the precepts of the multiple presidencies thesis, certain other secondary hypotheses present themselves for empirical testing. In this study, I will test some of the most profound of these statements based around the twin notions of an ongoing interaction between unit and structural level factors regarding the foreign policy divide between the president and the Congress throughout the Post War Era (1953-2004). Regarding presidential-congressional foreign policy construction, presidents tend to dominate the construction of issue area policies in the realms of national and domestic security as well as diplomacy, while other issue areas of foreign policy such as trade, foreign aid and immigration are more the province of a domestically dominant Congress. Additionally, these coming directly out of the multiple presidencies theory itself are notions that as the Cold War receded into the past the president lost power to successfully "securitize" issue areas outside of the high politics realm. Also, the Congress has become increasingly involved in the activities of high politics by "domesticating them" while continuing and even increasing its institutional dominance over the low politics issue arenas of economy and society. Finally, if it is true that the issue areas of foreign policy can be successfully arrayed along a spatial-dimension capturing their general locations as to the high and low politics arenas then it is true that differential levels of presidential success can be discerned as well as position taking itself. In fact, we can predict that presidents will take more positions in the high politics arenas relative to the low politics ones and will have significantly higher levels of success. Additionally, if it is also true that we can array those same issue areas along a spatial-dimension that captures their specific proximity to presidentialization/securitization and congressionalization/domestication (see Figure 2-2) then we can assert that presidential position taking as well as success rates are a function of the issue area's position along that continuum. These manifestations of issue area "location" can be interpreted from a presidentialist perspective as running from most to least securitized in potential (in other words, as the issue areas are arrayed by proximity to the president's security opportunity structure). Or, alternatively those same issue areas can be seen from a congressionalist perspective as moving from least to most in their potential for domestication (in other words, the issue areas can be seen as increasing in their intermestic composition as they move closer to the Congress's domestic opportunity structure). Therefore, presidents will take more positions and exhibit higher success rates among the issue areas most proximate to security (national security, domestic security and diplomacy). Finally, presidential success and position

80

taking will be less prevalent among the issue areas most removed from security and hence the most subject to routine congressionalization or in other words, domestication (those foreign issue areas that are by nature more intermestic).

A more specific hypothesis deals with the issue area of trade which potentially seems to represent somewhat of an outlier as popular notions support presidentialization of this normally low politics issue area. Presidential dominance of this issue area as a result of the Trade Act of 1934 was sold to the Congress as an "economic security issue" by FDR but this is only a period-specific account. Louis Fisher (2002) offers a more longitudinally oriented explanation by suggesting that congressional deference continued after the global "crisis" of the Great Depression as a by-product of Cold War necessities. However, the Congress has become increasingly active in this issue area since the end of the Cold War perhaps indicative of a change regarding the connection of trade to "high politics" with its return to a "low politics" issue area and hence congressional involvement. Of course, empirical validation is necessary for any of these contentions to be seen as systematically legitimate and the empirical chapters (4-7) will deal with this dilemma. For our purposes right now, we need to turn the discussion over to a methods-theory grounding by examining each in turn, the statist/state-centrist, domestic variables and finally the issue areas alternative as methodological frames for this and other foreign policy studies, especially those dealing with executive-legislative relations.

Issue Areas Methodology: A Transformative Historical-Institutional Analysis

The multiple presidencies thesis employs a type of transformative historical-institutional analysis applying it to executive-legislative foreign policy relations during the Post War Era (since 1953 in this study). Empirically, this type of study couches the presidential-congressional divide in foreign policy within two levels of analysis (the unit and the structural). This is done to account for within as well as across case stasis and dynamism simultaneously. Additionally, it accounts for the role of "political time" by suggesting that orders of executive-legislative relations rise remain and ultimately fall as the very political environment faced by the unit level actors in foreign policy evolves gradually or suddenly. The usage of the term "issue areas analysis" should be interpreted as a type of method from within a larger paradigmatic frame associated with the "New Institutionalist" approach to American politics. In utilizing that approach, I test a number of hypotheses relating to the role of both the structural (systemic) and unit (presidential-congressional) levels of analyses' impacts on presidential-congressional

81

international policy relations. I do this to measure the environmental impacts of historical and economic conditions across political time at the structural level of analysis (the political environment itself) with longitudinal study. Also, I look at the within political time effects on the units themselves' (the presidency and the Congress) using cross-sectional study of specifically political factors including popular, electoral and partisan/ideological forces. However, before introducing such things I must first answer the next logical question, "How to operationalize the variables of interest themselves?"

Fortunately, some of the groundwork has already been laid by previous research on related topics (particularly those emanating out of the two presidencies thesis). Since, 1953 the editors of the annual editions of the *Congressional Quarterly Almanac* have recorded roll call votes on policies/issues in which the president has taken a position. Furthermore, the *CQ Almanacs* have listed these votes by policy domain (foreign or domestic). Additionally, researchers have used these votes to develop either aggregate or individual level "success/support scores" in the perspective domains (i.e., Wildavsky 1966).

At this point some commentary is necessary regarding the employment of success versus support scores. First, the two scores derive from the same unit of analysis which is the roll call votes themselves but after that there is a wide divergence in their look and application. So much so, that it has been suggested as revealed in the introduction's critical literature review that differential impacts have been observed as the "level" of presidential success v. support. Second, the success scores are aggregate level scores as opposed to the support scores which are done at the individual level of analysis. The success scores are the victory percentages of presidents across all or some subset of position votes within the Congress. The sub-sets can be derived by using annualized, aggregated or within as well as across presidencies success scores. Another way of sub-dividing the data to achieve success scores is to develop "cut-points" for data inclusion which can be as arbitrary as a threshold for passage like excluding unanimous or near unanimous votes from one's analysis thus concentrating on contentious or close votes (Bond and Fleisher 1990 and Conley 1997). Another way is to utilize Congressional Quarterly's own method of vote division by restricting your data set to their "key votes" on important legislative issues (though you have to further discount the ones that are not position votes which restricts the size of your data set even further) (Sigelman 1979). Coming off CQ's method, you can create your own sub-sets of relevant position votes utilizing the divisions they keep by policy domain itself. Moving beyond the confines of CQ, you can utilize previous coding rules for deciding which votes are important versus which ones are not. A classic though now dated approach is to utilize William Riker's (1962) definition of an "important vote" as measured by the size of the minimum winning coalition necessary for passage. Or, a more recent effort by David Mayhew (1986) defines votes according to their relevance to the creation of "significant laws," this approach has been utilized in conjunction with another whereby you take the "last vote" as the significant vote for inclusion in your data set.

There are a number of problems with all of the data collection schemes ranging from their lack of comparability, to their lack of generalizability regarding the picture that they present for presidential-congressional relations and most important of all the fact that they reduce the population of presidential position votes down to samples.[2] Normally, this is par for the course, as seen in survey research because the population of anything is normally too large to adequately account for it in a single empirical study. However, in foreign affairs this is not the case. In fact, if you excessively utilize any of these data generating schemes what in fact you are doing is privileging the results of your study regarding some central facet like "significant laws" or "important/close votes." The entire population of foreign policy position votes between 1953 and 2004 is approximately 3300. While this seems high, painstaking content analysis of them is possible and in fact this is what I have done. This widens the lens of research so that the picture taken becomes a widescreen movie wherein presidential-congressional foreign policy relations can "play out across time."

The third feature of roll call voting as a primary means of analyzing the executive-legislative divide is the usage of the support score as an alternative to the success score as an indicator of presidential *influence* in what is generally seen as a *legislative arena* (Bond and Fleisher 1990). The support scores are gathered by finding the percentage of legislators supporting the same position as the president on each of the roll call votes. Then, usually some means of reducing the size of the data set is employed in a similar fashion as has already been detailed but in the case of support scores often the average support score rather than each score is what is used as the dependent variable. This of course produces the problem of the ecological fallacy as first pointed out in the literature review from the introductory chapter. Additional,

---

[2] See Literature Review Part I of the two presidencies thesis for more on these matters.

criticisms already detailed in the literature review have to do with the support scores' inborn bias toward congress-centered outcomes, its existence as a measure of support not success and its ultimately in-direct measure of presidential-congressional relations. The literature contrasting success v. support scores suggests that success scores generally tend to be higher and are not as subject to as much volatility both within and across presidencies (Shull and Shaw 1999). This same body of studies has also concluded that the success score tends to not be as subject to declination again both within and across presidencies (Edwards 1986). The principle reason for this is that the scores are generally lower and have less of a space within which to "fall" (Shull and Shaw 1999). Lastly, support scores are individual indicators of presidential support and to a lesser extent influence while success scores are aggregate factors providing an empiric for presidential success but not necessarily legislative support (Ragsdale 1998). In sum, I feel that the best dependent variable of interest for any study of presidential-congressional relations in foreign policy is the one which contains the most nuances within while capturing the widest scope from without. That is the success score, not the support score. The success score is presidentially oriented, measures success not support, and because of its aggregate nature allows for standard statistical procedures which limit the amount of variable transformations and hence holds model variance in check. Of course, it is also true that Wildavsky (1966) employed success not support scores as his dependent variable. Thus, studies which attempt to build on that original work should keep the success score for comparative-hypothesis reasons if nothing else. Finally, foreign affairs is the historic domain of presidential power at least in the time span of this study and as a measure the presidential success rate is the best indicator possible in order to capture this domain's uniqueness within the executive-legislative policy framework.

Finally the fourth feature of roll calls as a unit of analysis for presidential-congressional policy making has been seen in that, some later researchers have broken apart the domains into "sub-domains" or "issue areas." These researchers then developed new scores reflecting that effort (e.g., Conley 1997, Ragsdale 1998). Conley's (1997) effort utilized the notion of intermestic composition among issues that cross foreign and domestic affairs boundaries but limited it in practice. Ragsdale's (1998) systematic coding of support and congruence (success to us) across seven issue areas including four (security, trade, foreign aid and immigration—which she treats as a domestic issue area) is certainly the most developed treatment to date regarding issue areas analysis. However, Ragsdale (1998) lacks any theory to properly account for the differential patterns that she describes. Overall, the level of sophistication devoted to these "nuanced coding schemes" has been limited. Therefore I offer an alternative.

For ease, comparative research and the reasons I laid out previously I will utilize the "success score" method for operationalization purposes. However, I propose doing it more systematically and hopefully more objectively. Also, due to the "institutional" nature of the study as well as my previous commentary regarding this issue I will operate at the aggregate level of analysis as far as the roll call votes are concerned. I fundamentally believe it is a better "expression" of inter-institutional relations whereas individual level analyses on this subject test the actors within the institutions and not the institutions themselves. I believe evidence for that exists gathered from my critical literature review of the two presidencies thesis (see Literature Review) within notions of a "partisan two presidencies." The reader will remember that all of those studies were conducted at the individual level of analysis, whereas the institutional two presidencies was associated with aggregate level data. In my opinion then, previous comparisons of these groups of analyses by past researchers are open to being challenged as committing the "ecological fallacy." This methodological fallacy is built around the notion of making individual conclusions (like presidential support scores) from aggregate level data (like that used in presidential success scores) (Mannheim and Rich 1995). By remaining true to the aggregate level at least as far as the longitudinal analysis is concerned I will avoid this methodological "trap" (Mannheim and Rich 1995). What follows is the step-by-step plan of action that was utilized to test the various hypotheses related to the multiple presidencies thesis.

Data Gathering and Operationalization

First, I did a content analysis of the foreign policy presidential position votes themselves as recorded by CQ from 1953-2004. This was a huge undertaking that produced a data set which is as complete as is possible regarding this policy domain. Additionally, it covers the extant time frame in its *entirety* and allows for a true *population based analysis rather than a sample based one*. As previously stated, there are no less than 3300 data points listed in chronological order by day, month and year. Each vote is coded for presidential term, relevant Congress, legislative session, presidential position, presidential position outcome, vote outcome, number of yeas and number of nays. Furthermore, each vote accounts for the total number of partisans voting yea or nay in both the major congressional parties (the Democrats and the Republicans), partisans voting with as well as against the president's position, the presence or lack of regional/ideological coalitions in voting for or against a president's position as recorded by CQ. The coalitions recorded are the Conservative Coalition of Southern Democrats and Republicans as well as the Liberal Coalition of Northern Democrats and Republicans. In both cases, I also recorded whether or not the respective coalition's position triumphed on the vote.

At this point, I need to make a clarification regarding the coding of the Liberal Coalition. CQ never recorded the Liberal Coalition as I utilize the term. What the organization did was record an "anti-conservative coalition" from amongst the individual MC votes. The problem with using its data on this point is that it does not work well for aggregating purposes and it is not the traditional scholarly accepted definition of the Liberal Coalition as "the coalition of Northern Democrats with Republicans known to manifest itself along social issues in domestic affairs and foreign aid as well as immigration (at least in the past) within foreign policy" (Burns 1963). What CQ did record and which I could use was from 1958-1988 it recorded the "democratic-split votes" where the congressional Democratic Party split between its Northern and Southern wings (*CQ Almanac* 1958). Within those votes, the ones that were not also recorded as the Conservative Coalition were by default the Liberal Coalition. I then replicated the methodology for inclusion of cross-party coalition (when a majority of one intra-party faction votes with the majority of another intra-party faction (from *CQ Almanac* 1997, Appendix A; see also Bond and Fleisher 1990) for all votes from 1989-2004 in order to get a coherent set of coalition votes.

I coded each foreign policy vote along the dimension of issue areas discussed in chapter 2 from national security to immigration (see Figure 2-2). I quantified the foreign issue areas concept by developing a rank ordinal variable which utilized the presidentialized/securitized concept as its ordering principle. Issue areas that are most prone to being presidentialized/securitized can be said to be of the "highest natural ordering." What that means is that the issue area with the highest "value" on this scale is the one that is the most prone to being successfully presidentialized/securitized, in other words national security affairs. Also, issue areas that are least given to this process are of the "lowest natural ordering." For our purposes that means the most intermestic and hence congressionalized/domesticated issue area serves as the baseline for the variable's operationalization—immigration =0. The remaining categories then are presented in hierarchical order as: foreign aid=1, trade=2, diplomacy=3, domestic security=4 and national security=5. It needs to be remembered that this coding scheme is meant to capture the issue area's position relative to the historic domain of presidential

86

power—national security. Therefore, trade in practice is closer to the high politics arena than the other issue areas of foreign policy. Trade is fundamental to peace and often a precursor to war; it is fed by and in turn feeds the processes of security and diplomacy. Additionally, since the Trade Act of 1934, trade power has been largely *legislatively delegated* to the executive branch. According to Lindsay (1994), congressional resurgence of trade prerogatives did not occur until well into the Ford administration.

I also developed a coding scheme for mixed category votes where I took the mean of the two issue area values as the new value for the mixed category in question. Next, I looked at each vote and qualitatively reported its title, final result and type. Then, I created another rank ordinal variable which captured the inherent nuance that *"not all votes are the same in their qualitative impact."* For this purpose, I once again referenced the notion of presidentialization/securitization as my basic operating principle. Accordingly, votes that were least given to such activity, simple majority procedural votes (like a bill amendment), would serve as the baseline (0) and those most given to such a process, supermajority final votes (like a Constitutional Amendment) would receive a (3). Finally, those in the middle categories, majority final votes (like a bill passage/rejection) and supermajority procedural votes (like a vote to invoke cloture in the Senate or suspend the rules in the House) got a (1) and (2) respectively.

Another component of the data set was measures of partisanship and ideology that I included, especially to capture political effects. In order to examine the nuances within party control conditions, I established another rank ordinal variable again using the presidentialized/securitized condition as my operating principle. The variable is coded (0) for divided government when the Congress and the presidency are institutionally composed of different parties and (1) under split control government when the presidency and one branch of the national legislature are under the control of a single party. Lastly, the variable is coded as (2) in order to represent the condition of unified government when a single party controls both branches of the Congress and the presidency. This last condition provides the greatest party-centered orientation for presidential agency and even agenda setting in foreign affairs especially (from Shull 1997). Finally, I developed presidential success scores by annum out of the votes for foreign policy, the six issue areas and the mixed categories. These scores serve as the primary and secondary dependent variables for the study, upon which I conduct my hypothesis testing. The empirical models are specified as such to test the "contentions" of the multiple presidencies thesis at the unit and structural levels. The models do this by examining presidency-centered v. congress-centered "conditions" at each level of analysis. Simultaneously, they examine presidential success rates along three related but independent explanatory factors including macro-political, macro-economic and macro-historical contexts. Prior to specifying specific models, we need to first examine the variables themselves and the theoretical reasons behind their inclusion in this effort.

Dependent Variables

While I have already discussed the reasons for employing success over support scores as the primary and secondary dependent variables for this analysis, I have not discussed their division into first and second "tiers." Nor, have I explained the importance of the three "types" of outcome variables—foreign policy, issue area and mixed issue area as well as the usage of year for the baseline measure. It is to these issues that we now must turn.

The tracked annual foreign policy success score is the primary dependent variable of interest (the collection of annual presidential success scores on foreign policy votes from 1953-2004) for this study because it measures the widest scope of presidential "success" with the Congress regarding legislative productivity and especially outcomes. This variable is limited in its lack of capturing presidential influence over the legislative process until final outcomes. However, as Bond and Fleisher (1990) report if a researcher is studying presidential success and not support than there is no reason to worry about this limitation. Additionally, much of the legislative process is not only closed to public influence it is also closed to any external actor's potential for systematic influence due to wide disbursement of individual and group responsibility throughout including legislative initiation, committee/sub-committee activities, rule formation, position taking, logrolling, credit claiming and pork barrel legislating(Davidson and Oleszek 2006). Therefore, an analysis of outcomes rather than procedures is called for since this is the place where presidential agency is best recorded and in fact has been so by CQ for six decades now. The wide spread availability of this data and its base quantitative nature allow for the employment of statistical analysis in order to "tease out" readily identifiable empirical patterns.

I should make one final note about the nature of the annual foreign policy success score that I utilize which makes mine different from previous employments. In my case I have recalculated the annualized scores by including immigration as a foreign policy issue area.

Previous extant research that looks at the foreign policy success score does not include immigration as such an issue area, when used at all immigration is seen as an issue areas within domestic affairs not international relations (see Ragsdale 1998). I find this usage to be problematic at best because by excluding immigration but including trade within foreign policy you are probably not getting an accurate picture of intermestic characteristics within the foreign policy dimension. Finally, the exclusion of immigration has probably systematically inflated foreign policy success scores because of its highly domestic nature, the Congress has historically been very active in this issue area thus acquiescence to presidential "foreign policy prerogatives" has not been the norm (Gimpel and Edwards 1998).

The issue area and mixed issue area success scores were calculated by replicating the process for garnering the annualized foreign policy scores. This was done through finding the percentage of presidential "wins" on roll call position votes across the year for all years in the extant time frame 1953-2004. Thus, I have six issue area scores and where applicable mixed issue area scores for each year, these scores along with the aggregated foreign policy scores are included in the relevant tables differentiated throughout the empirical chapters (4-7). Together, these scores serve as the secondary dependent variables for this study within the cross-sectional aspect of this analysis. Additionally, these variables serve as explanatory factors in the longitudinal portion of the study. I will save discussion of basic trends within and across them for those chapters themselves and conclude this section with commentary on the employment of annualized as opposed to some other aggregation of "presidential success."

It may seem a bit arbitrary to locate presidential position vote success rates on a year-by-year basis since it is equally possible for other loci to be employed. For instance, why not utilize the bi-annual "congress" itself as the indicator, this certainly would increase the "n" especially for the issue area and mixed issue area scores. Also, it is conceivable to think of the presidential term or even an entire decade as an ordering principle for this kind of data. However, there is somewhat of an accepted norm among executive-legislative relations specialists as well as roll call analysts in general that the year is the best single indicator of presidential-congressional interaction (Shull and Shaw 1999). This being said, there are some profound methodological reasons for employing this measure including its ease for systematic time series analysis and its convenience as a regression outcome in cross-sectional study (Shull and Shaw 1999; Shull

1997). Now, we will engage in a more in-depth examination of the independent variables for this study.

Independent Variables

The explanatory variables of interest for this study measure macro-level characteristics of the internal and external political environment governing presidential-congressional foreign policy relations. These variables account for the political, economic and historical conditions which influence the day-to day as well as cross-time interactions between our national executive and legislative actors in American foreign policy. The political factors including public opinion, electoral, partisan and ideological forces provide evidence for the nuances of "power" directly impacting the institutions' proximity to one another on an issue-by-issue basis. The economic forces which are composed of national level measures for economic productivity/decline provide the underlying basis for presidential/congressional "agency" by establishing parameters for constraint. Finally, presidential/congressional "agency" is promoted by the overlying base conditions established through historical contexts. In other words, "agent-structures" are established indirectly by the historical-economic contexts that the unit level actors (the president and the Congress) find themselves in. Another way of thinking about this is that the economic conditions are establishing "agent-constraints," while the historical forces are providing for "agent-opportunities." In sum, these structures are in fact setting the static elements of foreign policy relations for the presidency and the Congress. Meanwhile, the more volatile political factors set the "agent-interaction processes" in a direct and far more dynamic fashion. It is among these factors that the daily "push and pull" of inter-institutional relations is seen rather than just felt. These factors capture the movement of presidential-congressional relations in foreign policy by tracking the "ebb and flow" of each "relational wave," however; the sea upon which these waves move is subject to the "tides" of the structural forces involved.

Beginning with the historical "structures," the major problem faced by any quantitative study is the restricted ability to capture temporal context itself. Previous research by both anecdotal and systematic analyzers has suggested that there are general ordering principles for American foreign policy history (Papp, Johnson and Endicott 2005). Both presidency as well as congressional researchers have developed periodization schemes, respectively, for the study of American national institutions. The goal has been to account for the development, stability and change in such institutions across time (i.e., Skowronek 1997 for the presidency and Stewart

90

2001 for the Congress). Finally, presidential-congressional relations itself have been subject to such periodizations (i.e., Lindsay 1994). However, these studies have employed a more Congress-centered perspective at the expense of a presidency-centered one. Furthermore, their degree of systematization is open to question as it is not robustly theorized at the level of the inter-institutional relationship itself (see Conley 2003 in Conley 2003; Lindsay 1994, Oldfield and Wildavsky 1989 as well as Malbin and Brookshire 2000). The periodization scheme I am using is a relatively accepted one within the literature at least as far as a broad view of American foreign policy is concerned. The early, late and post Cold Wars are accepted as the major environmental structures influencing the American state's interactions with the rest of the world both in the recent and distant past of the last fifty years (see Snow and Brown 1999). However, the 9/11 impact and recent development over the previous ten years to that time are not adequately reducible to a "post-Cold War" formulation and so I am treading new ground in this period of political time. Additionally, I have subsumed some elements of Davidson's (1996) periodization scheme regarding the ideological policy orientations of the Congress since the 1930's. Davidson's employment of conservative bipartisan (1938-1964), liberal partisan (1965-1978), post-reform (1979-1983) and conservative retrenchment periods (1984-present) is a profound systematization of not only congressional activities but also their ideological predilections. However, this theory does not adequately account for presidential agency in its scheme. Furthermore, despite Conley's (2002) updating through the lens of divided government foreign policy has not been exclusively examined in these periodized terms. Davidson's work does serve as an example of unit level systematization regarding the tracking of agency-behavior across time. It is from that perspective which I borrow his ideas. Replicating Conley's methodology from that work I have developed dummy variables to account for a synthesis of both the environmental setting (the Cold War and its Aftermath) with the agent-interactions (the presidential-congressional relationship) in US foreign policy construction. I code 1 for the presence of such an order including; the War Power Order (1953-1972), the Confrontation Politics Order (1973-1989), the Imperial Presidency Politicized Order (1990-2000) and the Extra-Systemic Dilemma Order (2001-present) as well as 0 for the lack thereof.

Furthermore, I attempt to account for another macro-historical condition which contains presidency-centered v. Congress-centered conditions-- the presence of war/peace. War is a phenomenon that lies at the heart of presidential power in foreign affairs, in fact, according to my

91

thesis it is the principle place of potential as well as realized presidentialized/securitized "power" in the executive-legislative divide. If war is such an empowering mechanism for presidential agency, then it is reasonable to expect that a systemic condition of "peace" serves the interests of the Congress often at the expense or at least the diminishing of presidential encroachment. Therefore, peace is a Congress-centered condition with certain expectations as to its influence of congressionalization/domestication of issue(s) within international relations. A final indicator emanating out of historical conditions is to be found in two related areas—the size of the armed forces on a year-by-year basis as well as the percentage of the federal budget dedicated to the Department of Defense (DoD). These of course are standard quantitative measures which do not require any transformations for asymptotic purposes.[3] These measures are indicative of the influence of the military-industrial complex in our society. They also suggest differential centering conditions for presidentialization/securitization and congressionalization/domestication of issue(s). When the size of the armed forces is high and a greater percentage of the budget is "given over" to the Department of Defense (DoD) then the environment is more favorable for presidential agency and vice versa.

Regarding the economic contexts of executive-legislative relations in foreign policy, I have gathered relatively standard macro-level indicators including the presence or absence of recovery/recessionary conditions as well as the size of the annual budget surplus/deficit. These two conditions work together to influence the amount of budgetary and general fiscal latitude allowed for policy making by both the president and the Congress. They also contain conditions which either constrain or provide opportunities for agency on either institution's behalf. For instance, recessions will be more negatively felt by presidents than by the Congress due to the influences of socio-tropic evaluations of the national economy on presidential elections and job approval ratings (Lewis-Beck 1989, Edwards 1980 and Fiorina 1981). Also, the Budget Reform and Impoundment Act of 1974 has brought the Congress "back in to the budget process" on a year-by-year basis being a central component to notions of both a resurgent as well as a redundant Congress in the foreign policy making process (Sundquist 1981 and Fisher 2000). Looking at recessions is difficult as there is a debate as to how to define them much less measure them. I employed the Department of Commerce's definition as being a "consecutive decline in

---

[3] Asymptotic relationships are direct linear correlations or associations between variables of interest like in ordinary least squares regression (OLS) models as an example.

Real Gross Domestic Product (GDP) for two quarters" (www.whitehouse.gov/doc 04-01-07).

Recognizing the difficulties of this definition I also included the period of "business cycle decline" as a proxy which along with the trough of the business cycle, the recession itself according to the Department of Commerce (DoC), would serve to represent "macro-economic recessionary conditions" as a whole (from Paterson 1993). I represented my combined measure as a dummy variable where 1 is indicative of recovery in the business cycle and 0 as recession. I operationalized in this manner for consistency sake with the project as a whole where I utilize notions of presidency-centered conditions as my base operating principle. The budgetary conditions variable has its own problems, in that it requires a log transformation in order to impose asymptotic properties within it for purposes of regression analysis. However, once accomplished it garners relatively easily interpretable findings. The percentage of Gross National Product (GNP) accounted for by trade as well as the percentage of the budget devoted to foreign aid programs are potential economic indicators of the level of presidential success and so are included as explanatory variables.

The political variables measure popular, electoral and partisan conditions which either favor or disfavor one or the other actors (the president or the Congress) in the foreign policy making endeavor. Public opinion has been shown to have differential effects relative to foreign policy construction with some concluding that it has an impact (Edwards 1980, Light 1983 and Page and Jordan 1993) while others suggest that no such influence is directly detectable (Bond and Fleisher 1990, Edwards 1989 and Almond 1950). Nevertheless, annual aggregate presidential public job approval ratings have been shown to have a direct and measurable impact on presidential roll call success (Edwards 1997). Light's (1983) work in particular is important to note since he concluded that public approval levels had differential impacts on presidential success by *issue area* which is something that Ragsdale and King (1989) also found. Therefore, I follow the examples of this previous research by incorporating the annual average presidential job approval rating (garnered by Gallup Polls and calculated by Ragsdale (1998) (1953-1997) as well as updated by me for 1998-2004) as a potential influencer on the international relations divide between the president and the Congress. While data limitations abound regarding the public opinion of the president's handling of foreign policy issues, some analysis is possible. From the *Hastings Polling Service*, I gathered data from 1975 on which shows public approval ratings of the president's handling of foreign policy as a domain specific activity. These data allow one to get past the Almond-Lippman thesis which has long suggested that the "public is largely unknowing and uncaring about politics, especially foreign affairs" (Almond 1950).

Electoral outcomes have the potential to influence the "internal environment" of presidential-congressional relations regarding the establishment of mandates or the lack thereof. High electoral conditions certainly favor the president, especially in an area of historic power like foreign affairs with the reverse being true among low electoral conditions. I utilized turnout rates in presidential as well as mid-term elections and the percentage victories for the president and his party in each (Dye 2007 and Boller 2006). Finally, I included a variable on Electoral College support in the most recent presidential election due to its notion as an "exaggerator of the winning candidate's performance in the election" (Edwards 2006 in Edwards 2006). Besides testing the obvious conditionality's involved, these variables also speak to the debate within the literature about the positive/negative effects of electoral support found in the mandate thesis (Gergen 1988), crisis re-election thesis (Huntington 1965), the decay curve thesis (Brace and Hinckley 1992), the coattails theses (Berelson et. al 1954 & Campbell et. al.1960) as well as the mid-term loss thesis (Fiorina 1981). Therefore, I have also developed dummy variables for "time in term" or proximity indicators including election years (both presidential and mid-term), first year of term, last year of term and first year after mid-terms (the third and seventh years). The basis for these is that the more proximate the president is to his election/re-election the more empowered he is for policy making in foreign policy in particular. Whereas, the more distal he is from that election or the more proximate to a mid-term election the less empowered he will be and hence the more emboldened the Congress in international relations.

I also look at partisan/ideological forces influencing the day-to-day foreign affairs relationship between the president and the Congress. I examine these forces by gathering data indicative of them including; the percentage of congressional seats held by the president's party in each session, the ideological rating by the Americans for Democratic Action (ADA) and the American Conservative Association/American Conservative Union (ACA/ACU) interest groups given to each president as well as both the percentage of party unity votes and partisan votes in the Congress he faces in both chambers per legislative session. Finally, the persistence of the Conservative and Liberal Coalitions as determinants in presidential position vote success/failure were also recorded as a measure of congressional ideology. Using the interest group ratings for presidents along with the CQ coalition voting may seem conflicting, however, studies have shown that these two rating systems roughly approximate one another and hence can be used simultaneously (see Bond and Fleisher 1990 & Poole and Rosenthal 1997). Likewise partisan voting and party unity scores track one another at least as far as previous trends analyses have shown; however there are some limitations with relying exclusively on party unity scores due to data gaps (Jacobson in Dodd and Oppenheimer 2005). As a final commentary on this topic, Jacobson (2006 in Edwards 2006) has discerned that partisanship as well as party unity voting has become closer in their ties to presidential support among roll call votes. However, this does not suggest a correlation with the success score itself which begs for a needed hypothesis test which I do in this study, albeit through the issue areas framework.

Additionally, in order to capture the ongoing influence of the opportunity structures at play in executive-legislative foreign policy relations I have coded for the presence/lack of securitization and domestication for each vote in the data set. I developed this measure from my content analysis of the individual roll calls themselves by looking at their vote summaries and determining if the issue covered within the vote had security or domestic aspects to it. I then created two dummy variables to capture these tendencies within the various issue area votes with the default (0) being the lack of their presence in both and (1) for its presence. I operationalized two other dummy variables to measure the presence or lack of securitization and domestication amongst the mixed issue area votes using the same operating principles. After reviewing these sets of variables, we must turn our attention to model specification issues.

Structural Level Models Testing Across Political Time

The structural level models will employ a time-series formulation with the dependent variable as the tracked annual presidential success rate in foreign and issue area affairs explained as a function of a *first order autoregressive trend* from the *base year of 2004* to the *origination year in 1953*. In other words, I will do a univariate regression of each annual presidential success score in foreign policy (the dependent-dependent variable) against the previous year's success score (the independent-dependent variable) in a time-sequential fashion from 2004 back to 1953. An *un-standardized ordinary least squares (OLS) longitudinal regression model* will look at the impacts of the proposed "orders" of executive-legislative relations on the success rate. Additionally, other *macro-level historical* conditions will be tested in another ordinary least squares (OLS) longitudinal model in order to discern the individual patterns of those relations as the opportunity structures are impacted by historical-contextual alteration. Also, another structural based ordinary least squares (OLS) model will employ various *macro-economic* variables in order to test the role of prevailing economic conditions on the executive-legislative foreign issue area relationship. Finally, the *securitization versus domestication phenomenon* is tested by another longitudinal ordinary least squares (OLS) regression on the presidential foreign issue area success rate.

Unit Level Models Testing Within Political Time

At the unit level, the presidential issue area/mixed issue area success rates are tested by using them as dependent variables in empirical models including individual differencing tests for presidencies within orders and aggregate differencing tests across orders. Next, simple *multivariate cross-sectional regression models* are specified in order to test the impacts of specifically *macro-level political* variables on the presidential-congressional foreign issue area divide. As previously discussed the political variables come in three distinct forms with each capturing a different aspect of the political forces at play in the executive-legislative foreign issue area relationship.

First the *popular determinants* measure the role, if any, of public opinion as an *external force* on presidential foreign issue area success vis-à-vis the Congress. And second, the *electoral determinants* operationalize the role played by voting outcomes as *setting conditions for policy making opportunities/constraints*. These are derived from American national presidential and mid-term elections. Finally third, the *partisan and ideological determinants* showcase the *internal forces* driving presidential-congressional interactions along the issue areas of foreign policy. Before laying out the map for how the empirical chapters will be presented, I must first discuss the major and minor hypotheses which the methods will test.

Hypotheses

As was previously discussed, the central hypotheses related to the development of the multiple presidencies thesis as an empirical theory of presidential-congressional relations in foreign policy suggest that differential issue area relationships exist. Furthermore, that those relationships are governed by the static forces of the political environment itself as well as the dynamic forces of the unit level factors involved. Accordingly, the primary hypothesis of concern to us is that *presidential power in foreign policy is a function of his primary opportunity structure which lies with security affairs*. A related hypothesis is that *congressional power in international relations is a function of the Congress's ability to domesticate issue area(s) of foreign policy by emphasizing their intermestic character.*

Other primary hypotheses deal with the longitudinal impacts of the presidential-congressional relationship in foreign affairs. Differential issue area success rates should be observed along a continuum of those that are closest to presidentialization/securitization and hence highest to those that are most distal (thus lowest) and hence subject to routine congressionalization/domestication. More specifically, high politics arena issue areas (national security, domestic security and diplomacy) will exhibit the least decline, have the most presidential position votes, have the higher general presidential position vote success rate, be the more static across political time and have the greatest influence overall in presidential success but be subject to the most "visible" decline—that occurring systematically as even the politics of war and peace become domesticized in later years. Likewise, the low politics arena (trade, foreign aid and immigration) will have the lower overall success rates, the fewest presidential position votes, be more dynamic in variability across political time but also subject to the most "visible" increase as the "politics of everything else" become the norm rather than the aberration in US foreign policy.

Furthermore, there should be an observable difference in the impact of political time itself as presidentialization/securitization will decline with a corroborating rise in congressionalization/domestication of issue areas as we move from the War Power Order into the Confrontational Politics Order. Lastly, a limited retrenchment of this phenomenon should characterize the Imperial Presidency Politicized Order with a somewhat uncertain outcome regarding the last Extra-Systemic Order.

The secondary hypotheses engendered by this research include the notions of the various macro-level historical, political and economic variables on the cross-sectional executive-legislative foreign policy relationship. Using Bond and Fleisher (1990) as a framework from which to proceed, the individual impacts of variables relating to presidency-centered and Congress-centered conditions can be systematically examined. I refer the reader back to the independent variables section for discussion of some of these specific hypotheses.

There are additional hypotheses not discussed in the previous section, I should like to develop them now. In addition to the suggested outcomes relating to political influences that I have already discussed, I would like to continue with contrasting presidency-centered v.

97

Congress-centered conditions regarding the role of public opinion. First, it should be axiomatic that high presidential popularity and its reverse have differential impacts on both foreign policy success rates in general as well as on the various issue area and mixed issue area success rates specifically. Second, popularity will matter the most where the issue areas are most visible, which is in the high politics arena. Third, lower presidential popularity and the prevalence of less visible issue areas of foreign policy (like those in the low politics arena) are associated with Congress-centered conditions. Hence, lower levels of general and specific presidential success in foreign relations as well as issue and mixed issue areas of foreign policy should be observed. The electoral-oriented statements have already been discussed, I now move to the partisan/ideological determinants.

First, partisanship should have a growing influence over presidential success in foreign policy as this domain becomes increasingly politicized over time. Second, what is true of partisanship in the last hypothesis is also true of ideology. However, it will not be as pronounced in its impacts due to its lower correlation with partisanship amongst the congressional party-in-government. Third, party unity works in favor of the Congress at the expense of the president in the low politics arena. And, a fourth related hypothesis is that party unity works in favor of the president at the expense of the Congress in the high politics arena. A fifth suggested outcome is that partisan voting follows the same patterns as party unity voting but will not be as pronounced in its impacts due to its more diffuse nature. At this point some clarification may be necessary regarding notions of party unity and partisan voting in relation to executive-legislative relations.

First, party unity and partisan voting are **not** the same thing, though they are related. *Party Unity* is a measure developed by the editorial staff at Congressional Quarterly, recording the proportion of votes in a legislative session that a majority of each party voted *together* (CQ Almanac 2004, vote studies appendix). Meanwhile, *Partisan Voting* is a measure first developed by James MacGregor Burns (1963, introduction) designating certain votes as having support thresholds where more than half of congressional partisans voted *against* more than half the congressional partisans in the *other* party. Therefore, partisan votes are a subset of party unity votes but not all party unity votes are correctly classified as partisan votes. The prevalence in the literature has been to rely on party unity scores rather than partisanship scores because they are easier to operationalize since CQ has recorded them since 1972 (Shull 1997). The difficulty is that they contain near-unanimous and unanimous votes which in a population study like this they remain self-contained. However, most extant research uses samples of votes thus the inclusion of party unity scores actually has votes which are not included in the rest of the indicators (Lindsay and Steger 1993). Unfortunately, partisan voting has its own set of problems, for instance, just because a vote is partisan does not mean it is important. Many, largely symbolic votes are taken in the Congress every year involving issues that are designed strictly to *promote* party solidarity by *demoting* the attributes of the other party. As an example of this, in the 1990's it was common for the Republican Party in Congress to promote legislation that placed restrictions on abortion access at overseas military hospitals (CQ Almanacs 1990-1998). First they did this to show party solidarity with President Bush and later to oppose President Clinton (CQ Almanac 1998, "abortions in military hospitals"). I believe that my employment of population data (the entire set of presidential position votes in foreign policy 1953-2004) offsets both party unity and partisan voting problems by capturing *all* nuances *simultaneously*.

Second, party unity and partisan voting have been seen to be on the rise in recent years, especially since the 1980's (Bond and Fleisher 1990, Shull and Shaw 1999). This comports with more general notions as to the rise of a more polarized politics in the Congress as well as between the executive and legislative branches (Bond and Fleisher 2000). Furthermore, if Conley (2002) is correct about a new environment for executive-legislative relations being hinged on the rise of partisanship. Then systematic quantitative measures of such phenomenon are directly found with the employment of party unity and partisan voting scores as they relate to presidential position voting. Specifically, Conley's (2002) work was devoted to domestic policy construction, a sphere more prone to congressionalization. In this work, I am operating in the international relations sphere of greater presidential authority (at least in theory). Thus, the rise of a more partisan Congress should be made manifest in the more domesticized low politics arena than in the high politics arena within foreign policy. In other words, presidential success will suffer a greater *negative* impact where it is most vulnerable in the low politics arena. While in the high politics arena such impact will be less pronounced, however, it will be more visible as any decline at all will be more significant since in this arena presidential success has further to fall.

Finally, securitization and domestication will show systematic relationships with their perspective institutional opportunity structures (the presidency for securitization and the Congress for domestication). Additionally, over time domestication will matter more as it is indicative of the environmental changes in the presidential-congressional foreign policy relationship, particularly after 1972. Suffice it to say, we can now discuss how this project will develop beginning with the report of longitudinal findings in the fourth chapter and concluding with the individuated cross-sectional chapters. These last three chapters are broken down according to the relevant order of presidential-congressional international relations policy making (5-7).

The empirical chapters that follow will each be premised with an introduction that provides an overall frame for the narrative and analysis. Next, there will be a section devoted to setting the broader historical, economic and political contexts. In the fourth chapter this will be a lengthy discussion of the macro-level structural developments influencing presidential-congressional relations across political time (1953-2004). In chapters 5-7 this narrative will look at the specific legislative interactions between the presidency and the Congress during each of the "orders" of political time including the War Power Order (1953-1972 in chapter 5), the Confrontation Politics Order (1973-1989 in chapter 6) and the Imperial Presidency Politicized Order (1990-2000 in chapter 7). Then, we will examine the relevant findings for the specified period of study, in other words, we will look at the outcomes of the empirical models associated with each frame of "political time." Likewise, chapter 4 will deal with the longitudinal findings examining the macro-level impacts of historical and economic forces on the structural level of the political environment in which executive-legislative foreign issue area relations takes place. And, chapters 5-7 will deal with the results from cross-sectional models looking at specifically political impacts regarding popular, electoral and partisan/ideological factors on annual presidential success vis-à-vis the Congress in foreign issue areas. After that, I will present a discussion of the relevance of each set of findings to the broader historical context they occur in by using the multiple presidencies thesis as a framing device and tabular analysis of the foreign issue area success rates. The eighth chapter, while a conclusion will contain a section devoted to findings relevant to the Extra-Systemic Dilemma Order (2001-2004) that we currently find ourselves in relative to executive-legislative foreign issue area relations. Finally, each chapter will conclude with a summary of the major points that have been previously dissected.

Summary

This chapter has attempted to put forward a new methodological synthesis which combines what is best out of the Realist oriented state-centrist and Liberal oriented domestic variables approaches to understanding US foreign policy. Accordingly, I have posited that an issue areas analysis is called for whereby the composite issue areas of foreign policy are examined separately in order to capture the inherent nuances within them. I suggest that in issue areas of foreign policy which are built around the traditional high politics arenas of presidential strength (as in national security, domestic security and diplomacy) a statist/state-centrist approach is called for. The reason for this is because foreign policy construction is largely reducible to and hence reliant upon central over adjacent decision makers. Furthermore, in issue areas of foreign policy where they are more subject to domestication due to their inherently "intermestic nature" as they are a part of the low politics arena (trade, foreign aid and immigration) a domestic variables approach is called for. Again, this is because adjacent decision makers will now have as much (and at times even more) influence over the construction of such policies.

The implications of the above proposed analysis suggest that a certain paradigmatic pluralism is possible for methodologies coming out of differing perspectives (i.e., state-centrism and domestic variables or even Realism and Liberalism themselves). More research should be done that attempts to amalgamate seemingly divergent perspectives in order to develop empirical or even normative research programs that are as diverse as the world that they find themselves trying to understand. Following the framework provided for by the issue areas approach, I have proposed a series of secondary methodological steps including content, time series and regression analyses on roll call presidential success rates. Such ancillary techniques naturally emanate out of the issue areas methodology as it is put into practice examining extant Post War Era executive-legislative foreign policy relations (1953-2004). Specifically, I utilize this process to test the explications of the multiple presidencies thesis and to develop implications out of the results themselves. These implications suggest not only the utility of the multiple presidencies thesis itself to examine and evaluate the presidential-congressional foreign affairs relationship. They also support the applicability of future use of an issue areas analysis as a methodological approach. It does this by allowing researchers to discern the contours of the American foreign policy landscape by capturing its inherent nuances but still promotes parsimonious mapping of that landscape's totality.

To this end, I have developed structural and unit level models which capture macro-level factors coming from historical, political and economic sources. These independent variables are to be regressed on the unit of analysis's (congressional roll call votes) primary and secondary dependent variables--the tracked annual presidential success rates on congressional roll call votes in foreign policy as well as the issue areas and mixed issue areas within the domain. Lastly, hypotheses emanating out of the multiple presidencies thesis are examined by the employment of the before-mentioned models with variable operationalization that looks at presidency-centered v. congress-centered conditions. I move now to an examination of the longitudinal findings regarding the "movie of the Post-War Era's executive-legislative relationship in foreign policy."

CHAPTER 4:

THE MULTIPLE PRESIDENCIES ACROSS THE ISSUE AREAS OF AMERICAN FOREIGN POLICY IN PRESIDENTIAL-CONGRESSIONAL RELATIONS

"Journeys, great and small, always begin at the beginning!"

—Mark Twain, *Tom Sawyer*

Introduction

In this chapter, we will examine the broad contours of the *multiple presidencies thesis's* findings by looking longitudinally across the 50 plus year history of the Post War Era (1953-2004). In that effort, I will follow the basic structure laid out in the previous chapters for report and analysis of the relevant findings including an introduction, followed by setting the historical contexts in political and economic terms for extant presidential-congressional foreign policy relations and then a dissection of the findings regarding the longitudinal models. Lastly, I will engage in a discussion of those base findings emanating out of the time series and regression analyses within the politico-economic historical contexts that they find themselves in. This chapter will close with a summary of the finer points of the study's findings and serve as a stepping stone into the cross-sectional analyses to come.

First of all, the historical context is more than just an anecdotal narrative of the presidential-congressional foreign affairs relationship. It is in fact a "setting event," which serves as the springboard for the quantitative modeling that follows it. Variables do not exist as phenomena unto themselves, rather they are themselves both products of and inhabitants within a certain context (or, in theory anyway multiple contexts). It is vitally important to remember that these variables are only indicative of their mutual and co-dependent interaction with the unit level actors (the president and Congress) within the specified timeframe of the study itself. The history is important because it provides for the appropriate selection of indicators and conditions their temporal impacts. With that in mind, I will concentrate on developing a narrative of the role played by the issue areas of foreign policy across political time.

The findings result from two general types of models, both of which are leveled at the structural impacts on presidential-congressional relations as measured by the dependent variable— the annual presidential success rate (in either foreign policy or the various issue areas of foreign policy—national security, domestic security, diplomacy, trade, foreign aid and immigration). One model type is a time series formation which tracks relations as either single entities (autocorrelations) or as groups (cross-correlations) across a given time frame by accounting for the role of time in a quantitative fashion (McClary and Hay 1975). I employ both in order to check for stasis and dynamism within as well as across the dependent variables.

Another model that I utilize is a simple multivariate regression of the role that the various issue area success scores (the secondary dependent variables) play in relation to overall presidential foreign policy success (the primary dependent variable).[1] This is important because it answers a basic contention of the multiple presidencies thesis that foreign policy is in actuality a polyglot of only loosely related issue areas. Other secondary support measures are also employed but I will discuss those within the text of the section itself. Finally, additional longitudinal regression models employing some of the secondary dependent variables are specified and run in order to look at basic patterns of relationships that were hypothesized in Chapter 2. These models look at certain historical and economic conditions operating at the macro-level whereby they exert a phenomenon-specific relationship influencing the structural settings of presidency-centered v. congress-centered conditions. In this effort, I also test for the influence of "periods of presidential-congressional foreign policy history" (War Power 1953-1972, Confrontation Politics 1973-1989, Imperial Presidency Politicized 1990-2000 and the Extra-Systemic Dilemma 2001-2004?). These last models serve as the starting off point for the cross-sectional analyses contained in the rest of this work.

Finally, the discussion section matches the empirics with the theory, by pulling together the elements of the historical context section with those of the empirical findings section. The history sets the context, while the models analyze it and then in this section, the two are brought together by the theoretical premises of the multiple presidencies thesis. Essentially, the two previous sections are re-discussed but under the framework of an analogy provided by the theory which not only suggests the utility of the theory but also brings what would otherwise be somewhat disparate analyses into a coherent systematized framework. Lastly, we take a final review of the chapter as a whole before moving on to the further articulations promised for in the cross-sectional portion of this study.

---

[1] See relevant portions of the methods chapter (3) for a deeper discussion of these contrasting dependent variables.

Issue Areas across Political Time

Throughout the "path of time" followed in this analysis, one overarching initial conclusion can be made regarding the role of the issue areas of foreign policy, that being—they matter and they do so in a systematic fashion. Having said that, how they matter, when they matter and their potential for mattering in the future is subject to a great deal of within and across case variance. The reason for this is simple; time itself has had a political impact on the executive-legislative relationship in foreign policy.

Our study begins in the year 1953, which was originally selected by me for methodological reasons since that is when the editorial staff at *Congressional Quarterly* began to systematically record presidential position voting within the Congress. It has proved to have a strong analytical prowess as well. In this year, we as a country saw the end of the first major point when the Cold War "got hot." The Korean War (1950-1953) was certainly not the first place of American-Soviet conflict but in the short decade after the end of the Second World War (the Post-War Era) it was the most intense by any measure of magnitude. Unlike the preceding Cold War conflicts of the late 1940's over Greece, Turkey and Germany; Korea was a major power war. This type of war not only reaches the magnitude measures of intensity and duration associated with designating major from minor wars (Singer and Small 1983).[2] It also has the characteristic of involving one or more major powers (states in the Westphalian system), in this case not only the US but also Britain and to a much reduced extent France (due to their protracted involvement in the Indochina War 1946-1954) (Cashman 1993). Furthermore, Communist China certainly qualified as a "quasi-major power" at least militarily and after the Yalu River intervention in late fall 1950 they took the place of the North Koreans as the central antagonists faced by the United Nations (UN).[3]

The Korean War arguably had almost as great an impact on the domestic populace of the United States as World War II, being the fact that, Truman utilized the war to engage in a partial mobilization of men and materiel (Milkis and Nelson 2003). This "partial" mobilization included

---

[2] These measure are usually indexes developed based around casualties, size of forces, duration of deployment, size and number of battles and material costs as well as the geographic scope of what must be seen as a type of "militarized dispute" (Singer and Small 1983, Vasques 1994, Cashman 1993, Singer 1999).

[3] While it is now known that the Soviets were directly involved militarily in the Korean and Vietnam Wars, such combat involvement was mostly constrained to air power and air defense in limited quantities.

a permanent extension of the draft, reserve and guard duration call-ups, increases in income and corporate taxes, rationing of industrial and consumer goods as well as perhaps most pervasively placing war economy controls over strategic resources like steel, coal and oil (Milkis and Nelson 2003). In fact, it was because of this mobilization activity that the United States economy suffered a severe retraction beginning in the summer of 1953 as the Armistice took effect and the country moved to a major de-mobilization of its war economy and conventional armed forces (Milkis and Nelson 2003). The corresponding "Korean War Recession," while not as pervasive in its impacts regarding the recessionary macroeconomic readjustments following each of the two World Wars (1919-1921 and 1946), this recession was deep enough and entrenched enough that it caused the Democratic Party to lose the Congress and was instrumental in Stevenson's defeat in the 1952 elections (Milkis and Neslon 2003 and Department of Commerce 2006, archive report).

While this was the first time in twenty years that the Republican Party had gained control of the White House as they did with Eisenhower's inauguration in 1953, just before between 1947 and 1948 the 80th Congress had been a Republican one. Therefore in the early days of the mid-1950s, notions of the entrenchment of the New Deal realignment were certainly not as powerful as they are now seen in retrospect to have been (from Mayhew 2002). A new "Red Scare" driven by the activities of Joseph McCarthy (R-WI) coupled with Eisenhower's "New Look" foreign policy with its emphasis on deterrence through "Mutually Assured Destruction" made the Cold War into an ever present and ominous everyday fear for the common man and woman in America (Snow and Brown 1999). In contrast to David Halberstam's (2000) picture of 1950s America as a lost age of innocence and opportunity, the 1950s from a foreign policy perspective were a series of crises some seen, some inferred.

The question of military intervention into the Indochina War at the Battle of Dien Bien Phu in 1954 split the Eisenhower "war cabinet" between Hawks calling for some form of military "solution" led by Vice-president Nixon and Doves cautioning against such an endeavor as led by a ground war weary Pentagon (Greenstein 1993). Eisenhower defected from direct intervention but set the US on a course for increased military, political and economic involvement in what would soon be the countries of North and South Vietnam (Ellsberg 1971). Real, though minor military intervention in Lebanon in 1958 as well as the diplomatic efforts during the Suez Canal Crisis of 1956 would foreshadow future American military adventures in years to come.

Additionally, shows of force in the South China Sea and the Black Sea by the US Navy against communist counterparts were flashpoints that bordered on the deadly during this time.

Despite recessions in 1953-54 and 1958, the American economy grew at unprecedented rates during the 1950's as it enjoyed the fruits of its Post-War position as the clear global economic hegemon. The other great powers were still rebuilding after the destruction of the Second World War including America's rivals in the Sino-Soviet bloc. The US economy accounted for about ½ of the world's GNP during this period, it had ½ the world's gold reserves, the US dollar was the de facto world currency upon which all others were pegged and the US enjoyed wide trade and international finance balances (Kegley and Wittkopf 2001; Department of Commerce 2006, archive reports). Finally, the United States had the highest industrial capacity and was the number one provider of global goods and services for all economic sectors (Papp, Johnson and Endicott 2006, Department of Commerce 2006, archive reports) Perhaps due to this as well as its free world leadership position, the US was the number one provider of foreign aid to both the First (though reconstructing) and Third Worlds (US AID 2006, archive reports and Snow and Brown 1999). As the fifties came to a close, the US looked ahead with promise as well as consternation to the decades to come—they would be both delighted and dejected by what they found.

The 1960's saw a return to Democratic control over the White House after regaining the Congress six years previously in 1954. Along with the arrival of Camelot, came an influx of liberal Northern Democrats in the 1958 mid-term elections, calling for the completion of Roosevelt's policy promises which included a more idealist-centered foreign affairs (from Davidson 1996 in Thurber 1996 and Papp, Johnson and Endicott 2006). The Kennedy doctrine's "flexible response" in combination with a more open diplomacy in the wake of the Bay of Pigs fiasco of 1961 and the hairbreadth nuclear showdown brought on by the Cuban Missile Crisis in 1962 saw the start of diplomatic accomodationism between the American and Soviet empires (Sorensen 1965 and Alison 1971). However, the dagger of Southeast Asia would plunge into the heart of such diplomatic accomplishments as the Open Air Test Treaty of 1963. At the time of the Kennedy assassination, a new optimism had developed regarding US foreign affairs but that optimism would be surely tested in the second half of the decade in the place called Vietnam.

The Vietnam War (1965-1973) amounted to a modern crucible at least as regards US foreign policy making. As the public opinion polls supporting "Johnson's War" declined, especially in the wake of the Tet Offensive in 1968—the Congress founds its voice in the vaunted realm of national security politics. First, a within party debate broke out between the Old Guard Democrats who would ultimately support Vice-president Hubert Humphrey's campaign for the White House in 1968 and the Young Turks rallying around such figures as Eugene McCarthy and Robert Kennedy. In the Congress, a politics of deference continued but extensions of Johnson's leadership outside of national security began to be questioned, especially in areas as diverse as immigration, foreign aid, trade and even Cold War diplomacy with the USSR itself (CQ Almanacs 1967-1968, various legislative histories and Sundquist 1981). After Tet not even national security was left to the purview of the president.

The return of divided government with the election of Republican Richard Nixon in 1968 exacerbated the conflict between the presidency and the Congress into an all out war of central v. adjacent decision makers in both foreign policy and domestic policy (from Fisher 2000, Aldrich and Rohde 2005 as well as Papp, Johnson and Endicott 2006). Specifically, regarding foreign policy this battle would lead to the resurgence of congressional authority both real and imagined in a fashion not seen since the revolt against Wilson's foreign policy Idealism in the 1920's ratification fight over the Treaty of Versailles.[4] The 1970s saw the immediate aftereffects of this protracted struggle with the War Powers Act of 1973 passed over Nixon's veto, the mid-1970s era congressional investigations of the CIA's covert activities both at home and abroad over the previous thirty years, the Jackson-Vanick Amendments regarding Jewish emigration from the USSR and the subsequent de-funding of the Vietnam War through the foreign aid appropriations process (Sundquist 1981).

The 1980s, which is sometimes viewed as a restoration of presidential power resulting from the prominence of the Reagan presidency, was in fact, a time of extended partisan conflict between the Republican president and the Democratic House of Representatives.[5] After the 1986 mid-term elections, a fully Democratic Congress offered routine foreign policy alternatives to Reagan's efforts in South Africa, military policy, defense budgets and perhaps most notably

---

[4] Idealism as a philosophy of foreign policy stresses cooperation through open diplomacy, international institutional development and nation-state adherence to the precepts and conditions of international law (Papp, Johnson and Endicott 2005).

[5] See Milkis and Nelson (2003) for this alternative viewpoint regarding the "Restoration Presidency" of Ronald Reagan.

Central America. Complicating all of this was that by the 1970s, US relative decline was pervasive and being felt by the domestic polity.

Dollar overhang, a condition where more US currency was "in float" in international markets than the US Mint could account for was in place as early as 1960 (Kegley and Wittkopf 2001). The pervasiveness of this problem led to the Nixonian scheme of dollar devaluation which ended formalized liquidity of international financial and currency markets (Kegley and Wittkopf 2001). Additionally, trade surpluses had turned into trade deficits by the mid 1960s, routine budget surpluses had become routine budget deficits after 1969. Then there was the emergent problem of First World competition from Japan and the European Community which placed the US industrial and agricultural sectors in tight economic straits as some worried that the American Eagle was being displaced by the Japanese economic Samurai (Kennedy 1986). Free trading presidents of both parties faced off against ever increasing numbers of protectionists in the Congress again of both parties (Lindsay 1994).

In the debate over the North American Free trade Agreement (NAFTA), the World Trade Organization (WTO) and the Free Trade Area of the Americas (FTAA) free trading regimes this familiar pattern of a protectionist Congress v. a free trading president continued well into the 1990s. However, the most prolific structural change to the international system was political not economic as the Soviet Empire collapsed into the dustbin of world history in late 1991. The end of the Cold War provided the opportunities of a "peace dividend" due to the decline of systemic conflict but this promise was left unfulfilled as the realities of a world without super power boundaries set in (Snow and Brown 1999, Papp, Johnson and Endicott 2006). War in the Persian Gulf followed by conflicts and potential conflicts brought on by the new security's ethno-political strife and the old security's concerns regarding the maintenance of a "national strategic interest" (from Mathews 1989 and Mearsheimer 2001). The Balkans, Somalia, the Sudan, Rawanda, Haiti, Liberia, Senegal, Russian descent, Chinese ascent and of course Iraq would test both the first Bush's "new world order" and Clinton's "selective engagement" foreign policy doctrines. However, that would only be the beginning of the real importance of a globalized world with its attendant forces on integration juxtaposed against the forces of fragmentation. These countervailing forces have led to creation of a political world that is unipolar only in military concerns, multipolar economically and most troubling for foreign policy decision makers and analysts polyglot socio-culturally (Papp, Johnson and Endicott 2006).

The foreign policy polity that we now occupy is one where diffusion and confluence go hand in hand on any array of issue areas from national security all the way to immigration. The aftermath of the twin towers attack on September the 11th 2001, have led us to re-evaluate the role of presidency-centered v. Congress-centered conditions regarding where the power in foreign policy lies, if it should lie there and why this is so. Recently, we have seen the securitization of immigration as a part of the "War on Terror" with prolonged employment of troops both regular and guard. Port and border security has brought trade into the security realm and an entirely new Cabinet Department devoted to domestic security has since been established. But, this has not necessarily led to a re-presidentialization of foreign policy as recent research has shown that the Congress has been heavily involved in the creation and implementation of these foreign policy efforts (Wolfsenberger in Dodd and Oppenheimer 2005). Nevertheless, W. Bush's "Bull Horn Moment" cannot be underestimated as to its initial and even long term impact as envisioned in the real Wars in Afghanistan and Iraq accomplished with overwhelming support/acquiescence by the Congress, including the opposition party. Finally, the Patriot Act and other domestic surveillance initiatives by the current administration have allowed for the development or at least the potential development of a domestic intelligence capability not seen since the height of the Soviet Union's Committee on State Security (KGB). And, again the Congress largely acquiesced to this "securitized" power into the domestic sphere. The ebb and flow of executive-legislative relations in foreign policy construction and implementation continues but it has been subject to some patterns and it is to these patterns that we now turn.

Empirical Findings

One of the central hypotheses that emanates out of the prescriptions of the multiple presidencies thesis is that the issue areas of foreign policy can be shown to manifest themselves in divergent patterns. The initial descriptive findings of the longitudinal analysis certainly support that contention. As Figures 4-1 and 4-2 suggest (see their supporting table in the appendix), the multiple issue areas of foreign policy whether as discrete or mixed entities appear in a robust fashion.[6] Taking a closer look at these two figures, we can see some significant differences in the distribution of the issue areas. First of all, the discrete issue areas: national security, domestic security, diplomacy, trade, foreign aid and immigration which are at the core

---

[6] All figures and tables relevant to this chapter are found in sequential order after the summary section.

of the theory's expectations regarding their presence as roll call phenomena are more prevalent in their presence within the data set than the mixed versions (which are composites of core categories). Second, among these core categories there are a "big three," composed of national security (31% of all votes), trade (23% of all votes) and foreign aid (20% of all votes). Third, national security is the category with the largest percentage of votes which is something that is consistent with hypothesized notions for the existence of an "opportunity structure" for presidential empowerment within this area of foreign policy.[7] Lastly, the lack of a sustained systematic presence regarding most of the issue areas, including the mixed issue areas rejects hypothesized conditions regarding the steady dispersion of foreign policy into a multiplicity of issue areas. I believe that the "core strength" exerted by national security, trade and foreign aid as points of ongoing confluence for issue development between the executive and legislative branches accounts for this finding but future research needs to be done in this area.

A related finding is the lack of a systematic role for the domestic security (5.9% of all votes) and diplomacy (7.7% of all votes) categories. As high politics arena categories, one would expect that they would be more prevalent within the data than they actually are. However, it is conceivable that the domestic security issue area has been largely over-shadowed by position taking in the national security category so much to the point that domestic security and to a lesser extent diplomacy is in effect a sub-category. If this is true, then the hypothesized relation between presidential position taking and success more generally is even more a function of the inherent opportunity structure that security represents for presidential power in foreign affairs.

Moving on to more analytical findings, we discern differential patterns as to the longitudinal success rates of presidents regarding the core issue areas. I concentrated on these at the expense of the mixed formulations because of their stronger appearance, analytical role within the theory and easier methodological interpretability. I will save discussion of the mixed issue areas for the cross-sectional chapters where they become most manifest (chapters 6-8). As Tables 4-1 and 4-2 indicate, there are statistically significant differences in the mean percentage success rates for presidents across the three main issue areas—national security (74% success), trade (71% success) and foreign aid (72% success). This not only supports hypothesized contentions, it also follows the expected patterns of success with presidents routinely doing

---

[7] See Chapter 2's extended discussion of the importance of opportunity structures' role within the multiple presidencies thesis.

better in the high politics arena than in the low politics one, however this is offset by the lack of sustained presence of three of the issue areas across time—domestic security, diplomacy and immigration. It also follows expected patterns with national security as the single most successful issue area for presidential foreign policy position vote "wins" (74% overall). Additionally, as the table points out the mean success rate for presidents is greater on national security than on trade and foreign aid. A means test confirms a statistically significant difference in success between the issue areas (p=.05). It is a debatable question as to the substantive significance of such an empirical claim, therefore deeper analytical inquiry is necessitated.

Standard deviations and standard mean errors are quite small, which is indicative of the fact that I am employing *population* rather than *sample* statistics. As an implication, it is entirely possible that much of the variation or lack thereof noted in the two presidencies literature is a result of its overwhelming reliance on samples and even sub-samples as opposed to the population data which is available, just painstaking to get at (see Bond and Fleisher 1988, Malbin and Brookshire 2000 and Conley 1997 for some relatively recent "sampling" endeavors). One major analytic finding out of this table is that despite hypothesized claims there is no marked difference in the "degree" of presidential success relative to the non-security issue areas (see Tables 4-1 and 4-2). We would expect a variation in the success rate regarding comparisons between national security success-trade and national security success-foreign aid. However, these expectations were not born out; in fact there is no discernible difference in the success rates in trade (71%) v. foreign aid (72%) (Again, see Tables 4-1 and 4-2). There are two possible explanations, one is methodological and the other theoretical.

Methodologically, it is conceivable that the sheer number of "data points" is overwhelming any inherent differences that "lie below the surface" due to the reliance on population data. A future research project may differentiate these votes out along "types" based on the relative value of the vote itself (majority procedural, majority final, supermajority procedural and supermajority final). I do this in the cross-sectional chapters, but looking at it longitudinally is certainly something to examine at a later date. Theoretically, if we are keeping in mind the notion that what is presidency-centered serves as the base ordering principle for the study overall, then the further we "move" away from security (e.g., the low politics arenas) the less subject issue areas are to the ordering principle itself and hence "within low politics arena" variance may not be able to be discerned with this type of research program. Not only is this a point for further study unto itself, it also provides an empirical referent which in large measure supports the basic thesis regarding the role of issue areas and opportunity structures in the president's foreign policy success rate (Chapter 2). So far, the study is supported by basic descriptive and minor analytic empirics but what happens when those empirics are examined in a more robustly systematic manner?

Time series analysis examines data longitudinally with the specific contribution that it accounts mathematically for the "impact of time" itself on the phenomenon of interest (from McCleary and Hay 1975). Its principal limitation is its tendency to develop systematic error over time which is referred to by time series analysts as "serial autocorrelation of the disturbance term" (McCleary and Hay 1975, introduction). While this problem is particularly endemic to ordinary least squares (OLS) models, the relatively limited nature of this study's application of such analyses should serve to limit the negative impacts at least generally. Looking at a base univariate ARIMA model tracking the foreign policy success and core issue area success scores across time we can gain at least a modest systematic perspective on the executive-legislative foreign affairs relationship. The models specified take on the following characteristics:

Model 1 $FPn{\sim}(1,0,0)$

Where $o>0$

Model 2 $NSn{\sim}(1,0,0)$

Where $o1>0$

Model 3 $DSn{\sim}(1,0,0)$

Where $o2>0$

Model 4 $Dn{\sim}(1,0,0)$

Where $o3>0$

Model 5 $Tn{\sim}(1,0,0)$

Where $o4>0$

Model 6 $FAn{\sim}(1,0,0)$

Where o5>0

Model 7 IMMn~(1,0,0)

Where o5>0

Lags for all models= 50, where each lag is an annualized measure beginning with 2004 as the base year of interest and closing with the year 1953 (the origination point).

What the above is referring to is the statistical distribution of each of the time series models as to their specific type and character of the observations being tracked across time. For instance, model 1 is specified as *FPn~(1,0,0) where o>1*. What this is referencing is that the time series model for the dependent variable presidential foreign policy success is distributed (represented by the tilda symbol ~) as a population (represented by the capital letters *FP*) of all presidential position votes on foreign policy between 1953 and 2004 (represented by the letter *n*). Furthermore, the numbers contained within the parentheses *(1,0,0)* indicate the type of time series model being employed as a first-order autoregressive model. In this case, the dependent variable is regressed against itself at descending intervals beginning at the base year of 2004 and working back in time (the notions of t and t-minus) to the origination point for the study in 1953. Finally, the concept of θ is the Greek letter theta and is a statistical convention for any number or integer. But, in this analysis the numbers employed as primary and secondary dependent variables (the respective 1953-2004 annual presidential success rates in foreign, national security, domestic security, diplomacy, trade, foreign aid and immigration policies) are always greater than zero.

The models are of the type first-order autoregressive and measure the alteration in the various core success rates across time. One limitation of this type of autoregressive integrated moving average (ARIMA) modeling is that it has limited forecasting abilities because it only accounts for within rather than across case variance over time (McCleary and Hay 1975, introduction). However, as Figure 4-1 indicates the models "map out" in an expected fashion with some interesting twists which previous non-time series analysis neglected. This type of time series model is best thought of as a "regression on itself," whereby the current observation (presidential success in some issue area of foreign policy in 2004) is seen as the "outcome" of previous annualized presidential success rates back in de-sequential order to the year 1953 (McCleary and Hay 1975, chapter 2). Finally, since seasonality is not of concern due to the

114

annualized nature of the data, simple first differencing is all that is necessary to re-impose stationarity on the series' of concern by accounting for natural drift in the respective trend lines (from McCleary and Hay 1975, chapter 2).

First of all, model stationarity is met in the first 20 lags within foreign policy as well as national security, trade and foreign aid success rates. Stationarity is a time series concept that roughly approximates a model fitness test like the *F-test* in regression analysis. It is referring to the lack of natural *drift* or seasonal presence of *trend* within the data. This means that the model can be said to be actually *explaining* an outcome as opposed to one appearing by mere chance. In other words, the sooner a time series attains stationarity the stronger the model is as an explanatory device. This is an indicator of the systemic presence that the "big three" have as indicators of foreign policy interaction between the president and the Congress. On the other side of the coin, diplomacy does not attain stationarity until the thirty-seventh lag, well over halfway into the distribution of the data and most importantly, domestic security as well as immigration *never* attains stationarity (Figure 4-3). Two immediate conclusions can be drawn from these empirics. First, security abroad is a place of presidential power not security within. Second, the dominant presence of the "big three" (national security, trade and foreign aid) are once again limiting the potential for the "lesser three" (domestic security, diplomacy and immigration) as places of presidential-congressional interaction.

Following the issue of stationarity, we see the pattern repeat itself when analyzing the modified Q statistics (the Box-Ljung statistic). The modified Q statistic measures each autocorrelation for its probability of difference from zero and the presence of a "white noise" phenomenon amidst the stochastic and trend process terms (together they amount to the measure of endogenous variance in a time series) (Box and Ljung 1978). As Table 4-3 indicates, measurable autocorrelations are present in all of the models except immigration and somewhat surprisingly domestic security. However, a second look at the domestic security category does indicate a high probability for rejecting the null hypothesis that all inferred autocorrelations will be 0 and just the opposite conclusion is reached by interpreting the probabilities emanating out of the immigration modified Q statistics (Appendix Table 4-1 data).

Additionally, Figure 4-3 indicates that there are two general trends prevalent among the "big three" (national security, trade and foreign aid) regarding the movement of the respective success rates across time. The first major trend is that national security tends to be relatively steady state and since foreign policy success is high (also revealed in this figure) then that means that variation in the overall success rate is more associated with non-security oriented issue areas. This confirms a major hypothesis of the multiple presidencies thesis and even identifies those issue areas responsible for the before mentioned variance (Figure 4-3). It is in the "low politics arena" of trade and foreign aid where such variations in the series' trends are observed. For instance, while the trend line for national security success has only a single major break in it after stationarity, trade has four (Figure 4-3). And, in both trade and foreign aid, the success rates are subject to a high rate of increase in the size of the Q statistic relative to national security which follows a more incremental pattern that is easier to explain through the increase in T—the total number of observations (Appendix Table 4-1 data) (Box and Ljung 1978). The foreign policy success rate series has two major breaks and since these are at distal places in the time series itself, this indicates that the foreign policy success rate today is not as correlated with that of the past. What explains this? From our analysis so far, change in trade and foreign aid seems more likely candidates than national security but let us take a closer look with some cross-correlations.

The cross-correlations look at *between* case differences across time and project inferences regarding the overall relationships between the elements of the series themselves (McCleary and Hay 1975, chapter 5). As Figure 4-4 shows, foreign policy success is a *function of* national security success (model A), ceteris paribus due to its high correlation coefficient function (CCF) of .564. However, as the figure also shows a case can be made for trade given its equally high CCF of .525 (model B). Foreign aid places in third with a CCF of .24 but from a time series perspective we cannot discern the *exact determinant mechanism* for presidential foreign aid success (see Appendix Table 4-2). We can only eliminate foreign aid and all other issue areas by implication as contenders. So, the question remains—is it national security or is it trade? Simple multiple regression models applied longitudinally can shed some light on this question.

For this portion of the analysis, I specify two models, the first is a multivariate ordinary least squares regression (OLS) employing foreign policy success as the dependent variable and both national security success as well as trade success as the explanatory factors with a disturbance term for error. All of the three variables are the full cross-time annualized position vote success scores with no attention paid to political time differences—those will be dealt with in coming chapters. Therefore the first model takes the form:

116

Foreign Policy =National Security + Trade + E

Where all variables are population indicators

The second model is posited in order to test two of the fundamental hypotheses coming from the multiple presidencies thesis. That issue area success is indicative of the degree of "presidentialization/securitization v. congressionalization/domestication of the specific votes themselves within the foreign policy domain. With that in mind, this model takes two forms with the first as:

Model 2-A1:

National Security=Securitization + Domestication + e

Where securitization and domestication are dummy variables coded as a result of the content analysis of the relevant vote summaries.

Model 2-A2:

Trade =Securitization + Domestication + e

Model 2-B

Foreign Policy=Securitization + Domestication + e

Where this serves as the baseline model for comparison relative to notions of presidency-centered v. Congress centered conditions.

As Table 4-3 tells the findings are within the expected range for the predictions of the theory. According to the results of the first model, while both explanatory variables correlate positively and robustly (p-value=0) with foreign policy success, the un-standardized correlation coefficient is significantly higher for national security *beta=.42* than for trade *beta=.364*. When the model is re-specified to include all issue areas the results are even more emblematic of a multiple presidencies interpretation of executive-legislative relations in foreign policy. As Table 4-4 indicates, while trade has the highest correlation value, the two security oriented issue areas together trump it by a significant amount (.31 for trade, .22 for national security and .19 for domestic security). Also, in general trade is the only substantively significant factor amongst the "low politics arena," although it is true and also supportive of the larger theory that all issue areas of foreign policy enjoy a "statistically" significant relationship (alpha set at .05) with the dependent variable (Table 4-4).

The second model(s)' shows a clear role for securitization in the success rate of president's in foreign policy along predicted directions. As a presidency-centered condition, securitization has a significant relationship with national security and foreign policy success, however the correlations are relatively weak (Tables 4-5—4-6). Even more troubling, as Tables 4-5—4-6 reveal the relationship is negative suggesting that as the presence of securitization among foreign policy votes increases there is a corresponding *decrease* in the success rate whether foreign or national security in orientation. Why is this so? Perhaps, it is because of the longitudinal aspect of the data itself since actual variance within is not captured by this particular model. Therefore, we will leave this topic for now and re-address it in the cross-sectional models where a more specified approach is possible. Additionally, when securitization is utilized in the trade version of the success model and subject to a backwards elimination technique for model specification, it is maintained in the re-specified model (Table 4-7). As a side note, this also occurs when the formulation is run with foreign aid success as the secondary dependent variable in place of the trade success rate.

When taking the view of Congress-centered conditionality, similarly supportive yet *qualified* results are also found. Domestication of votes serves the same role in influencing the foreign policy success rate and non-security issue area success rates (measured with trade success as a proxy) for the Congress as the securitization phenomenon dies for the presidency (Table 4-7). Whereas securitization does not "drop" out of the model for trade (and foreign aid as well), it is domestication that "drops" out of the national security model but remains as a strong and negative indicator of trade (and foreign aid) success (Table 4-7). What this really means is that domestication is inherent to the low politics arena (with trade as the proxy *beta= -.07*) and likewise, securitization holds a similar position in both politics' arena (with national security as the proxy *beta=-.019*). Lastly, as you can see in Table 4-7, a negative relationship between domestication and trade success is found. Unlike the results for securitzation's impact, these findings are in comportment with the precepts of the multiple presidencies. It is to be expected that as an issue is subject to successful domestication (read congressionalization) then the president will have a more difficult time getting his way on the vote in question due to the nature of the Congress' opportunity structure in domestic (read more intermestic) types of foreign policies.

The last set of longitudinal empirics deals with the role played by the concept of "political time" as an explanatory (potential or real) of presidential success rates in foreign policy and its component issue areas. The model uses our standard dependent variable of annual presidential success in foreign policy and regress the impacts of the four periods of political time. Therefore, the model is specified as follows:

Foreign Policy=War Power Order + Confrontation Politics Order + Imperial Presidency Politicized Order + Extra Systemic Dilemma Order + E

Where each order is operationalized by a dummy variable.

The results as seen in Table 4-8, portray the start of a complex story that the rest of this work attempts to clarify. Three of the four periods have a statistically significant relationship with foreign policy success. This is a fascinating finding and difficult to interpret but as an initial observation the one period that lacks significance, the Confrontation Politics Order 1973-1989, is the one most associated within the literature as congressional resurgence in foreign policy. If anything the association ought to be negative but it is simply non-existent. Or, is it? Think about this. A large amount of scholarship on roll call analysis has found that during the 1970s and 1980s there was something of a "roll call boom." The Congress as part of its reform efforts began to record more and more votes, especially on procedural mechanisms which themselves increased during this time (Shull and Shaw 1999, Rohde 1991, Page and Jordan 1992, Lindsay and Steger 1993). Therefore, it is possible that the votes during this time are "flooding the data set," essentially "polluting the observations" leading to counterintuitive inferences in a population based model that is longitudinal in its composition (from Enders 2004, chapter 5).

Another interesting finding is that despite only being four years in length, the last period—the Extra-Systemic Dilemma has a significant relationship with position vote success in foreign policy. While this does support the expectations of the theory, the reader should take this finding with some caution as our current president is well known for *not* taking positions on roll call votes (Leloup and Shull 2003). Therefore, this period may have the same problem as the previous one discussed but only from the opposite direction. Too few position votes, just like too many may also cause this period of time to not be directly comparable with ones around it (see Shull and Shaw (1999) for an extended discussion on the "comparability" of presidential position voting across different periods of time).

A final finding that comports well with expectations of the multiple presidencies thesis but may seem counterintuitive relates to the Imperial Presidency Politicized (1990-2000). As Table 4-8 suggests, there is a negative significant relationship between this period of time and the success rate in foreign policy. While some may feel this is not in keeping with the theory, I can assure them that it is. Here is why. What was once freely given for extended periods of time is now quickly taken away (see the difficulties our current president is having relative to the Iraq War). Furthermore, the highly politicized nature of the executive-legislative divide that has been particularly pervasive since the late Reagan administration has worked in general against presidents and for the Congress. This is because divided government is best seen as a Congress-centered condition and unified as a presidency-centered. However, W. Bush's year and a half of split control government between May of 2001 and December of 2002 might represent something of an aberration from the norm. Of course, much of that time saw an unusually high level of of bi-partisanship in the wake of 9/11. But, even during this time the Congress was already returning to its partisan roots as the 2002 mid-term campaign season came under way (CQ Almanac 2002, "election report").

Finally, we need to examine the role of other historical and economic indicators exerting a macro-level impact on the extant executive-legislative foreign policy relationship. The first such model tests the historical conditionality regarding the size and scope of the US military establishment's role in determining national security success. This model is specified in the following manner:

Model 1

National Security=War + Armed Forces + Defense Budget + E

What this model's findings portray, as shown in Table 4-9, is a mixed bag, as to the applicability of the theory across time. For instance, while the base hypothesis of the military establishment as measured by the size of the armed forces and the percentage of the budget allocated to it is upheld. Only size of the armed forces is in the expected direction wherein, as the size of the armed forces increases there is a corresponding increase in the national security success rate. And, the budget measure is actually in a reverse relationship regarding expected outcomes where as the percentage increases, there is a corresponding systematic declination in the president's rate of success in national security votes. What might be most interesting is the fact that the war dummy variable has a negative relationship with national security. However, in this case it could be that the limited amount of actual war during the timeframe of the analysis might be limiting the inferential capacities of this measure. I should also like to point out that while the relationship is negative and passes statistical significance ($p=.05$) it is quite weak (*beta*=-.07) so how reliable the interpretation is certainly open to question. Cross-sectional study with this variable should lead to a truer assessment of this variable's impact (see Chapter 5).

The next two models within Tables 4-10—4-11 examine the impacts of macro-level economic indicators and presidential success in trade and foreign aid respectively. Accordingly, each model is specified as such:

Model 2

Trade=Budgetary Conditions + GDP + Business Cycle + International Finance/Trade + E

And

Model 3

Foreign Aid= Budgetary Conditions + GDP + Business Cycle + International Finance/Trade + E

The second model, which correlates the economic indicators with trade success across time, finds statistically significant relationships across the board. These results support the broad hypothesis regarding macro-level impacts on issue area success rates. The signs are in the expected directions with one exception. Regarding the general condition of the economy, when it is healthy (read non-recessionary), when the budget deficit is low or even in surplus conditions and when the level of economic interdependence is low (as measured by trade/finance surpluses (or at least only modest deficits), then presidents have more success in trade votes. But when the opposite is true, such success is in decline due to the emergence of congressional conditionality over presidential conditionality within the variables (Table 4-10, Model 2). The deviating factor is economic growth (in this case measured as Real GDP), these results suggests that as real gross domestic product (GDP) grows success in trade declines. This is a bit counterintuitive, however, it can be explained on methodological grounds as a "proxy" or "indirect" variable which cannot adequately capture the "real" relationship with trade success as the more direct observations in the other variables do.

Model 3 offers up an interesting set of findings by replicating the previous model's independent variables and looking at their relationship with foreign policy success. Only Real GDP and business cycle conditions have demonstrable impacts on presidential success in foreign aid across time. Additionally, the correlations are modest among both variables and only the business cycle behaves in expected ways (*beta*=.04). Of course, remember that Real GDP (*beta*=-.031) had a similar "deviating" impact on trade success and due to a smaller proportion of foreign policy votes related to foreign aid; this deviation impact would be even more decisive (Table 4-11, Model 3). Now, let us return to the "movie" of executive-legislative foreign policy relations and bring it all together.

The Multiple Presidencies across the Issue Areas of Foreign Policy

So how do we relate the events of the contextual narrative with the systematic findings of the longitudinal study? The answer is the multiple presidencies thesis. The story of executive-legislative relations in foreign policy during the Post-War Era is a long and extremely complex one, however, if viewed from the perspective of multiple sets of presidential-congressional relations across the component issue areas of foreign affairs it is not nearly as complex as first thought. The reason for this is that security serves somewhat as an anchor to the ship of state steered by the president and crewed by the Congress. As this analogy goes, when the ship hits troubled waters in the sea of foreign policy, then the president-captain is in charge like in the time of the War Power Order 1953-1972 with its heightened Cold War tensions that led immediately out of one hot war in Korea and into another in Vietnam. Meanwhile, as détente became the diplomacy of the day, Vietnamization and the Nixon Doctrine became focal points for future Cold War strategy the waters of the foreign policy sea calmed down but the crew got antsy.[8] The captain(s) (in the form of Nixon himself and later at least in an electoral fashion Ford and Carter) were displaced in mutinies by a recalcitrant Congress. Finally, a moderated status quo develops wherein the president-captain and the Congress-crew develop a tandem institutional relationship where storms rise (like wars in the Middle East) with a congressional rally-round-the president phenomenon. However, as quickly as the crisis comes it begins to fade and the calm waters bring about congressional-crew discontent with the president-captain's day-to-day voyaging in the foreign policy sea. Keep this rough analogy in mind, as we move into the cross-sectional chapters and take snapshots of the executive-legislative foreign policy relationship. The album that will ultimately result will provide a companion to the movie of presidential-congressional longitudinal foreign relations that was offered in this chapter.

---

[8] Vietnamization refers to a strategic policy initiated by the Nixon administration in 1969 to gradually drawdown American forces in the Vietnam War and ultimately lead to a "peace with honor" as America would retreat from active participation in Southeast Asian conflict. The strategy was built around a combination of aggressive diplomacy with the enemy and the simultaneous movement toward turning over first combat and ultimately logistical operations against the North Vietnamese Army and the Viet Cong to the South Vietnamese government.

Summary

This chapter has discussed the longitudinal analysis and findings relative to the multiple presidencies across the issue areas (national security, domestic security, diplomacy, trade, foreign aid and immigration) of foreign policy. In this effort, I have started with an opening historical narrative regarding the broad contours of executive-legislative relations in this domain of policy making. Next, we examined the findings related to such foreign affairs relations by employing time series, mean percent differencing and simple multiple regressions. While not all of the findings support the thesis, most of them do and they do so in both general as well as specific ways. Essentially, foreign policy success is a function of the component issue area success rates, especially those in the high politics arena (national security, domestic security and diplomacy). Within that, national security has the most privileged position and hence impact on positively influencing presidential success as hypothesized by the notion of presidency-centered conditions. However, it was found that the negative impact of securitization on foreign and national security success is a major impediment for the theory's general application. Clearly, more research needs to be done in order to explain this discordant finding or at least account for its presence within the established framework of the multiple presidencies.

Likewise, the low politics arena (trade, foreign aid and immigration) are least associated with presidential success as they are Congress-centered conditions. This is especially true of foreign aid and immigration but trade is also quite limited in its systematic impact as well. Finally, the big three of national security, trade and foreign aid seem to be the driving forces within the foreign policy domain, something vitally important to realize for this and other studies employing an "issue areas analysis."

Then, we examined the quantitative indicators for periodicity regressed against the dependent variable and found significant if not always intuitive relationships. Coming out of these findings, we saw how the multiple presidencies thesis, as a theory of presidential-congressional foreign policy relations can be shown to provide a strong heuristic for bringing together the qualitative narrative with the quantitative indicators themselves through analogous reasoning. And, now let the War Power Cometh!

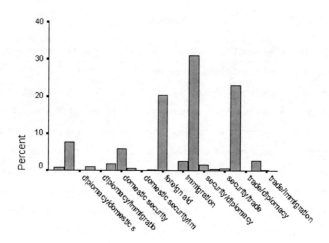

Figure 4-1. Issue Areas of Foreign Policy Bar Chart Across Political Time (1953-2004)

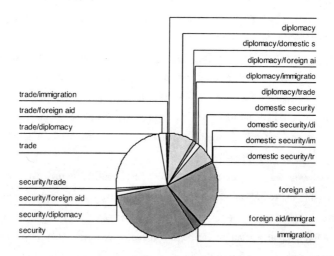

Figure 4-2. Issue Areas of Foreign Policy Pie Chart Across Political Time (1953-2004)

Table 4-1. National Security v. Trade Policy Success across Political Time (1953-2004)

	t	df	Sig. (2-tailed)	Mean Difference	95% Confidence Interval of the Difference	
					Lower	Upper
Annual presidential success score in national security policy	266.943	3142	.000	.746402	.740919	.751884
Annual presidential success score in trade policy	196.990	3343	.000	.713475	.706374	.720576

Table 4-2. National Security v. Foreign Aid Policy Success across Political Time (1953-2004)

	t	df	Sig. (2-tailed)	Mean Difference	95% Confidence Interval of the Difference	
					Lower	Upper
Annual presidential success score in national security policy	266.943	3142	.000	.746402	.740919	.751884
Annual presidential success score in foreign aid policy	217.138	3197	.000	.723677	.717143	.730212

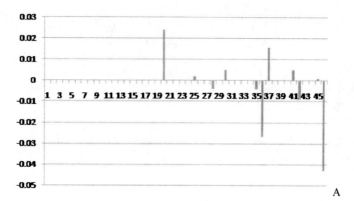

A

Figure 4-3. Models of Foreign and Issue Area Presidential Success Relative to Congress Time
Series Autocorrelation Analysis. A) Across Political Time (1953-2004): Annual
Presidential Foreign Policy Success Time Series Autocorrelation Analysis. Note: see
Appendix Table 4-1 data for readout of this and the following six models. B) Across
Political Time (1953-2004): Annual Presidential National Security Success Time
Series Autocorrelation Analysis. C) Across Political Time (1953-2004): Annual
Presidential Domestic Security Success Time Series Autocorrelation Analysis. D)
Across Political Time (1953-2004): Annual Presidential Diplomatic Policy Success.
Time Series Autocorrelation Analysis. E) Across Political Time (1953-2004): Annual
Presidential Trade Policy Success Time Series Autocorrelation Analysis. F) Across
Political Time (1953-2004): Annual Presidential Foreign Aid Policy Success Time
Series Autocorrelation Analysis. G) Across Political Time (1953-2004): Annual
Presidential Immigration Policy Success Time Series Autocorrelation Analysis.

B

C

Figure 4-3. Continued

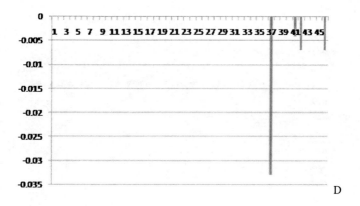

D

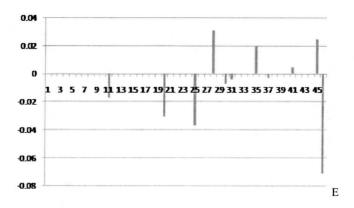

E

Figure 4-3. Continued

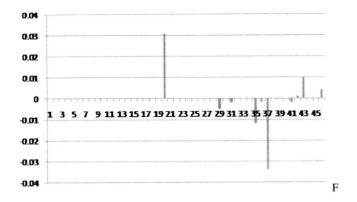

F

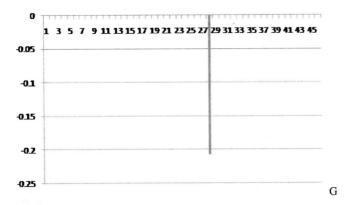

G

Figure 4-3. Continued

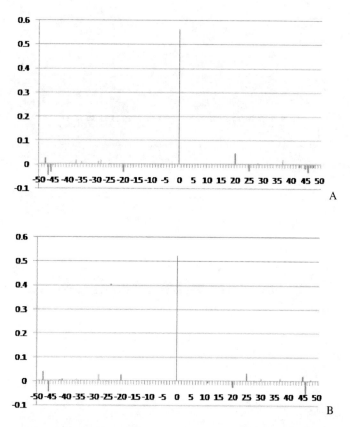

Figure 4-4. Models of Presidential Foreign National Security and Trade Success Relative to Congress Time Series Cross Correlation Analysis. A) Across Political Time (1953-2004): Annual Presidential Foreign and National Security Policy Success Time Series Cross-Correlation Analysis. B) Across Political Time (1953-2004): Annual Presidential Foreign and Trade Policy Success Time Series Cross-Correlation Analysis. Note: see Appendix Table 4-2 data for readouts of this and the other cross-correlation analyses (A, B and C—only shown in the appendix).

Table 4-3. Foreign Policy Success Regression Analysis of Central Core Issue Area Success (National Security and Trade) Across Political Time (1953-2004)

Foreign Policy=National Security + Trade + E	Un-standardized Coefficients		Sig.
	B	Std. Error	
(Constant)	.155	.007	.000
annual presidential success score in national security policy	.420	.009	.000
annual presidential success score in trade policy	.364	.006	.000

R Square	Adjusted R Square	Std. Error of the Estimate	Durbin-Watson
.702	.702	.072	.026

Predictors: (Constant), Annual Presidential Success Score in Trade Policy, Annual Presidential Success Score in National Security Policy
Dependent Variable: Annual Presidential Success Score in Foreign Policy
N=3335

Table 4-4. Foreign Policy Success Regression Analysis of All Issue Area Policy Success (National Security, Domestic Security, Diplomacy, Trade, Foreign Aid and Immigration) Across Political Time (1953-2004)

	Un-standardized Coefficients		Sig.
	B	Std. Error	
(Constant)	.126	.011	.000
annual presidential success score in trade policy	.314	.008	.000
annual presidential success score in foreign aid policy	.044	.008	.000
annual presidential success score in immigration policy	.020	.005	.000
annual presidential success score in national security policy	.222	.011	.000
annual presidential success score in domestic security policy	.196	.007	.000
annual presidential success score in diplomatic policy	.068	.005	.000

R Square	Adjusted R Square	Std. Error of the Estimate	Durbin-Watson
808	.807	.046	.036

Predictors: (Constant), Annual Presidential Success Score in Immigration Policy, Annual Presidential Success Score in Diplomatic Policy, Annual Presidential Success Score in National Security Policy, Annual Presidential Success Score in Trade Policy, Annual Presidential Success Score in Domestic Security Policy, Annual Presidential Success Score in Foreign Aid Policy
Dependent Variable: Annual Presidential Success Score in Foreign Policy

Table 4-5. Models of the Impacts of Securitization and Domestication of Foreign Policy Votes on Various Annual Presidential Success Rates. Model 1 Foreign Policy Success Regression Analysis of Securitization and Domestication of Foreign Policy Votes across Political Time (1953-2004)

Foreign Policy=Securitization + Domestication + E	Un-standardized Coefficients		Sig.
	B	Std. Error	
(Constant)	.753	.004	.000
Securitization of Vote	-.030	.006	.000
Domestication of Vote	-.034	.005	.000

R Square	Adjusted R Square	Std. Error of the Estimate	Durbin-Watson
.013	.013	.131	.034

Predictors: (Constant), Domestication of Vote, Securitization of Vote
Dependent Variable: Annual Presidential Success Score in Foreign Policy

Table 4-6. Models 2a & 2b National Security Policy Success Regression Analysis of Securitization and Domestication of Foreign Policy Votes across Political Time (1953-2004)

Models	Model 2a: National Security=Securitization + Domestication + E Model 2b: National Security=Securitization + E	Un-standardized Coefficients		Sig.
		B	Std. Error	
2a	(Constant)	.759	.005	.000
	Securitization of Vote	-.023	.007	.001
	Domestication of Vote	-.008	.007	.250
2b	(Constant)	.754	.003	.000
	Securitization of Vote	-.019	.006	.002

R Square	Adjusted R Square	Std. Error of the Estimate	Durbin-Watson
.004	.003	.155	.035

Predictors: (Constant), Domestication of Vote, Securitization of Vote
Dependent Variable: annual presidential success score in national security policy

Table 4-7. Model 2c Trade Policy Success Regression Analysis of Securitization and
Domestication of Foreign Policy Votes across Political Time (1953-2004)

Model	Trade=Securitization + Domestication + E	Un-standardized Coefficients		Sig.
		B	Std. Error	
2c	(Constant)	.760	.006	.000
	Securitization of Vote	-.047	.009	.000
	Domestication of Vote	-.076	.009	.000

R Square	Adjusted R Square	Std. Error of the Estimate	Durbin-Watson
.024	.023	.206	.052

Predictors: (Constant), Domestication of Vote, Securitization of Vote
Dependent Variable: Annual Presidential Success Score in Trade Policy

Table 4-8. Foreign Policy Success Regression Analysis of Executive-Legislative Orders of
Political Time in Foreign Affairs across Political Time (1953-2004)

	Un-standardized Coefficients		Sig.
	B	Std. Error	
(Constant)	.700	.016	.000
War Power Order 1953-1972	.134	.016	.000
Confrontation Politics Order 1973-1989	.005	.016	.777
Imperial Presidency Politicized 1990-2000	-.125	.016	.000
Extra-Systemic Dilemma 2001-2004	.143	.018	.000

R Square	Adjusted R Square	Std. Error of the Estimate	Durbin-Watson
.479	.478	.095	.030

Predictors: (Constant), Extra-Systemic Dilemma 2001-2004, Imperial Presidency Politicized
1990-2000, War Power Order 1953-1972, Confrontation Politics 1973-1989
Dependent Variable: Annual Presidential Success Score in Foreign Policy

Table 4-9. Macro-Level Historical-Economic Conditions as Determinants of Presidential Core
Issue Area Success. Model 1 National Security Success Regression Analysis of
Macro-Historical Determinants across Political Time (1953-2004)

National Security = War/Peace + Armed Forces + Defense Budget + E	Un-standardized Coefficients		Sig.
	B	Std. Error	
(Constant)	.386	.013	.000
war	-.072	.006	.000
Annual Size of US Armed Forces in millions	.239	.012	.000
Defense Outlays as a % Annual Federal Budget	-.518	.060	.000

R Square	Adjusted R Square	Std. Error of the Estimate	Durbin-Watson
.223	.222	.132	.032

Predictors: (Constant), Defense Outlays as a % Annual Federal Budget, war, Annual Size of US
Armed Forces in millions
Dependent Variable: Annual Presidential Success Score in National Security Policy

Table 4-10. Model 2 Trade Policy Success Regression Analysis of Macro-Economic
Determinants across Political Time (1953-2004)

Trade=Budgetary Conditions + GDP + Business Cycle + International Finance/Trade + E	Un-standardized Coefficients		Sig.
	B	Std. Error	
(Constant)	.766	.008	.000
Annual Trade and International Finance Balance in Billions	-3.286E-05	.000	.000
Annual Real GDP as measured by current dollars in trillions	-.015	.001	.000
Business Cycle Conditions	.074	.008	.000
Budgetary Conditions in Billions of current dollars	.001	.000	.000

R Square	Adjusted R Square	Std. Error of the Estimate	Durbin-Watson
.252	.251	.180	.030

Predictors: (Constant), Budgetary Conditions in Billions of current dollars, Business Cycle
Conditions, Annual Trade and International Finance Balance in Billions, Annual Real GDP as
measured by current dollars in trillions
  Dependent Variable: Annual Presidential Success Score in Trade Policy

Table 4-11. Model 3 Foreign Aid Policy Success Regression Analysis of Macro-Economic Determinants across Political Time (1953-2004)

Foreign Aid= Budgetary Conditions + GDP + Business Cycle + International Finance/Trade + E	Un-standardized Coefficients		Sig.
	B	Std. Error	
(Constant)	.778	.007	.000
Annual Trade and International Finance Balance in Billions	1.179	.000	.622
Annual Real GDP as measured by current dollars in trillions	-.031	.001	.000
Business Cycle Conditions	.047	.007	.000
Budgetary Conditions in Billions of current dollars	2.844	.000	.444

R Square	Adjusted R Square	Std. Error of the Estimate	Durbin-Watson
.177	.176	.173	.036

Predictors: (Constant), Budgetary Conditions in Billions of current dollars, Business Cycle Conditions, Annual Trade and International Finance Balance in Billions, Annual Real GDP as measured by current dollars in trillions
Dependent Variable: Annual Presidential Success Score in Foreign Aid Policy

CHAPTER 5
THE WAR POWER COMETH!: THE SECURITIZED TIME OF THE EARLY COLD WAR,
1953-1972

Introduction

In this chapter, we examine the War Power Order from 1953-1972, a time when the president's opportunity structure in security reaches its zenith. The early days of the Cold War provide an almost perfect instrument for the presidency to orchestrate the conduction of foreign policy. The reason for this is simple, the "crisis" mentality of these times had taken on a structural level impact whereby the Congress (and for that matter all other relevant members of the American polity) had essentially acquiesced to the presidency's force of will in foreign policy. In particular, the Congress had become the "servant" of a "securitized" presidential "master."[1]

The question, is how the presidents whether Eisenhower, Kennedy, Johnson or early Nixon were able to effectively reduce all of the disparate six issue areas of foreign policy into a "securitized" domain of high over low politics. The answer is provided by the president's opportunity structure in national security in combination with the structural "securitized" political environment offered by the early Cold War. These two factors, operating in concert at both the unit and systemic levels made this period of US foreign policy executive-legislative history into one where the "two presidencies" was prominent to the point of being axiomatic (Wildavsky 1966). The problem of course was that this period of time proved to be more the aberration than the norm for the presidential-congressional foreign policy relationship. This is especially true when foreign affairs are viewed across its component issue areas and the perspective arenas that differentiate them one from another.

This chapter will follow a similar structure as the last one by opening with an encompassing narrative built around executive-legislative foreign policy relations across the issue areas and the timeframe they are found in. The narrative will be divided by presidency in sequential order beginning with Eisenhower's two terms and ending with Nixon's first. Specific attention will be given to the role of security in influencing overall foreign policy development including seemingly ancillary issue areas like foreign aid, trade and not so ancillary domestic security. Next, it will move on to an examination of the empirical findings emanating out of the

---

[1] See the outline for the War Power Order, in particular its Hegelian dialectical structure in Chapter 1.

remaining longitudinal and the first set of cross-sectional studies. These studies will look specifically at the unit level relationship between the president and the Congress in foreign affairs by studying the impacts of political factors including public, electoral and partisan/ideological forces. The longitudinal regressions are employed in order to establish a baseline for comparison with the cross-sectional findings. This will showcase both the continuities and even more importantly the differences regarding the presidential-congressional relationship from across time and within time frameworks. Then, I will attempt to once again bring the narrative into systematic synthesis with the findings through a tabular analysis of the various presidential success rates across the component issue areas of foreign policy as provided by the multiple presidencies thesis. Of course, I will conclude with a brief summary of the chapter's major discussion points. And, now for Act I Scene I of the executive-legislative foreign affairs relationship—The War Power Cometh!

Foreign Issue Areas under Security's Yoke

The first thing to remember about the War Power Order 1953-1972 is the privileged role that security has during this time. This early period in Cold War history reduces all other potential conflicts and channels all potential confluences through the lens of the US-Soviet superpower struggle. Older readers may recall as children having their parents build fall out shelters or experience the civil defense emergency drills. Younger readers may not be as able to appreciate how "real" the Cold War was made in everyday political, economic and even socio-cultural "life." Too often we remember these times as an idyllic period of plenty, already reduced to nostalgia in the early seventies movie *American Graffiti* (1972). Or, we only remember the second half of this period as a time when the very traditions of our society were questioned as a result of the masses movements for change and the inevitable counter-reaction that arose against them. In this case, one may find themselves re-reading their copy of Hoffman's *Steal this Book!* or Kerouac's *The Road Less Traveled*. But, the fact of the matter is that, all of the above are true statements of this period of American history. So, the real question for us is, "Where do we find the president, the Congress and foreign policy during this time?

The answer is that presidential-congressional relations in foreign policy were not very visible to the outside observer and so they were somewhat hidden. Where they were visible and most important where they remained invisible, the president clearly dominated and the Congress routinely if somewhat masochistically was subordinated. Things did not have to be that way but they were. This was not because presidents were so great as to be unquestioned in foreign policy nor that the Congress was incompetent in international relations and hence inconsequential. No, it was that way because people, the president, the Congress and the polity writ-large wanted it to be that way.

While a fully developed normative analysis of this subject is beyond the scope of this particular research, it needs to be addressed that power is only held (at least in democracies like ours) through acceptance by the followers and persuasion by the leaders (from Neustadt 1960). During the War Power Order, the polity itself was enraptured by the messianic virtues of the modern presidency as ushered in by no less than FDR. America could do anything, it should do everything and such a virtuous people were clearly led by a virtuous leader—the president of the United States. In no where was this more true than in foreign policy, as the Congress was characterized by a domestic liberal economic agenda, a socially conservative tradition and most importantly for us, virtually absolute acquiescence to executive leadership in the "politics that lie beyond the water's edge" (Dodd 2005 in Dodd and Oppenheimer 2005, Snow and Brown 1999, Davidson 1996 in Thurber 1996 and Sinclair 2005 in Dodd and Oppenheimer 2005). Now let us study the War Power Order by its component presidencies and the issue areas of foreign policy that they dealt with in their interactions with the Congress.

Eisenhower 1953-1961

From an issue areas perspective, non-security was for all intents and purposes non-existent during the Eisenhower years. This was observed not only in openly national security oriented policies like the size of the armed forces or the percentage allocated to defense within the federal budget (both high during this time) but also domestic security (the Subversives Activities Act and Amendments), trade (restrictions placed on East-West trade and sanctions to those who traded with the Warsaw Pact—The Eisenhower Doctrine came out of this), immigration (checks against "communist" infiltrations) and foreign aid (the "Mutual Security Acts"). What tied all of these disparate legislative initiatives together was the overwhelming employment of a "securitized" language in their construction and purpose. This study is not subject to linguistic analysis; however, it would be an area of fruitful research for the future. For our purposes, it can be thought of as a major empirical referent in support of the thesis for this section that "it was all about security and hence presidentialization of foreign policy." It also needs to be noted that fully constituted legislative histories of these and other initiatives during this period need to be

139

conducted in order to get a true sense of their contribution to this research program. However, for the purposes of this project such analyses will have to wait and we will instead concentrate on detailing enough of the narrative necessary for an initial understanding of executive-legislative foreign policy relations during this crucial time. In this effort, I will concentrate on issue areas exclusive of security because they showcase the pronounced impact that the national security issue area had on *all* issue areas of foreign policy.

During the Eisenhower years, domestic security became a pronounced issue area of foreign policy unto itself. The investigative oversight of the House Un-American Activities Committee as well as McCarthyism in the Senate placed the executive branch of first Truman and later Eisenhower under the watchful eyes of a "fire alarm" Congress.[2] As the reader should recall from the last chapter, Eisenhower was swept into office on an electoral strategy which emphasized "Corruption, Communism and Korea." His early experience with unified Republican government for the first time since Hoover's first two years (1929-1931) was certainly emblematic of a "mandate," at least as regards foreign policy. However, as the Almond-Lippman (1950) thesis suggested regarding the lack of public attention to foreign affairs issues how long such a mandate could be capitalized on by President Eisenhower in his relationship to the Congress was certainly questionable. Within two years the 84th Congress opened with divided government and Eisenhower's control over the public policy agenda was no longer absolute as 1954 returned a "normal" vote outcome, which for Eisenhower disfavored him at least as far as partisanship was concerned.[3] It is an interesting side note that a modest review of the legislative history involving the Subversive Activities Act and its subsequent Amendments suggests the appearance of certain coalitions of interest diversified by both region and ideology. Essentially, an "order promoting" Conservative Coalition (Republicans and Southern Democrats) acts in opposition to Ike's interests and a more "liberty positing" Liberal Coalition (Republicans and Northern Democrats) manifests itself in support of the ideologically moderate president (CQ Almanacs 1958-59, vote studies appendices). We will see this appearance of countervailing

---

[2] See McCubbins & Scwartz (1984) "Congressional Oversight Overlooked: Police Patrol versus Fire

　　　Alarm," *AJPS* vol.1, pages 165-177, Mid-West Political Science Association, University

　　　Of Indiana, IN: Blackstone Publishing.

[3] See Campbell et. al. (1960) for a fuller discussion of the "normal" vote.

forces manifesting itself routinely, if not always systematically, across other issue areas of foreign policy regarding the president's legislative agenda(s). What explains it best seems to be the president's relative position to the various coalitions regarding the issue area of concern; presidents (even Eisenhower) seem to engage in strategic alliance making much in support of broader coalition formation theories (Riker 1962, Burns 1963, Bond and Fleisher 1990).

Thinking about the above statements, we see a similar though at first thought counter-intuitive pattern of alliance making regarding the Conservative and Liberal Coalitions and presidential success. Particularly in the areas of foreign aid and to a lesser extent in trade and immigration at least anecdotal patterns of coalitional formation appear, albeit not necessarily in any fully systematized fashion. Regarding foreign aid, the various Mutual Security Acts formalize the granting of Post-Marshall Plan aid to the new arena of Cold War conflict—the Third World. In this effort, the Conservative Coalition manifests itself in a neo-isolationist fashion opposing Eisenhower's expansions into this issue area as even after the death of Robert Taft (R-OH) in 1953 a fully interventionist Republican Party has not yet manifested itself (CQ Almanac 1959, vote summary appendix). Meanwhile, the Liberal Coalition shows itself in support of the president's agenda regarding this attempt to win the Cold War through economic and political development of the Third World over the force of arms (CQ Almanac 1959, vote summary appendix). Relatively modest measures in trade and immigration follow the patterns observed in foreign aid as to coalition formation; however, there infrequent appearance makes any inferences drawn open to severe question.

Moving back into the relatively exclusive arena of high politics, we see that national security policies are places of overawing opportunity for presidential agency. The extension of "war economy controls" well after the end of the Korean War, continuance of the system of conscription, expansion of the military reserve forces and procurement policies favoring the "New Look" (expansion of the strategic nuclear forces into the "triad" as well as the creation of the strategic air and sea lift capabilities) tended to be overwhelmingly supported in a bi-partisan fashion. These tendencies were offset by the emergence of a "hawkish" Conservative Coalition in support of the Eisenhower national security program and a "dovish" Liberal Coalition opposed to it but again, its systematic appearance is not as robust (from CQ Almanacs 1958-60, vote summary appendices). In a last bit of national security dominance, it should be noted that all troop deployments and doctrine applications (like the Eisenhower Doctrine for the Middle East) were overwhelmingly supported by a Congress that was usually controlled by the opposition party. Finally, national security was so prominent in the Eisenhower White House that domestic initiatives like the Highway Act of 1956 (the largest publics works project in American public policy history) was "sold" as a means for swift military transit during conditions of systemic war (see CQ Almanac 1956, legislative history for Highway Act).

JFK & LBJ 1961-1969

The Kennedy and Johnson presidencies saw a foreign policy focus which has two somewhat contradictory trends, at the superpower level conflict was actually reduced after the "world blinked," at the end of those fateful 13 days in October of 1962 (see Alison 1971 for a systematic analysis of the Cuban Missile Crisis). The Open Air Test Treaty in 1963 and a return to "summitry" with the USSR after the U-2 spy plane incident during the late Eisenhower administration would if nothing else be a precursor for the détente to come (see May 1969 for a cogent and somewhat contemporized review of these). However, at the level of "proxy actors" in the Cold War struggle no such reduction was present; in fact a major increase in the intensity of relations to the point of open confrontation is what occurred. The Gulf of Tonkin incident and its corresponding congressional resolution in 1964 led the United States down a foreign policy path to open warfare with the communists over a piece of Southeast Asia called Vietnam (see Elsberg 1971 for a review of this process). While it is easy to see this "as the beginning of the end," it was in fact far from that. Public approval of US action in Vietnam would remain high until the Tet Offensive and the Congress would not begin to seriously defect from stated administration policies relative to Southeast Asia until well into 1968 (from Sundquist 1981 and CQ Almanacs 1966-68, congressional debates over Vietnam policy). In fact, continued congressional acquiescence to presidential dominance regarding the war was the norm throughout this time (CQ Almanac 1967, Fulbright committee statements). However, some "chinks" in the presidential foreign policy armor were being exposed once one leaves the safety of the national security issue area.

For instance, the Conservative Coalition, while continuing to support presidential national security policies in Vietnam, the Dominican Republic and elsewhere balked against the Great Society prescriptions for opening immigration through increases in quota allowances for immigrants (CQ Almanac 1965, vote summary appendix). Also, the Liberal Coalition a hallmark of support for civil rights advances in the domestic sphere parts way with the Kennedy and

142

Johnson administrations' emphasis on military aid over economic development and humanitarian aid to the "Group of 77" Non-Aligned Nations (NAM) of the Third World (from Axelrod 2007, Morrison 1990 and CQ Almanacs 1962 and 1968, congressional debates over the Foreign Assistance Act of 1962 and subsequent Amendments).

In fact, the Foreign Assistance Act of 1962 is somewhat of a bridge between the two contradictory developments in foreign policy during the Kennedy and Johnson years. The reason for this is that, the codification of US foreign aid as an ongoing permanent instrument of the Cold War via the Foreign Assistance Act of 1962 at first dictated a continued presidentialization of foreign policy through the national security lens. However, by the end of the 1960's this same instrument would be the vehicle by which the Congress would reassert itself as an institutional alternative to the presidency in foreign policy construction. With the return of divided government after the 1968 presidential election, that vehicle would take on a life all its own as the Congress specifically drove into the quagmire of Vietnam War policy.

Nixon I 1969-1973

The first term of Richard Nixon's presidency, represented the "setting sun" of a fully presidentialized and securitized foreign policy. While presidential success remained high in foreign policy it was now due primarily to the offsetting impact of the Conservative Coalition supporting Nixon's policies in foreign affairs, especially regarding Vietnam (see Malbin and Brookshire 2000). The days of complete bi-partisanship, when the president, the Congress and the rest of the polity spoke with a "single voice" (through the mouth of the presidency) were now a thing of the past. The fact that we are almost forty years removed from this time and the past has yet to reassert itself, shows the longstanding impact of this "sea change" in presidential-congressional relations where foreign affairs are concerned. It might be helpful to conceptualize the Nixon years as exhibiting "two presidencies" all their own, one for his first term which will be articulated here and another for his second term which is presented (along with Ford's) in the next chapter (see chapter 6).

The first Nixon presidency represents continuity with the immediate past, like the Eisenhower through Johnson years; Nixon dominates foreign policy albeit through a modified technique (reliance on the Conservative Coalition's ongoing "securitized" support as a base). The Cold War Consensus on foreign policy, especially regarding security and "securitized" policies was still the predominant force in presidential-congressional relations. But, the "chinks" first exposed in the late Johnson administration regarding foreign aid applications to Southeast Asia opened up into fissures and finally cracks in the executive-legislative Cold War Consensus.

A systematic review of the foreign aid appropriations process in particular during this time is beyond the scope of this study's examination, however, a cursory glance is revealing in itself. By the early 1970's, the foreign aid appropriations process had become a place of intense floor battles between the Conservative (supporting Nixon) and Liberal (opposing the president) Coalitions over the increasing proclivity and scope of the Cooper (R-KY)-Church (D-MA) Amendments. These amendments came out of the Appropriations Committee in the House of Representatives and had corollaries with various senatorial amendments offered during floor debate by Fulbright (D-AR), Proxmire (D-WI) and others mostly Northern Democrats and a small faction of Northeastern Republicans. Supporting Nixon was Senators such as "Scoop" Jackson (D- WA) and Michael Mansfield (R-MI) and of course others, mostly Republicans and Southern Democrats (CQ Almanacs 1971-1972, vote summaries). It needs to be noted that these procedural maneuvers appeared after the escalations of ground and air US combat operations by Nixon in Cambodia in 1970 and Laos 1971. Those two operations and the domestic protests that led out of them across American university campuses need to be understood as what they actually represented—a fundamental "revolution" in how foreign policy was constructed regarding the locus of institutional power. Essentially after 1972, the president would no longer hold a hegemonic position because after 1972 foreign affairs were no longer reducible to the needs and dictates of national security.

Empirical Findings I: The Longitudinal Political Determinants of Presidential Foreign Policy Success

The results for this section come in two related but differentiated forms. First, for the purposes of continuity with the previous chapter as well as to set baseline conditions for comparative purposes I will continue with longitudinal study of foreign policy and relevant issue area success. In this case, though we will look at specifically political factors roughly differentiated along three dimensions public, electoral and partisan/ideological. Together these forces can be seen to be driving the unit level relationship between the president and the Congress in foreign policy. The longitudinal findings provide useful empirical referents for how the multiple presidencies have played out across time as unit level phenomenon; however they are limited in their inability to be utilized as explanatory devices for *within time* study—that is where the cross-sectional regressions come in.

These regression models will further illuminate the executive-legislative foreign policy relationship by looking at the unit level interactions within the specified time frame of the War Power Order. By comparing similarly constituted models based around the three dimensions of the political forces, we can determine what the *nuances* of the presidential-congressional relationship *really* were during this dynamic period of US foreign policy history. But, first let us look at the longitudinal relationships of these political forces on presidential success in foreign and issue area policies. Similar to the last chapter, all relevant tables are found at the end of this chapter in sequential order with the longitudinal empirics reported first and then followed by the cross-sectionals.

Tables 5-1 through 5-4 cover the longitudinal analyses regarding the influence of public opinion factors on the foreign policy and relevant issue area success rates. For these and all other analyses in this chapter, I chose the national security, trade and foreign aid success rates as emblematic of all issue area success. My reason, for doing this is found in the last chapter's results regarding the strong presence of the "big three" foreign policy issue areas, which I referred to as the "core issue areas" (see Chapter 4). Accordingly, the explanatory factors for all of these models include: annual presidential job approval ratings, annual presidential foreign policy approval ratings, annual congressional job approval ratings and annual congressional job disapproval ratings. The dependent variables are of course the annual presidential position vote success rates in foreign policy, national security policy, trade policy and foreign aid policy.

As Table 5-1 reveals, all four independent variables have significant as well as relatively robust correlations with foreign policy success. Two of the variables, congressional job approval and presidential job approval are signed in the right directions as far as expectations are concerned. Using the working framework of presidency-centered versus Congress-centered conditions as our guide, we can see that increases in congressional job approval will have a depressed effect on foreign policy success because higher congressional job approval is a congress-centered condition. Likewise, higher presidential approval is a presidency-centered condition which exerts a positive and strong relationship on the presidency's overall foreign policy success rate.

145

However, contradictory findings result from the other two variables congressional disapproval as well as presidential foreign policy approvals has strongly negative correlations with foreign policy success. This stands in direct contradiction to hypothesized effects and seems to be somewhat counterintuitive because you would think that presidential approval in foreign policy would "track" with overall presidential public approval and that the disapproval rating for Congress would have an inverse relationship with its approval rating. While the R square for the model as a whole is modestly robust (.408), perhaps the inclusion of such related factors as the two presidential approval ratings and the two congressional approval ratings is causing a multicollinearity effect. Since this is a baseline measure only, I will not indulge in further model manipulation but it is a place for further study.

Table 5-2, measures the impacts of the forces of public opinion on presidential national security success with expected results once one takes into account the findings in Table 5-1. Due to the high rate of presence that national security success has in foreign policy success writ large, it should not surprise anyone that the findings largely "track" each other with a slight decrease in the R square (.338). This decrease is to be expected since success in this category is actually a sub-set of success in the other. Also, the reader should note that the model still fits very well; this is a strong indicator of national security's role in "dictating" foreign policy success in general.

Regarding trade success, as Table 5-3 suggests only the two congressional public approval ratings follow expected predictions out from a congress-centered versus a presidency-centered perspective. It is clear that as an inherently "intermestic" issue, trade substantively affects presidential success and latitude vis-à-vis Congress. It is also indicative that the "contradictory" findings in the negative relationship between presidential approval even in foreign policy and trade success, suggest that in fact presidents are not as advantaged under presidency-centered conditions in the more "congressionalized" issue area of trade.

As Table 5-4 indicates, there is an across-the-board negative (yet still significant) correlation between the public opinion factors and presidential success in foreign aid. While congressional approval is in the expected direction as premised by our bifurcation into presidency-centered and congress-centered conditions, the weak R square (.19) limits the utility of this model as far as inferential and even explanatory purposes are concerned. Again, it is conceivable that presidency-centered conditions are playing less and less a role as the issue area of concern moves further out of the high politics arena. However, the fact that congressional

146

disapproval continues to have a negative relationship is disconcerting. But, it is conceivable that congressional disapproval is offset by presidential disapproval which could explain this outcome, particularly given the widespread evidence that Americans do not like foreign aid as an instrument of foreign policy (from Kegley and Wittkopf 2001).

The next set of tables (Tables 5-5 — 5-8), deal with the longitudinal effects of electoral forces on presidential success relative to the Congress regarding foreign affairs policy making. As before, the dependent variables are the perspective presidential position vote success rates in foreign policy, national security, trade and foreign aid relative to the Congress. The independent variables for each of the models are: presidential popular vote percentage victories, Electoral College percent victories, turnout rates for presidential elections, turnout in House elections during mid-terms, turnout in House elections during quadrennial elections and dummy variables indicating whether it is a presidential or a mid-term election year.

Table 5-5 shows the relationship between the electoral forces and the overall foreign policy success rate, turnout has an expected relationship with it being positive for presidential elections and negative in mid-term elections (turnout is insignificant regarding the within case relationship of House turnout in presidential elections). Somewhat unexpectedly, Electoral vote has a negative (albeit weak) correlation with foreign policy success but this is offset by the positive (and stronger) effect seen with the popular vote. This probably says more about the in-directness of the Electoral College as a vote function than any real impact on roll call position vote outcomes. Lastly, presidential election years have a negative (though weak) impact on foreign policy success over time. Despite its appearance, this is probably a campaign effect due to the increased role of presidential "issues" (like foreign policy) in presidential election years. In other words, during the presidential campaign season normally non-politicized issues of foreign policy will tend to become salient with the public and hence take on a more politicized (read partisan) character in ongoing presidential-congressional relations. Therefore, presidential success in foreign policy will systematically decline during presidential election years but then re-bound somewhat when the status quo of governing begins again in the next year after the presidential election.

When examining the effects of electoral forces on national security success, as in Table 5-6 we see similar results as in the foreign policy writ-large category. Again, see the commentary on the last set of findings for why this is probably the case. However, the within case scenario of

147

turnout in House races during the presidential election now appears as a significant indicator and follows an expected negative direction. The reason for this is that turnout in these elections which is high would be indicative of a congress not a presidency-centered condition. Electoral forces do not seem to have the "staying impact" which public opinion does. As we start to break apart the "foreign policy box" into its component elements a massive increase in the level of variance takes place. The R square for this model is still relatively strong (.250); however, this is a decline from the previous model's robust (.444). What explains this? Probably, it is due to the more anecdotal appearance of electoral forces, they are more dynamic, less routine and hence more variable in the degree and level of their "impacts" as determinants of presidential-congressional relations, especially in foreign policy.

Table 5-7 looks at the electoral determinants and presidential trade success. Both electoral year variables are statistically significant, however, the weakness of their respective correlations is such that they are questionable at best as strong (or even weak) determinants of executive-legislative trade relations. The rest of the variables perform in unexpected ways, having uniformly negative relationships with trade success despite hypothesized conditions. The only outlier to this phenomenon is House turnout in presidential elections; in this case it is strong and positive. Perhaps, this is due to "presidential pork" regarding the construction of trade policy with individual representatives and senators in mind. Again, as so much is true about any initial endeavor this is a case worthy of further study.

The last table that interprets the role of electoral forces in foreign policy success takes aim at presidential success in foreign aid policy. Table 5-8 shows that four of the six variables behave in the predicted direction, however presidential vote turnout is just short of statistical significance (.09). Of the remaining two variables, one electoral vote defects from hypothesized conditions (though this is probably offset by the popular vote anyway) and the other House turnout in presidential elections is insignificant.

Despite the fact, that this model has fairly strong results largely corroborating the multiple presidencies thesis it is somewhat weakly specified with a modest R square (.174). Of course, it needs to be stated that R squares are not perfect predictors of model strength. The limited number of variables in this and other regression models in these cross-sectional studies is probably the main reason for the decline in the size of the R squares. As you decrease the size of your models as to variable count you will tend to produce *underspecified* outcomes, which are

148

manifest in lower R square values. However, you will simultaneously *increase* the precision of your model regarding overall *inference capacity* relative to its specific variables. Therefore, as the *generality* of your model as a device for explanation decreases with the lowering of R squares (due to the increase in model variance left unexplained) it actually increases as to its *specificity* for explaining individual independent-dependent variable interactions. What this means is that the average *individual* residual distance decreases while the average *aggregate* residual distance increases (Agresti and Finlay 2001, chapter 11).

The next set of tables (Tables 5-9—5-12) explore the role of partisanship as an across time determinant of the character of the foreign policy relationship shared between the executive and the legislature. As always, the outcome variables are the annualized success scores for the president across foreign, national security, trade and foreign aid policies in his relationship with the Congress. For these analyses, the input variables are partisan indicators including: unified government, percent president's party in House and Senate, percentage partisan roll calls in House and Senate and the various party unity scores for the House and Senate by their respective major parties (the Democrats and the Republicans).

Regarding the presidential success rate in foreign policy, Table 5-9 indicates that there are three basic interpretations emanating out of the impact of partisan factors. First, partisanship in general is deleterious for presidential success in foreign policy as indicated by the percent partisan roll call measures for both the House and the Senate. This is to be expected for bi-partisanship and to a lesser extent cross-partisanship is more associated with congressional deference to presidential leadership in foreign affairs policy construction. Second, also, following the prescriptions of a presidency-centered condition is that partisanship has a more positive impact relative to presidential success in the Senate than in the House. The reason is that in the Senate the strength of the parties is naturally lower than in the House due to their more egalitarian and individualist make-up (from Davidson and Oleszek 2005). Therefore, in the Senate partisan activity in foreign affairs is used to create presidential support rather than offset it as occurs in the House. The Senate can be thought of as a more presidency-centered legislative institution than the House, thus the parties are a source of power. However, the opposite is true in the House which is institutionally more congress-centered and its parties are sources then of congressional not presidential empowerment in foreign policy. In a related finding the differential impacts of the relative strength of the president's party in the two chambers also

149

provides corroborating support for a presidency-oriented Senate in foreign policy and a congressionally-oriented House. Third, unified government itself follows predicted patterns with a positive and significant impact on foreign policy success. The real strength of this model can be found in its measure of variance control. The R square is a very robust .68 which suggests that the impact of partisanship may deserve independent study itself.

Table 5-10 looks at partisanship and national security success. It follows a similar pattern as the foreign policy model with the exception that the relationship with partisanship generally is not quite as strong (the Senate partisanship indicator reduces to statistical insignificance). However, all other variables are in the predicted direction and this model is as robust as the previous with a .67 R square.

As expected, once we leave the presidentially oriented confines of the national security issue area there is a perceptible decline in the congressional political party as an organizing instrument for presidential governance in foreign policy. While partisan roll call voting and president's party percentages in each chamber follow expected patterns, party unity and unified government diverge. Party Unity divides out along a left-right basis, wherein Republican unity is positively associated with presidential trade success regardless of chamber and Democratic unity has a negative association (though in one case it is insignificant). In other words, the strength of the hypothesis that the Senate is some bastion of strength for presidential success in foreign policy only seems to hold in the high politics arena. In the more intermestic low politics arena, of which trade is the most prominent issue area, no such case can be made for a presidential-senatorial "special relationship." Finally, unified government drops out as a significant indicator suggesting that its role as a presidency-centered indicator is in question once we leave the vaunted realm of security politics. The over arching role of security during the War Power Order may actually be masking some level of presidential-congressional discord regarding the non-securitized issue areas of foreign policy. The bedrock of security may be so "thick" that the more naturally politicized (and hence partisan) issue strata of executive-legislative foreign policy relations are actually hidden from systematic view.

Table 5-12 studies foreign aid success as a function of partisan forces. The result is somewhat of a mixed bag. Unified government returns to statistical significance and has a predicted positive relationship with foreign aid success but has a weak correlation (*beta*= .161). Meanwhile, as with the above table, any sense of a presidential-senatorial special relationship in foreign aid is lost as the sign reverses to a negative direction. In fact, if anything there seems to be a modest presidential-House relationship positively influencing foreign aid success. This is a strong indicator that by looking at the component issue areas of foreign policy we can garner interesting patterns that are nuanced to the point of contradiction as this presidential-House foreign aid relationship is juxtaposed against the presidential-senatorial national security finding. Again, this is a place for further inquiry; however it currently lies beyond the scope of this project.

The last set of longitudinal findings (Tables 5-13—5-16) discusses the role of ideology on our four dependent variables of interest. Accordingly, the explanatory variables employed in these analyses were: the Conservative Coalition votes for the president's foreign policy position and those against, the Liberal Coalition's votes for the president's foreign policy position and those against as well as the annualized ideological assessment of the president's legislative positions by the liberal interest group the Americans for Democratic Action (ADA). Essentially, this is a proxy measure as it captures the foreign policy votes contained within the data set but it also is based off all position votes each year including those in domestic and economic policies. Together these measures are giving us a picture of the ideological distribution between as well as within the presidency and the Congress across time.

Regarding overall foreign policy success, ideology tends to support hypothesized conditions; wherein presidential success is positively associated with coalition voting in support of presidential positions and negatively correlated with opposition coalitional conditions. It is also, telling that the stronger correlation coefficients are among the supporting coalitions, in fact the Conservative Coalition votes against the president's position fail to meet statistical significance. While the model is instructive overall as to its basic support for the multiple presidencies thesis, it is offset by the fact that there is a high level of unaccounted for variance contained within (R square=.19). However, I would repeat that as with my previous explanation regarding a similar matter this may be due to the decrease in the number of variables involved. Which actually means that the specific variable relationships are stronger than one might first believe. Additionally, there are two possibilities driving this outcome, one theoretical the other methodological. From a theoretical perspective, ideology is subsumed within more generally consistent partisan voting (from Poole and Rosenthal 1997). Meanwhile, methodologically speaking the coalitional voting (whether liberal or conservative) is in fact only a small sample of the position roll call vote population and hence might be subject to being "lost" in the "residual white noise" of the massive amount of foreign policy voting contained within the data set itself. This, by the way, could also be accounting for the low R square in the model as a whole.

Finally, the rating of presidential ideology is interesting, in that it suggests that more liberal presidents have higher foreign policy success rates than conservative ones. This is fascinating because it places doubt in the notion of a "partisan two presidencies" which is suggested to help Republican presidents only due to the Conservative Coalition's more pronounced presence as a foreign policy support device for presidential position taking (Bond and Fleisher 1988). Again, I think that a theoretical as well as a methodological explanation possibly accounts for this outcome. Theoretically, liberal presidents tend to be associated with broader legislative agendas in general, thus there are just more legislative "items" for the Congress to address in all domains of policy (Pika and Maltese 2006). Likewise, as reported by Shull and Shaw (1999), methodologically liberal presidents take more roll call positions and given the generally high success rate in presidential roll call voting, it makes sense that they would conceivably have a "higher success rate." As further evidence of this hypothesis, look at the correlation coefficient at (.127) it is relatively low even though it is statistically significant (p=.05). Therefore, at least in the aggregate, the real difference between conservative and liberal president's success rates in foreign policy may not be as great as these results seem to suggest at first glance.

Moving on to the issue areas studies, we first examine ideology's impact on national security success. As Table 5-14 reveals, the results are in the "right" direction as far as the predictions emanating out of the multiple presidencies thesis is concerned. But the model is too weak statistically to be taken seriously (R square = .011). However, regarding substantive interpretations it is interesting to note that the weakness of the model may actually be *in-direct* evidence of the thesis as a whole. What I mean by this is that national security success can be inferred form this model to *not* be subject to ideology. This is important because it suggests that this domain is not as *politicized* across time as some of the other issue areas and thus it supports the prolonged existence of a bi-partisan non-ideological consensus around presidential prerogatives in the national security issue area.

In contrast to the above conclusions, trade is indeed subject to such politicization as measured by ideology (R square=.513). In this case, the Conservative Coalition drops out of statistical significance as does the Liberal Opposition Coalition. This is important because it is suggesting that the Conservative Coalition is more high politics (security driven—see Table 5-14) and the Liberal Coalition is more low politics (non-security driven—see Table 5-15). Taking an ideological view of the foreign affairs issue areas, this makes sense given the philosophical predilections of the two ideologies as far as foreign policy is concerned (conservatives tend toward Realist (read "Hawkish") assessments of world politics while liberals tend to a more Idealist (read "Dovish") conception of the US's position in world affairs) (Papp, Johnson and Endicott 2005). Looking at the results regarding foreign aid success (Table 5-16) we can see continued support for the above hypotheses. However, the correlations weaken considerably with the two opposition coalitions falling to statistical insignificance. The poor showing of the R square (.025), while in general support of the notion that "things get political" as we move away from the presidentialized high politics arena leaves any stronger inferences from this model open to question.

Before finishing this section of the chapter, I must discuss a somewhat ancillary topic that is only *indirectly* related to the political determinants of the unit level foreign policy relationship between the American executive and national legislative branches. The questions of influence regarding "type of vote" and "value of issue area" serve at the heart of the mechanistic or instrumental process represented by executive-legislative relations. While a complete examination of this issue is beyond the scope of this present study, it still needs to be addressed in at least a modestly systematic fashion. As the reader may recall, presidency-centeredness would imply that the more high politics arena the vote and the more super-majoritarian as well as final the vote the more likely the outcome will favor the president's previously stated position. A cursory examination of these trends (see Tables 5-17—5-20), indicates weak support for hypothesized conditions regarding trade and foreign aid success but no support for expected patterns in national security or foreign policy success. The overwhelmingly weak strength of any of these models as shown in their low R squares suggests that in practice type of vote and issue area value have little to do with presidential position success rates in foreign policy relations with the Congress. This is instructive because it reveals a weakness in prior roll call analysis. Populations are just better to utilize than samples. Much prior research has utilized various "ordering rules" whether they are contentious votes, close votes, significant votes, non-unanimous votes or something else in roll call analysis. All of these operate from a basis that the "type of vote" matters. However, my findings suggest otherwise; in fact, the true picture of roll call relations at least as far as foreign affairs is concerned is left *unrevealed* when such ordering schemes are employed. Clearly, this is a place for further inquiry as I have thrown down a gauntlet which gets at the heart of presidential-congressional roll call research but that will have to wait for further study and debate. For, at this point in time we must move on to the cross-sectional findings relative to foreign, issue and now *mixed* issue area presidential success relative to the Congress.

Empirical Findings II: Cross-Sectional Political Determinants of Presidential Success in Foreign Policy during the War Power Order 1953-1972

By way of review regarding the last section's overall results, it is important to recall that amongst the various political determinants of foreign and issue area success only the partisan factors exerted a consistently strong longitudinal correlation. Therefore, for this next analysis I have limited my inquiry to a re-examination of those partisan factors as determinants of the *within political time* framework provided by the War Power Order, 1953-1972. Tables 5-21—5-25 contain the relevant findings; regarding overall foreign policy success during this time (see Table 5-21) we see results that strongly comport with the basics of the multiple presidencies thesis. For starters the model is extremely robust with 96% of the variance accounted for (see the R square). Secondly, all variables are significant and "signed" in the right direction with strong correlations. From these findings, we can strongly infer that partisanship when unified (the unified government variable) served as a source of presidential empowerment in foreign affairs. We can also suggest that when the parties-in-the Congress diverged (as indicated by the other variables) it had little detrimental impact on presidential success because the increase in partisan roll calls is offset by the differential impact of party unity voting within the chambers themselves. Therefore, the president during the War Power Order was in a "win-win" situation where presidential-congressional foreign policy relations were concerned. Essentially, where partisanship was shown to be *least* beneficial to the presidency-centered position (in the Senate) is precisely where partisanship has long been known to matter the least amidst the two chambers (from Leloup and Shull 2003). Thus, we can suggest that partisanship was a source of strength in presidential-House relations during this time and bi-partisanship was the main source of power for the foreign affairs presidential-Senate relationship.

154

Table 5-22 details the national security success relationship among executive-legislative affairs during the War Power Order. Though partisanship plays a positive role in the presidency's congressional relationship with the Senate it has an almost uniformly *negative* impact on War Power Order national security success. Why is this so? Well, if you keep in mind the fact that this is a time in US foreign policy history dominated by the Conservative Coalition's support for national security policies then it makes sense that this phenomenon would "push out" the forces of partisanship in this domain. As Table 5-23 portrays, this phenomenon continues in trade with the exception that now it is party unity that is offsetting partisan roll call voting but the interpretation is largely the same. As the multiple presidencies would predict, during this period of *political time* security is so pronounced that trade has been largely "securitized" this is shown in its distributional impact which follows what occurred in the national security issue area. Finally, foreign aid success (see Table 5-24) follows the established pattern with the exception that unified government returns as a positive indicator of presidential success. Even though the power of security is overawing during this time, we must remember that foreign aid is much further removed from the high politics arena than trade. Thus, its greater intermestic congress-centered conditionality makes it more politicized and hence given to partisanship (which the unified government variable is indicating in this case).

So where do we go from here? As was indicated in the previous chapter (4), the mixed issue areas of foreign policy do not assert themselves well in a longitudinal fashion. However, it is conceivable that a within time formulation like the War Power Order will shed some systematic light on this until now only anecdotal subject. Comparing the partisan factors findings from Table 5-25's mixed issue area success with those of overall foreign policy success (Table 5-21) we can see that there is little discernible difference between the two. This is indicative of the fact that at least as far as the War Power Order is concerned, the same partisan factors that impact presidential success in foreign policy as a whole also work in favor (and disfavor) of mixed issue area success. This is telling because, it means that there just may not be anything distinctive about mixed issue areas, another point for future research's departure but beyond our present concerns.

The Multiple Presidencies during the War Power Order

So how do we make sense out of all this? Well, the first step is to take a broader view regarding the differential "rates" of foreign policy and issue area success enjoyed by the various presidencies that held office during the War Power Order. As Tables 5-26 — 5-29 indicate presidential success in foreign policy is high throughout, in both chambers and regardless of president or Congress. However, these tables also indicate that across the various issue areas of foreign policy there is some not so subtle variation in the level of success. National security and the high politics arena in general tend to exhibit high patterns of success. The great outlier though is trade, technically a part of the low politics arena it routinely exhibits success rates on a par with those found in the high politics arena. A final conclusion that can be drawn from these tables is the substantive lack certain issue areas like immigration have in their systematic appearance.

However, diplomacy and domestic security which tend to "fall out" as issue areas under longitudinal circumstances do exhibit a robust showing in this cross-sectional, albeit descriptive account. Foreign aid is present as expected given its role as one of the "core" issue areas of foreign policy but it is not as subject to variation as one might expect (roughly on par with trade and diplomacy to a lesser extent). Again, this is probably due to the massive presence of security and its environmental potential to "securitize/presidentialize" all other issue areas of foreign policy. Lastly, there is a trend for greater variation amidst the issue area success rates as time in an individual presidential term goes by. But, this phenomenon does not seem to impact national security or domestic security (though the lesser appearance of this issue area throughout leads to some questions about this particular "descriptive inference"). Of course, this is in keeping with the precepts of the multiple presidencies thesis, particularly during this extant period of political time.

Summary

In this chapter, I have discussed the War Power Order's impact on the multiple presidencies across the issue areas of foreign policy. The dominance of the national security issue area (and to a lesser extent the high politics arena in general) was so pervasive that most of foreign policy became a "securitized/presidentialized" domain. The narrative discussed the subordination and later rumblings of the Congress as it and the presidency dealt with the various issue areas of foreign affairs. Then, we looked at the unit level relationships between the presidency and the Congress over those same issue areas by first continuing with longitudinal studies of various political factors including popular, electoral and partisan/ideological aimed at the success rates in the "core" issue areas (national security, trade and foreign aid) as well as foreign policy itself. The longitudinal findings pointed us in the direction of partisan factors as determinative of the presidential-congressional international relations policy dynamic. Cross-sectional analyses of these political factors and the four dependent variables led to a look at the various individuated success rates for the various presidencies of the War Power Order. Security can be said to be king during this time, however does it hold across time or was it an artifact of Cold War contingency? The answer to this question awaits us in the next chapter.

Table 5-1   Foreign Policy Success Regression Analysis of Popular Determinants across Political Time (1953-2004):

	Un-standardized Coefficients		Sig.
	B	Std. Error	
(Constant)	1.984	.045	.000
Public Approval of Presidential Foreign Policy	-.512	.027	.000
Congressional Job Disapproval Ratings	-1.107	.050	.000
Congressional Job Approval ratings	-2.134	.080	.000
Average Annual Presidential Public Approval	.363	.030	.000

R Square	Adjusted R Square	Std. Error of the Estimate	Durbin-Watson
.409	.408	.105	.064

Predictors: (Constant), Average Annual Presidential Public Approval, Congressional Job Disapproval Ratings, Public Approval of Presidential Foreign Policy, Congressional Job Approval Ratings
Dependent Variable: Annual Presidential Success Score in Foreign Policy
N=3335

Table 5-2. National Security Policy Success Regression Analysis of Popular Determinants across Political Time (1953-2004)

	Un-standardized Coefficients		Sig.
	B	Std. Error	
(Constant)	2.191	.053	.000
Public Approval of Presidential Foreign Policy	-.331	.031	.000
Congressional Job Disapproval Ratings	-1.468	.059	.000
Congressional Job Approval ratings	-2.253	.094	.000
Average Annual Presidential Public Approval	.345	.035	.000

R Square	Adjusted R Square	Std. Error of the Estimate	Durbin-Watson
.338	.336	.1226539	.046

Predictors: (Constant), Average Annual Presidential Public Approval, Congressional Job Disapproval Ratings, Public Approval of Presidential Foreign Policy, Congressional Job Approval ratings
Dependent Variable: Annual Presidential Success Score in National Security Policy
N=3335

Table 5-3. Trade Policy Success Regression Analysis of Popular Determinants across Political
Time (1953-2004)

	Un-standardized Coefficients		Sig.
	B	Std. Error	
(Constant)	.977	.073	.000
Public Approval of Presidential Foreign Policy	-.411	.043	.000
Congressional Job Disapproval Ratings	.369	.081	.000
Congressional Job Approval ratings	-.270	.129	.036
Average Annual Presidential Public Approval	-.492	.048	.000

R Square	Adjusted R Square	Std. Error of the Estimate	Durbin-Watson
.274	.272	.168	.049

Predictors: (Constant), Average Annual Presidential Public Approval, Congressional Job
Disapproval Ratings, Public Approval of Presidential Foreign Policy, Congressional
Job Approval ratings
Dependent Variable: Annual Presidential Success Score in Trade Policy
N=3335

Table 5-4. Foreign Aid Policy Success Regression Analysis of Popular Determinants across
Political Time (1953-2004)

	Un-standardized Coefficients		Sig.
	B	Std. Error	
(Constant)	1.938	.080	.000
Public Approval of Presidential Foreign Policy	-.186	.046	.000
Congressional Job Disapproval Ratings	-1.159	.092	.000
Congressional Job Approval ratings	-1.531	.140	.000
Average Annual Presidential Public Approval	-.226	.050	.000

R Square	Adjusted R Square	Std. Error of the Estimate	Durbin-Watson
.195	.193	.175	.038

Predictors: (Constant), Average Annual Presidential Public Approval, Congressional Job
Disapproval Ratings, Public Approval of Presidential Foreign Policy, Congressional
Job Approval ratings
Dependent Variable: Annual Presidential Success Score in Foreign Aid Policy
N=3335

Table 5-5. Foreign Policy Success Regression Analysis of Electoral Determinants across
           Political Time (1953-2004)

	Un-standardized Coefficients		Sig.
	B	Std. Error	
(Constant)	-.147	.032	.000
% of Voting Age Population participation in House elections during presidential election years	-.198	.202	.329
% Voting Age Population participation in most recent House Mid-term Election	-.846	.078	.000
% Voting Age Population participation in most recent Presidential Election	2.523	.216	.000
Presidential Electoral Vote Victory in Most recent election	-.319	.018	.000
Presidential Popular Vote Victory in Most recent election	.285	.052	.000
Mid-Term Election Year	.006	.004	.175
Presidential Election Year	-.036	.005	.000

R Square	Adjusted R Square	Std. Error of the Estimate	Durbin-Watson
.444	.442	.099	.023

Predictors: (Constant), presidential election year, % voting age population participation in most
           Recent presidential election, presidential electoral vote victory in most recent
           Election, mid-term election year, presidential popular vote victory in most recent
           Election, % voting age population participation in most recent House mid-term
           Election, % of voting age population participation in House elections during
           Presidential election years
Dependent Variable: Annual Presidential Success Score in Foreign Policy
N=3335

Table 5-6. National Security Policy Success Regression Analysis of Electoral Determinants across Political Time (1953-2004)

	Un-standardized Coefficients		Sig.
	B	Std. Error	
(Constant)	-.348	.046	.000
% of Voting Age Population participation in House elections during presidential election years	-3.621	.285	.000
% Voting Age Population participation in most recent House Mid-term Election	-1.748	.111	.000
% Voting Age Population participation in most recent Presidential Election	6.057	.302	.000
Presidential Electoral Vote Victory in Most recent election	-.349	.025	.000
Presidential Popular Vote Victory in Most recent election	1.010	.071	.000
Mid-Term Election Year	.012	.006	.034
Presidential Election Year	-.089	.007	.000

R Square	Adjusted R Square	Std. Error of the Estimate	Durbin-Watson
.250	.249	.135	.035

Predictors: (Constant), presidential election year, % voting age population participation in most Recent presidential election, presidential electoral vote victory in most recent Election, mid-term election year, presidential popular vote victory in most recent Election, % voting age population participation in most recent House mid-term Election, % voting age population participation in House elections during Presidential election years

Dependent Variable: Annual Presidential Success Score in National Security Policy
N=3335

161

Table 5-7. Trade Policy Success Regression Analysis of Electoral Determinants across Political Time (1953-2004)

	Un-standardized Coefficients		Sig.
	B	Std. Error	
(Constant)	-.190	.044	.000
% of Voting Age Population participation in House elections during presidential election years	7.500	.277	.000
% Voting Age Population participation in most recent House Mid-term Election	-1.499	.107	.000
% Voting Age Population participation in most recent Presidential Election	-3.684	.295	.000
Presidential Electoral Vote Victory in Most recent election	-.265	.024	.000
Presidential Popular Vote Victory in Most recent election	-.213	.071	.003
Mid-Term Election Year	.052	.006	.000
Presidential Election Year	.014	.006	.028

R Square	Adjusted R Square	Std. Error of the Estimate	Durbin-Watson
.583	.582	.135	.042

Predictors: (Constant), Presidential Election Year, % voting age population participation in most recent
Presidential election, presidential electoral vote victory in most recent election, mid-Term election year, presidential popular vote victory in most recent election, % Voting age population participation in most recent House mid-term election, % of Voting age population participation in House elections during presidential election years
Dependent Variable: Annual Presidential Success Score in Trade Policy
N=3335

Table 5-8. Foreign Aid Policy Success Regression Analysis of Electoral Determinants across Political Time (1953-2004)

	Un-standardized Coefficients		Sig.
	B	Std. Error	
(Constant)	-.055	.063	.379
% of Voting Age Population participation in House elections during presidential election years	.296	.378	.434
% Voting Age Population participation in most recent House Mid-term Election	.609	.143	.000
% Voting Age Population participation in most recent Presidential Election	.696	.410	.090
Presidential Electoral Vote Victory in Most recent election	-.180	.032	.000
Presidential Popular Vote Victory in Most recent election	.282	.095	.003
Mid-Term Election Year	-.059	.008	.000
Presidential Election Year	.018	.008	.025

R Square	Adjusted R Square	Std. Error of the Estimate	Durbin-Watson
.174	.172	.171	.034

Predictors: (Constant), presidential election year, % voting age population participation in most Recent presidential election, presidential electoral vote victory in most recent Election, mid-term election year, presidential popular vote victory in most recent Election, % voting age population participation in most recent House mid-term Election, % of voting age population participation in House elections during Presidential election years

Dependent Variable: Annual Presidential Success Score in Foreign Aid Policy

N=3335

Table 5-9. Foreign Policy Success Regression Analysis of Partisan Determinants across Political
Time (1953-2004)

| | Un-standardized Coefficients | | Sig. |
	B	Std. Error	
(Constant)	1.066	.026	.000
Unified Government	.147	.004	.000
Senate Party Unity (R)	.240	.038	.000
Senate Party Unity (D)	1.549	.071	.000
House Party Unity (R)	-.362	.049	.000
House Party Unity (D)	-1.474	.078	.000
Senate Partisan Roll Calls	-.614	.031	.000
House Partisan Roll Calls	-.170	.024	.000
Presidential Party Seat % in House of Representatives	-.650	.048	.000
Presidential Party Seat % in Senate	.518	.060	.000

R Square	Adjusted R Square	Std. Error of the Estimate	Durbin-Watson
.676	.675	.077	.031

Predictors: (Constant), Presidential Party Seat % in Senate, House Partisan Roll Calls, Senate
Partisan Roll Calls, House Party Unity (R), House Party Unity (D), Unified
Government, Senate Party Unity (R), Presidential Party Seat % in House of
Representatives, Senate Party Unity (D)
Dependent Variable: Annual Presidential Success Score in Foreign Policy
N=3335

Table 5-10. National Security Policy Success Regression Analysis of Partisan Determinants across Political Time (1953-2004)

	Un-standardized Coefficients		Sig.
	B	Std. Error	
(Constant)	1.253	.030	.000
Unified Government	.219	.005	.000
Senate Party Unity (R)	-.842	.044	.000
Senate Party Unity (D)	2.458	.080	.000
House Party Unity (R)	-.593	.055	.000
House Party Unity (D)	-1.129	.087	.000
Senate Partisan Roll Calls	.050	.036	.162
House Partisan Roll Calls	-.493	.027	.000
Presidential Party Seat % in House of Representatives	-2.099	.056	.000
Presidential Party Seat % in Senate	1.270	.072	.000

R Square	Adjusted R Square	Std. Error of the Estimate	Durbin-Watson
.668	.667	.086	.033

Predictors: (Constant), Presidential Party Seat % in Senate, House Partisan Roll Calls, Senate Partisan Roll Calls, House Party Unity (R), House Party Unity (D), Unified Government, Senate Party Unity (R), Presidential Party Seat % in House of Representatives, Senate Party Unity (D)
Dependent Variable: Annual Presidential Success Score in National Security Policy
N=3335

Table 5-11. Trade Policy Success Regression Analysis of Partisan Determinants across Political Time (1953-2004)

	Un-standardized Coefficients		Sig.
	B	Std. Error	
(Constant)	-.040	.050	.426
Unified Government	-.015	.008	.060
Senate Party Unity (R)	.737	.074	.000
Senate Party Unity (D)	-.068	.136	.616
House Party Unity (R)	.471	.094	.000
House Party Unity (D)	-.626	.149	.000
Senate Partisan Roll Calls	-.412	.060	.000
House Partisan Roll Calls	-.424	.045	.000
Presidential Party Seat % in House of Representatives	.698	.092	.000
Presidential Party Seat % in Senate	.809	.116	.000

R Square	Adjusted R Square	Std. Error of the Estimate	Durbin-Watson
.495	.493	.147	.035

Predictors: (Constant), Presidential Party Seat % in Senate, House Partisan Roll Calls, Senate Partisan Roll Calls, House Party Unity (R), House Party Unity (D), Unified Government, Senate Party Unity (R), Presidential Party Seat % in House of Representatives, Senate Party Unity (D)

Dependent Variable: Annual Presidential Success Score in Trade Policy

N=3335

Table 5-12. Foreign Aid Policy Success Regression Analysis of Partisan Determinants across
Political Time (1953-2004)

| | Un-standardized Coefficients | | Sig. |
	B	Std. Error	
(Constant)	2.093	.058	.000
Unified Government	.161	.009	.000
Senate Party Unity (R)	-.130	.082	.113
Senate Party Unity (D)	-.822	.160	.000
House Party Unity (R)	.748	.109	.000
House Party Unity (D)	-.701	.173	.000
Senate Partisan Roll Calls	-.870	.068	.000
House Partisan Roll Calls	.804	.052	.000
Presidential Party Seat % in House of Representatives	.651	.103	.000
Presidential Party Seat % in Senate	-2.379	.130	.000

R Square	Adjusted R Square	Std. Error of the Estimate	Durbin-Watson
.298	.296	.161	.035

Predictors: (Constant), Presidential Party Seat % in Senate, House Partisan Roll Calls, Senate
Partisan Roll Calls, House Party Unity (R), House Party Unity (D), Senate Party
Unity (R), Unified Government, Presidential Party Seat % in House of
Representatives, Senate Party Unity (D)
Dependent Variable: Annual Presidential Success Score in Foreign Aid Policy
N=3335

Table 5-13. Foreign Policy Success Regression Analysis of Ideological Determinants across
Political Time (1953-2004)

| | Un-standardized Coefficients | | Sig. |
	B	Std. Error	
(Constant)	.674	.004	.000
ADA Presidential Interest Group Rating	.127	.006	.000
Conservative Coalition For	.009	.003	.006
Conservative Coalition Against	.007	.005	.171
Liberal Coalition For	.040	.007	.000
Liberal Coalition Against	-.015	.016	.336

R Square	Adjusted R Square	Std. Error of the Estimate	Durbin-Watson
.191	.189	.108	.048

Predictors: (Constant), Liberal Coalition Against, Liberal Coalition For, Conservative Coalition
Against, Conservative Coalition For, ADA Presidential Interest Group Rating
Dependent Variable: Annual Presidential Success Score in Foreign Policy
N=3335

167

Table 5-14. Presidential National Security Policy Success Regression Analysis of Ideological Determinants across Political time (1953-2004)

	Un-standardized Coefficients		Sig.
	B	Std. Error	
(Constant)	.748	.005	.000
ADA Presidential Interest Group Rating	.027	.008	.000
Conservative Coalition For	.005	.004	.183
Conservative Coalition Against	.010	.007	.137
Liberal Coalition For	.023	.009	.017
Liberal Coalition Against	-.035	.020	.083

R Square	Adjusted R Square	Std. Error of the Estimate	Durbin-Watson
.011	.009	.135	.028

Predictors: (Constant), Liberal Coalition Against, Liberal Coalition For, Conservative Coalition Against, Conservative Coalition For, ADA Presidential Interest Group Rating
Dependent Variable: Annual Presidential Success Score in National Security Policy
N=3335

Table 5-15. Trade Policy Success Regression Analysis of Ideological Determinants across Political Time (1963-2004)

	Un-standardized Coefficients		Sig.
	B	Std. Error	
(Constant)	.530	.005	.000
ADA Presidential Interest Group Rating	.342	.007	.000
Conservative Coalition For	.007	.004	.092
Conservative Coalition Against	.005	.007	.440
Liberal Coalition For	.046	.008	.000
Liberal Coalition Against	-.024	.020	.224

R Square	Adjusted R Square	Std. Error of the Estimate	Durbin-Watson
.513	.512	.135	.059

Predictors: (Constant), Liberal Coalition Against, Liberal Coalition For, Conservative Coalition Against, Conservative Coalition For, ADA Presidential Interest Group Rating
Dependent Variable: Annual Presidential Success Score in Trade Policy
N=3335

Table 5-16. Foreign Aid Policy Success Regression Analysis of Ideological Determinants across Political Time (1953-2004)

	Un-standardized Coefficients		Sig.
	B	Std. Error	
(Constant)	.671	.006	.000
ADA Presidential Interest Group Rating	.069	.010	.000
Conservative Coalition For	.013	.005	.016
Conservative Coalition Against	.000	.009	.987
Liberal Coalition For	.037	.011	.001
Liberal Coalition Against	-.035	.028	.203

R Square	Adjusted R Square	Std. Error of the Estimate	Durbin-Watson
.025	.023	.187	.040

Predictors: (Constant), Liberal Coalition Against, Liberal Coalition For, Conservative Coalition Against, Conservative Coalition For, ADA Presidential Interest Group Rating
Dependent Variable: Annual Presidential Success Score in Foreign Aid Policy
N=3335

Table 5-17. Foreign Policy Success Regression Analysis of Issue Area of Foreign Policy Value and Type of Foreign Policy Vote across Political Time (1953-2004)

	Un-standardized Coefficients		Sig.
	B	Std. Error	
(Constant)	.751	.005	.000
Value for Type of Vote	-.002	.002	.476
Issue Area of Foreign Policy Value	-.007	.001	.000

R Square	Adjusted R Square	Std. Error of the Estimate	Durbin-Watson
.007	.006	.131	.024

Predictors: (Constant), Issue Area of Foreign Policy Value, Value for Type of Vote
Dependent Variable: Annual Presidential Success Score in Foreign Policy
N=3335

Table 5-18. National Security Policy Success Regression Analysis of Issue Area of Foreign
Policy and Type of Foreign Policy Vote across Political Time (1953-2004)

	Un-standardized Coefficients		Sig.
	B	Std. Error	
(Constant)	.760	.006	.000
Value for Type of Vote	-.008	.003	.002
Issue Area of Foreign Policy Value	-.001	.002	.388

R Square	Adjusted R Square	Std. Error of the Estimate	Durbin-Watson
.003	.002	.155	.034

Predictors: (Constant), Issue Area of Foreign Policy Value, Value for Type of Vote
Dependent Variable: Annual Presidential Success Score in National Security Policy
N=3335

Table 5-19. Trade Policy Success Regression Analysis of Issue Area of Foreign Policy Value
and Type of Foreign Policy Vote Across Political Time (1953-2004)

	Un-standardized Coefficients		Sig.
	B	Std. Error	
(Constant)	.751	.008	.000
Value for Type of Vote	.012	.003	.000
Issue Area of Foreign Policy Value	-.015	.002	.000

R Square	Adjusted R Square	Std. Error of the Estimate	Durbin-Watson
.019	.019	.206	.043

Predictors: (Constant), Issue Area of Foreign Policy Value, Value for Type of Vote
Dependent Variable: Annual Presidential Success Score in Trade Policy
N=3335

Table 5-20. Foreign Aid Policy Success Regression Analysis of Issue Area of Foreign Policy Value and Type of Foreign Policy Vote across Political Time (1953-2004)

	Un-standardized Coefficients		Sig.
	B	Std. Error	
(Constant)	.739	.007	.000
Value for Type of Vote	.008	.003	.007
Issue Area of Foreign Policy Value	-.008	.002	.000

R Square	Adjusted R Square	Std. Error of the Estimate	Durbin-Watson
.007	.006	.187	.037

Predictors: (Constant), Issue Area of Foreign Policy Value, Value for Type of Vote
Dependent Variable: Annual Presidential Success Score in Foreign Aid Policy
N=3335

Table 5-21. Foreign Policy Success Regression Analysis of Partisan Determinants War Power Order (1953-1972)

	Un-standardized Coefficients		Sig.
	B	Std. Error	
(Constant)	3.642	.075	.000
House Partisan Roll Calls	1.020	.036	.000
Senate Partisan Roll Calls	.696	.037	.000
House Party Unity (D)	2.767	.058	.000
House Party Unity (R)	-.891	.054	.000
Senate Party Unity (D)	-1.842	.101	.000
Senate Party Unity (R)	.421	.053	.000
Presidential Party Seat % in Senate	-9.688	.295	.000
Presidential Party Seat % in House of Representatives	1.467	.044	.000
Unified Government	.791	.024	.000

R Square	Adjusted R Square	Std. Error of the Estimate	Durbin-Watson
.960	.959	.013	.030

Predictors: (Constant), Unified Government, Senate Party Unity (D), Senate Partisan Roll Calls, Senate Party Unity (R), House Party Unity (R), House Partisan Roll Calls, Presidential Party Seat % in House of Representatives, House Party Unity (D), Presidential Party Seat % in Senate
Dependent Variable: War Power Order Annual Foreign Policy Success Score
N=1157

Table 5-22. National Security Policy Success Regression Analysis of Partisan Determinants War Power Order (1953-1972)

	Un-standardized Coefficients		Sig.
	B	Std. Error	
(Constant)	.354	.329	.283
House Partisan Roll Calls	-.650	.160	.000
Senate Partisan Roll Calls	-1.695	.176	.000
House Party Unity (D)	-4.908	.308	.000
House Party Unity (R)	-2.457	.235	.000
Senate Party Unity (D)	6.102	.455	.000
Senate Party Unity (R)	-1.463	.249	.000
Presidential Party Seat % in Senate	10.424	1.270	.000
Presidential Party Seat % in House of Representatives	-3.629	.210	.000
Unified Government	-.502	.103	.000

R Square	Adjusted R Square	Std. Error of the Estimate	Durbin-Watson
.796	.793	.056	.094

Predictors: (Constant), Unified Government, Senate Partisan Roll Calls, Senate Party Unity (D), Senate Party Unity (R), House Party Unity (R), House Partisan Roll Calls, Presidential Party Seat % in House of Representatives, House Party Unity (D), Presidential Party Seat % in Senate

Dependent Variable: War Power Order Annual National Security Policy Success Score
N=1157

Table 5-23. Trade Policy Success Regression Analysis of Partisan Determinants War Power
Order (1953-1972)

| | Un-standardized Coefficients | | Sig. |
	B	Std. Error	
(Constant)	-2.016	.180	.000
House Partisan Roll Calls	-2.475	.085	.000
Senate Partisan Roll Calls	-1.068	.089	.000
House Party Unity (D)	3.978	.138	.000
House Party Unity (R)	-7.292	.129	.000
Senate Party Unity (D)	2.937	.240	.000
Senate Party Unity (R)	-1.449	.127	.000
Presidential Party Seat % in Senate	13.676	.704	.000
Presidential Party Seat % in House of Representatives	-1.305	.105	.000
Unified Government	-1.096	.057	.000

R Square	Adjusted R Square	Std. Error of the Estimate	Durbin-Watson
.944	.943	.031	.148

Predictors: (Constant), Unified Government, Senate Party Unity (D), Senate Partisan Roll Calls,
Senate Party Unity (R), House Party Unity (R), House Partisan Roll Calls,
Presidential Party Seat % in House of Representatives, House Party Unity (D),
Presidential Party Seat % in Senate

Dependent Variable: War Power Order Annual Trade Policy Success Score
N=1157

173

Table 5-24. Foreign Aid Policy Success Regression Analysis of Partisan Determinants War
Power Order (1953-1972)

	Un-standardized Coefficients		Sig.
	B	Std. Error	
(Constant)	7.628	.135	.000
House Partisan Roll Calls	4.019	.064	.000
Senate Partisan Roll Calls	2.307	.067	.000
House Party Unity (D)	5.291	.103	.000
House Party Unity (R)	-.317	.097	.001
Senate Party Unity (D)	-5.404	.180	.000
Senate Party Unity (R)	-.483	.096	.000
Presidential Party Seat % in Senate	-22.711	.528	.000
Presidential Party Seat % in House of Representatives	3.688	.079	.000
Unified Government	1.707	.043	.000

R Square	Adjusted R Square	Std. Error of the Estimate	Durbin-Watson
.975	.975	.023	.033

Predictors: (Constant), Unified Government, Senate Party Unity (D), Senate Partisan Roll Calls,
Senate Party Unity (R), House Party Unity (R), House Partisan Roll Calls,
Presidential Party Seat % in House of Representatives, House Party Unity (D),
Presidential Party Seat % in Senate
Dependent Variable: War Power Order Annual Foreign Aid Policy Success Score
N=1157

Table 5-25. Mixed Issue Area Policy Success Regression Analysis of Partisan Determinants
War Power Order (1953-1972)

	Un-standardized Coefficients		Sig.
	B	Std. Error	
(Constant)	1.948	.000	.000
House Partisan Roll Calls	.301	.000	.000
Senate Partisan Roll Calls	1.254	.000	.000
House Party Unity (D)	3.261	.000	.000
House Party Unity (R)	1.868	.000	.000
Senate Party Unity (D)	-3.536	.000	.000
Senate Party Unity (R)	1.741	.000	.000
Presidential Party Seat % in Senate	-10.270	.000	.000
Presidential Party Seat % in House of Representatives	2.100	.000	.000
Unified Government	.680	.000	.000

R Square	Adjusted R Square	Std. Error of the Estimate	Durbin-Watson
1.000	1.000	.000	.026

Predictors: (Constant), Unified Government, Senate Partisan Roll Calls, Senate Party Unity (D), Senate Party Unity (R), House Party Unity (R), House Partisan Roll Calls, House Party Unity (D), Presidential Party Seat % in House of Representatives, Presidential Party Seat % in Senate

Dependent Variable: War Power Order Annual Mixed Issue Area Success Score
N=96

175

Table 5-26. Annual Presidential Success Scores in Foreign Policy & Issue Areas*+- 1953-1961 Eisenhower Presidency across 83rd-86th Congresses

Year	Foreign Policy	Security	Domestic Security	Diplomacy	Trade	Foreign Aid	Immigration	N
1953	C=80% (20:5)	C=100% (5:0)	C=20% (1:4)	C=100% (2:0)	C=83% (5:1)	C=100% (5:0)	C=100% (2:0)	N=25
	H=100% (10:0)	H=100% (3:0)	H=n/a (0:0)	H=n/a (0:0)	H=100% (1:0)	H=100% (5:0)	H=100% (1:0)	N=10
	S=66% (10:5)	S=100% (2:0)	S=20% (1:4)	S=100% (2:0)	S=80% (4:1)	S=n/a (0:0)	S=100% (1:0)	N=15
1954	C=67% (24:12)	C=n/a (0:0)	C=41% (5:7)	C=100% (1:0)	C=92% (12:1)	C=80% (4:1)	C=n/a (0:0)	N=36
	H=85% (11:2)	H=n/a (0:0)	H=67% (4:2)	H=n/a (0:0)	H=100% (4:0)	H=100% (3:0)	H=n/a (0:0)	N=13
	S=57% (13:10)	S=n/a (0:0)	S=17% (1:5)	S=100% (1:0)	S=89% (8:1)	S=50% (1:1)	S=n/a (0:0)	N=23
1955	C=86% (57:9)	C=85% (22:4)	C=n/a (0:0)	C=80% (4:1)	C=91% (21:2)	C=83% (10:2)	C=n/a (0:0)	N=66
	H=86% (20:3)	H=90% (9:1)	H=n/a (0:0)	H=n/a (0:0)	H=89% (8:1)	H=75% (3:1)	H=n/a (0:0)	N=23
	S=86% (36:6)	S=81% (13:3)	S=n/a (0:0)	S=80% (4:1)	S=93% (13:1)	S=88% (7:1)	S=n/a (0:0)	N=43
1956	C=79% (33:9)	C=38% (3:5)	C=n/a (0:0)	C=100% (1:0)	C=100% (8:0)	C=85% (17:3)	C=n/a (0:0)	N=42
	H=75% (9:3)	H=40% (2:3)	H=n/a (0:0)	H=n/a (0:0)	H=100% (4:0)	H=100% (3:0)	H=n/a% (0:0)	N=12
	S=80% (24:6)	S=33% (1:2)	S=n/a (0:0)	S=100% (1:0)	S=100% (4:0)	S=82% (14:3)	S=n/a (0:0)	N=30
1957	C=91% (43:4)	C=86% (12:2)	C=n/a (0:0)	C=75% (3:1)	C=100% (10:0)	C=94% (15:1)	C=100% (2:0)	N=47
	H=80% (12:3)	H=67% (4:2)	H=n/a (0:0)	H=100% (1:0)	H=100% (2:0)	H=80% (4:1)	H=100% (1:0)	N=15
	S=97% (31:1)	S=100% (8:0)	S=n/a (0:0)	S=67% (2:1)	S=100% (8:0)	S=100% (11:0)	S=100% (1:0)	N=32

Table 5-26. Continued

Year	Foreign Policy	Security	Domestic Security	Diplomacy	Trade	Foreign Aid	Immigration	N
1958	C=79% (45:12)	C=73% (11:4)	C=70% (7:3)	C=50% (1:1)	C=94% (15:1)	C=86% (12:2)	C=n/a (0:0)	N=57
	H=78% (21:6)	H=70% (7:3)	H=100% (4:0)	H=50% (1:1)	H=83% (5:1)	H=80% (4:1)	H=n/a (0:0)	N=27
	S=75% (9:3)	S=80% (4:1)	S=50% (3:3)	S=n/a (0:0)	S=100% (10:0)	S=89% (8:1)	S=n/a (0:0)	N=30
1959	C=75% (45:15)	C=100% (6:0)	C=70% (7:3)	C=75% (3:1)	C=63% (5:3)	C=86% (19:3)	C=n/a (0:0)	N=60
	H=75% (12:4)	H=100% (1:0)	H=40% (2:3)	H=100% (1:0)	H=n/a (0:0)	H=100% (7:0)	H=n/a (0:0)	N=16
	S=70% (31:13)	S=100% (5:0)	S=100% (5:0)	S=67% (2:1)	S=63% (5:3)	S=80% (12:3)	S=n/a (0:0)	N=44
1960	C=83% (34:7)	C=n/a (0:0)	C=50% (1:1)	C=100% (3:0)	C=88% (14:2)	C=80% (16:4)	C=n/a (0:0)	N=41
	H=85% (11:2)	H=n/a (0:0)	H=50% (1:1)	H=n/a (0:0)	H=100% (4:0)	H=86% (6:1)	H=n/a (0:0)	N=13
	S=82% (23:5)	S=n/a (0:0)	S=n/a (0:0)	S=100% (3:0)	S=83% (10:2)	S=77% (10:3)	S=n/a (0:0)	N=28

*Annual foreign policy percentage success of presidential position roll call votes as recorded by CQ Almanacs 1953-1960 (Issue area success scores compiled by author from content analysis of vote summaries in the relevant almanacs).
+ratios of counts wins to losses in parentheses
-Some years' votes contain mixed categories—those votes are individuated on another set of tables but are included in the aggregate annual foreign policy success scores of this table.

177

Table 5-27. Annual Presidential Success Scores across Issue Areas of Foreign Policy For Kennedy Administration (1961-1963), 87th-88th Congresses*

year	Foreign Policy	Security	Domestic Security	Diplomacy	Trade	Foreign Aid	Immigration	Totals
1961	C=89% (58:7)	C=89% (8:1)	C=50% (1:1)	C=89% (8:1)	C=94% (15:1)	C=89% (24:3)	C=n/a (0:0)	N=65
	H=96% (23:1)	H=100% (4:0)	H=n/a (0:0)	H=100% (3:0)	H=100% (7:0)	H=90% (9:1)	H=n/a (0:0)	N=24
	S=85% (35:6)	S=80% (4:1)	S=50% (1:1)	S=83% (5:1)	S=89% (8:1)	S=88% (15:2)	S=n/a (0:0)	N=41
1962	C=92% (59:5)	C=73% (8:3)	C=100% (1:0)	C=100% (4:0)	C=96% (27:1)	C=90% (18:2)	C=n/a (0:0)	N=64
	H=95% (20:1)	H=80% (4:1)	H=n/a (0:0)	H=100% (2:0)	H=100% (6:0)	H=88% (7:1)	H=n/a (0:0)	N=21
	S=91% (39:4)	S=67% (4:2)	S=100% (0:0)	S=100% (2:0)	S=95% (21:1)	S=92% (11:1)	S=n/a (0:0)	N=43
1963a[1]	C=86% (59:10)	C=95% (18:1)	C=100% (1:0)	C=100% (4:0)	C=75% (9:3)	C=81% (25:6)	C=n/a (0:0)	N=69
	H=70% (14:6)	H=83% (5:1)	H=n/a (0:0)	H=100% (1:0)	H=75% (3:1)	H=56% (5:4)	H=n/a (0:0)	N=20
	S=92% (45:4)	S=100% (13:0)	S=100% (2:0)	S=100% (3:0)	S=75% (6:2)	S=91% (20:2)	S=n/a (0:0)	N=49

*All position votes, including mixed categories are contained in the annual aggregate foreign policy success scores but mixed category votes are excluded from the individuated issue area scores and are included on another table.

---

[1] 1963a contains all position votes on foreign policy that Kennedy took including the ones that Johnson also took to ensure continuity with Kennedy administration policy after LBJ's assumption to office.

Table 5-28. Annual Presidential Success Scores across Issue Areas of Foreign Policy. Johnson Administration (1963-1969) 88th-90th Congresses*

year	Foreign Policy	Security	Domestic Security	Diplomacy	Trade	Foreign Aid	Immigration	Totals
1963b[2]	C=86% (18:3)	C=n/a (0:0)	C=n/a (0:0)	C=100% (2:0)	C=100% (4:0)	C=80% (12:3)	C=n/a (0:0)	N=21
	H=67% (6:3)	H=n/a (0:0)	H=n/a (0:0)	H=n/a (0:0)	H=100% (2:0)	H=57% (4:3)	H=n/a (0:0)	N=9
	S=100% (12:0)	S=n/a (0:0)	S=n/a (0:0)	S=100% (2:0)	S=100% (2:0)	S=100% (8:0)	S=n/a (0:0)	N=12
1964	C=83% (45:9)	C=86% (6:1)	C=100% (1:0)	C=50% (1:1)	C=86% (18:3)	C=84% (16:3)	C=n/a (0:0)	N=54
	H=79% (15:4)	H=100% (2:0)	H=100% (1:0)	H=0% (0:1)	H=80% (4:1)	H=83% (5:1)	H=n/a (0:0)	N=19
	S=86% (30:5)	S=80% (4:1)	S=n/a (0:0)	S=100% (1:0)	S=88% (14:2)	S=85% (11:2)	S=n/a (0:0)	N=35
1965	C=89% (74:9)	C=60% (6:4)	C=100% (1:0)	C=86% (6:1)	C=94% (17:1)	C=92% (33:3)	C=100% (5:0)	N=83
	H=96% (24:6)	H=75% (3:1)	H=n/a (0:0)	H=100% (3:0)	H=100% (4:0)	H=100% (9:0)	H=100% (4:0)	N=25
	S=86% (50:8)	S=50% (3:3)	S=100% (1:0)	S=75% (3:1)	S=93% (13:1)	S=89% (24:3)	S=100% (1:0)	N=58
1966	C=73% (47:17)	C=69% (9:4)	C=100% (1:0)	C=100% (1:0)	C=91% (10:1)	C=61% (14:9)	C=n/a (0:0)	N=64
	H=80% (24:6)	H=80% (4:1)	H=n/a (0:0)	H=100% (1:0)	H=86% (6:1)	H=88% (7:1)	H=n/a (0:0)	N=30
	S=68% (23:11)	S=63% (5:3)	S=100% (1:0)	S=n/a (0:0)	S=100% (4:0)	S=43% (6:8)	S=n/a (0:0)	N=34

---

[2] 1963b these votes are recorded as having been taken by Kennedy and Johnson—Johnson took these positions to ensure continuity in administration policy in the wake of President Kennedy's assassination.

179

Table 5-28. Continued

year	Foreign Policy	Security	Domestic Security	Diplomacy	Trade	Foreign Aid	Immigration	Totals
1967	C=80% (75:19)	C=89% (24:3)	C=80% (4:1)	C=100% (9:0)	C=73% (8:3)	C=60% (12:8)	C=n/a (0:0)	N=94
	H=76% (22:7)	H=82% (9:2)	H=n/a (0:0)	H=n/a (0:0)	H=25% (1:3)	H=70% (7:3)	H=n/a (0:0)	N=29
	S=82% (53:12)	S=94% (15:1)	S=80% (4:1)	S=100% (9:0)	S=100% (7:0)	S=50% (5:5)	S=n/a (0:0)	N=65
1968	C=82% (75:17)	C=96% (27:1)	C=44% (4:5)	C=100% (1:0)	C=90% (19:2)	C=64% (7:4)	C=n/a (0:0)	N=92
	H=81% (22:5)	H=100% (5:0)	H=33% (1:2)	H=n/a (0:0)	H=67% (2:1)	H=83% (5:1)	H=n/a (0:0)	N=27
	S=82% (53:12)	S=96% (22:1)	S=50% (3:3)	S=100% (1:0)	S=94% (17:1)	S=40% (2:3)	S=n/a (0:0)	N=65

*Some votes are in mixed categories which are in a separate table but are included in the aggregate foreign policy success scores but not in the individuated issue area success scores.

Table 5-29. Annual Presidential Success Scores across Issue Areas of Foreign Policy. Nixon Administration (1969-1974) 91st-93rd Congresses*

Year	Foreign Policy	Security	Domestic Security	Diplomacy	Trade	Foreign Aid	Immigration	Totals
1969	C=93 (40:3)	C=91% (20:2)	C=100% (3:0)	C=100% (4:0)	C=100% (5:5)	C=88% (7:1)	C=n/a (0:0)	N=43
	H=89% (8:1)	H=100% (3:0)	H=n/a (0:0)	H=100% (1:0)	H=100% (1:0)	H=75% (3:1)	H=n/a (0:0)	N=9
	S=94% (32:2)	S=89% (17:2)	S=100% (3:0)	S=100% (3:0)	S=100% (4:0)	S=100% (4:0)	S=n/a (0:0)	N=34
1970	C=93% (27:2)	C=75% (6:2)	C=100% (1:0)	C=100% (8:0)	C=100% (7:0)	C=100% (4:0)	C=n/a (0:0)	N=29
	H=90% (9:1)	H=0% (0:1)	H=n/a (0:0)	H=100% (3:0)	H=100% (3:0)	H=100% (3:0)	H=n/a (0:0)	N=10
	S=95% (18:1)	S=86% (6:1)	S=100% (1:0)	S=100% (5:0)	S=100% (4:0)	S=100% (1:0)	S=n/a (0:0)	N=19
1971	C=84% (57:11)	C=87% (45:7)	C=n/a (0:0)	C=100% (1:0)	C=60% (3:2)	C=89% (8:1)	C=n/a (0:0)	N=68
	H=95% (19:1)	H=100% (18:0)	H=n/a (0:0)	H=n/a (0:0)	H=0% (0:1)	H=100% (1:0)	H=n/a (0:0)	N=20
	S=79% (38:10)	S=79% (27:7)	S=n/a (0:0)	S=100% (1:0)	S=75% (3:1)	S=88% (7:1)	S=n/a (0:0)	N=48
1972	C=70% (26:11)	C=65% (15:8)	C=n/a (0:0)	C=50% (1:1)	C=66% (2:1)	C=50% (1:1)	C=n/a (0:0)	N=37
	H=92% (12:1)	H=100% (7:0)	H=n/a (0:0)	H=0% (0:1)	H=100% (1:0)	H=n/a (0:0)	H=n/a (0:0)	N=13
	S=58% (14:10)	S=50% (8:8)	S=n/a (0:0)	S=100% (1:0)	S=50% (1:1)	S=50% (1:1)	S=n/a (0:0)	N=24

Table 5-29. Continued

1973	C=60%	C=47%	C=50%	C=100%	C=51%	C=75%	C=0%	N=123
	(74:49)	(23:26)	(1:1)	(7:0)	(18:17)	(9:3)	(0:1)	
	H=46%	H=26%	H=100%	H=100%	H=50%	H=86%	H=0%	N=41
	(19:22)	(5:14)	(1:0)	(1:0)	(6:6)	(6:1)	(0:1)	
	S=67%	S=60%	S=0%	S=100%	S=52%	S=60%	S=n/a	N=82
	(55:27)	(18:12)	(0:1)	(6:0)	(12:11)	(3:2)	(0:0)	
1974a[3]	C=59%	C=71%	C=n/a	C=100%	C=48%	C=67%	C=n/a	N=49
	(29:20)	(12:5)	(0:0)	(2:0)	(10:11)	(4:2)	(0:0)	
	H=50%	H=100%	H=n/a	H=100%	H=38%	H=50%	H=n/a	N=18
	(9:9)	(3:0)	(0:0)	(1:0)	(3:5)	(2:2)	(0:0)	
	S=65%	S=64%	S=n/a	S=100%	S=54%	S=100%	S=n/a	N=31
	(20:11)	(9:5)	(0:0)	(1:0)	(7:6)	(2:0)	(0:0)	

*Some votes are in mixed categories, which are in a separate table but are included within the aggregate annual foreign policy success scores but not individuated in the issue area scores.

---

[3] 1974a refers to Nixon's position votes during the year of his resignation from office the rest of the position votes for that year are recorded under the new president Gerald R. Ford and hence, not included in this table.

CHAPTER 6
CONFRONTATION POLITICS: THE RISE OF THE DOMESTICATING FOREIGN POLICY CONGRESS DURING DÉTENTE AND IN THE AFTERMATH OF THE VIETNAM WAR, 1973-1989

Introduction

Now, we enter the second act of our movie regarding presidential-congressional foreign policy relations by looking at the extant inter-institutional relationship during the years 1973 and 1989. This period of political time is being referred to as the "Confrontation Politics Order" and its dominant characteristic is the increased role of the Congress as a factor in dictating the issue area success rates of the presidencies beginning with Nixon's second term and ending with the start of the first Bush administration. The fact that this period of US foreign policy executive-legislative history is not well demarcated by its component presidential administrations is instructive in itself. The simple fact of the matter is that during this time, presidents did *not* govern foreign policy themselves but rather in tandem with (and often against) the Congress (from Sundquist 1981). Why, this is so will be revealed in the narrative's descriptive account in combination with the cross-sectional regression analyses that follow this introduction.

Speaking of the narrative, it will emphasize the changed role of the Congress in its interactions with the executive across the issue areas of foreign policy. For starters, the role played by internal reforms in combination with legislative critique of executive foreign policy dominance will be looked at. Then, we will examine certain specific issue areas including domestic security, diplomacy, trade and foreign aid policy that exemplified congressional attempts to "de-securitize" or in other words "domesticate" foreign policy.

The systematic study will be leveled at presidential success in core issue areas and foreign policy itself as a function of partisan and to lesser extent ideological factors. These should be seen in comparative terms with the cross-sectional as well as longitudinal findings from the last chapter's empirical studies. The picture will come in to full light by another tabular based analysis of the differentiated success rates across the component issue areas of foreign policy and then we will conclude with a small summary of the chapter's basic points.

The Confrontation Politics Order, 1973-1990: Executive-Legislative Conflict across the Issue Areas of Foreign Policy

The most dramatic change in the executive-legislative foreign policy relationship occurred in the environmental changes regarding the development of détente, the aftermath of the Vietnam War and the emergence of a fully integrated world economy (Rosati 2005). However, I dealt with these in the third chapter so instead we will concentrate on the unit level alterations. There are two of significance which need to be "mapped out." First, change in extant executive-legislative relations was a phenomenon internal to Congress that stemmed from organizational reforms in the committee and leadership structure (Rohde 1991). Second was an exogenous development whereby the Congress began to routinely re-assert and in many cases assert its institutional, partisan and to some extent ideological prerogatives in foreign policy construction relative to the presidency (Sundquist 1981). This last point was of course exacerbated by the persistence of divided and split control government throughout the Confrontation Politics Order, in fact only Jimmy Carter had unified government and analyses have indicated that even he did not enjoy as many of the "fruits" of such a condition as the presidencies of the War Power Order had under similar circumstances (see LeLoup and Shull 2003, Shull and Shaw 1999 & Shull 1997).

Regarding the reforms themselves, collectively they amounted to a re-distribution of internal power in the Congress, especially in the House of Representatives by moving it away from the congressional committees (especially their chairs) and placing it within the sub-committees and the parties-in-Congress (Rohde 1991, Dodd 1986, Smith 2000 & Cox and McCubbins 1993). These early seventies era reforms, while not specifically done to influence foreign policy construction had a direct influence nonetheless. As Lindsay (1994) has shown, at least trade policy was given over to what I would call a "congressionalization/domestication" phenomenon as the Trade Act of 1934 while not rescinded was after the early 1970s subject to intense congressional involvement. This is especially true among members of Congress with high levels of international trade in their respective states and districts (Lindsay 1994). Specifically relative to the increased role of the parties, especially in the House these instruments provided a mechanism whereby proactive speakers such as Tip O'Neil, Jim Wright and to a lesser extent Tom Foley could serve as their parties' alternative spokesmen for a number of issues in foreign policy by the 1980's. Such activities occurred in the area of sanctions policy regarding South Africa, MX missile development, the "star wars" defense initiative and perhaps most pervasively the Boland (D MA) Amendments to defense and foreign aid authorization and appropriations bills (CQ Almanacs 1985-89, various legislative histories). Any one of these would be an instructive case study for deeper evaluation, however that would take us away from the more general purposes of this research project so further study will have to wait.

As to the more directed issue of congressional resurgence in foreign affairs during this period of political time (1973-1989). The unit level interactions between the executive and the legislature were intense, conflictual and more politicized as partisanship intensified and ideology began to manifest itself more profoundly. The most pervasive example of this conflict occurred in the aftermath of the Vietnam debacle as the War Powers Act of 1973 was passed over President Nixon's veto with a "near-unanimous" support rate in excess of 80% (CQ Almanac 1973, War Powers Resolution study). The Church (D-AR) Committee investigations into the CIA's domestic and foreign intelligence operations are emblematic of a "domestication" of domestic and even national security (CQ Almanac 1975, committee reports). Despite Fisher's (2000) dismissal of the Church Committee activities' bans such as President Ford's executive order proscribing assassination as "a tool of foreign policy" can be seen from the perspective of a congress-centered issue promotion with presidential acquiescence. This reverses the dominant trend of the War Power Order where it was the president proposing and the Congress disposing (though often supporting) foreign affairs legislative initiatives.

In the realms of diplomacy and foreign aid, the Congress shut off military aid to Southeast Asia during the North Vietnamese mechanized offensive in the spring of 1975 (CQ Almanac 1975, Vietnam War study). They also prevented the Ford administration from providing military aid overt or covert to anti-communist forces (both state and non-state in form) in Uganda, Mozambique, South Africa, Namibia and Zimbabwe (Sundquist 1981, Lowi 1985 and CQ Almanac 1976, foreign aid reports). Finally, the Carter administration faced back-to-back battles with the Conservative Coalition of Southern Democrats and Republicans over the Panama Canal Treaties of 1978 and their empowering acts in 1979 (CQ Almanacs 1978-79, Panama Canal Treaties studies). The conservative opposition to Carter was so pervasive, that it caused a record number of mostly procedural roll calls during these two years (Shull and Shaw 1999). While Carter won these, what he lost was more important as he himself admits the Republicans were able to so effectively "chip away" at the Democratic Party's strength in the 1978 elections as a result of the divisive Panama Canal debates. This action set the stage for an eventual Republican take over of the Senate two years later (Carter 1982). From this survey it should be easy to see that the "politics of foreign policy" were no longer what "the president made of them" but were now subject to a push and pull as the two proactive national institutions of American government jockeyed for positional power. However, this survey needs to be emboldened by more systematically based analysis and to that we now turn.

Empirical Findings

Given the notions about the Conservative Coalition's role as a device of both congressionalization (read domestication) of issue areas during the Confrontation Politics Order and for that matter its perceived impact on limiting partisanship, it is instructive to look back at the impact of ideological factors during the previous War Power Order. Looking at tables 6-1 — 6-4, we can see that ideology of the Congress or for that matter the presidency had little systematic impact on presidential success in foreign policy or any of the core issue areas during the War Power Order. This is not surprising for two reasons; first the overwhelming Cold War consensus around foreign policy writ large which included deference to presidential leadership would mean that ideological conflict was *reduced* during the 1953-1972 timeframe. Second, *bi-partisanship* not *cross-partisanship* would be the norm of the day under such non-ideological conditions. In other words, presidency-centered conditions (bi-partisanship and consensus ideology) would predictably trump Congress-centered (cross-partisanship/partisanship and internally divided ideology within each party) throughout the War Power Order.

From a comparative perspective we should see some alterations in the role of ideology as a determinant of presidential success with the Congress in foreign policy and its component issue areas. And as detailed in Table 6-5, this is true. Ideology is a relatively strong predictor of presidential success in foreign policy writ large as a coalitional *support* phenomenon but not as a coalitional *opposition* factor. What is important about this as far as the multiple presidencies is concerned is that presidency-centered conditions are still dominant; however they are beginning to take on a *politicized* aspect. This is particularly shown in the model's strong R square (.393), but it is offset by the relative weakness of the correlations overall (see Table 6-5). Nonetheless, it does at least call for further inquiry and that it what the next three tables do.

In national security success (Table 6-6), the same elements which factor into general foreign policy success repeat themselves, except that the Liberal Coalition becomes lost as a

186

support (or opposition) mechanism. This is probably due to the increases in partisanship that begin to take effect, even in foreign policy voting in the Congress by the late 1970's and that impact was *first* felt in the decline of the liberal coalition (CQ Almanac 1978, coalition voting study). Finally, the strength of the model overall as an explainer of the outcome variable is in itself problematic due to the severe decline in the variance control element (R square=.119). In fact, this is the kind of variance control levels associated with the War Power Order tables where ideology was shown to largely be negligible as a factor in dictating presidential roll call success with the Congress (see Tables 6-1 — 6-4). Looking specifically at trade and foreign aid success during the Confrontation Politics Order (Tables 6-7 — 6-8), we see a familiar pattern of variables not being significant and having low correlation coefficients when they do. Additionally, despite model strength for trade outcomes, the model for foreign aid is not very robust at all (compare the R squares in Tables 6-7 and 6-8). Therefore, despite alternative hypothesized conditions, ideology is still not a strong determinant in presidential success; at least as far as the more nuanced view of the issue areas perspective is concerned. President's still "get their way" in foreign policy, however we can say that the Cold War Consensus is in jeopardy because when viewed holistically, foreign policy is increasingly becoming politicized. However, the ideological politicization of foreign policy tended to *help* not *hurt* presidential position success as a basis for *coalitional support* during this extant period of political time. The real question emanating out of these sets of empirical findings is what changed? The answer could lie in the parties-in-Congress themselves and that is where we now turn.

When examining partisanship, the first overwhelming factor is the general strength of all the models (Tables 6-9 — 6-12), using variance control as a measure of model strength (the R squares) one can see that all of the models account for in excess of 2/3 of the variance factor. For social scientific statistical models this is impressive indeed. Furthermore, there seems to be a pattern that exhibits itself in the following manner: Republican party unity is positively associated with presidential foreign policy success and corresponding Democratic unity (in the House) has a negative association. In addition to a partisan divide, there is also a chamber differentiation wherein the president's party strength matters more in the House than in the Senate. This is probably due to the Senate's increased role in foreign policy generally as well as the peculiarities of the Senate where party does not matter as much due to a lack of limitations on procedural measures like floor debate and amendment recommendation (from Sinclair 2000).

But it is instructive in suggesting that things are "heating up" from a partisan perspective because conflict is increasingly becoming a function of the party divide itself. It is this last reason why the unified government variable has such a weak outcome (r=.08) relative to presidency-centered predictions. Basically, the unified government of the Carter presidency and the split control government of the Reagan years worked to embolden presidential partisan/coalitional *support* in the Senate and *opposition* in the House. Finally, the election year measures support predictions regarding a positive relation between presidential elections and foreign policy success but defy such expectations from a congress-centered perspective relative to mid-term elections. These election years are *also* positively associated with foreign policy success, however as with presidential elections the correlations are on the whole weak (r=.078 and .035 respectively). Furthermore, the increase in the number of partisan roll calls in both chambers is standing juxtaposed to the previous statements as a *negative* relationship develops in presidential-senatorial foreign affairs relations and a corresponding *positive* (though weaker) relationship develops between the executive and the House (see Table 6-9). So, what are the nuances of this period's executive-legislative issue area dynamic?

In national security (see Table 6-10), the president's success rate seems immune to the presence of mid-term elections as deviating outcomes appear (thus, being positively rather than negatively associated with annual national security success). Additionally, the pronounced patterns regarding party and chamber that were so important in foreign policy success do not seem to reappear in any systematized fashion. In fact, party strength seems to matter more in the House than it does in the Senate, which is somewhat counterintuitive. However, it could be that the increased role of the procurement and basing policy among the roll call votes is driving a "domestication" process all its own in the House at this time.

The model predicts extremely well for trade (see Table 6-11), with the previously observed patterns in foreign policy writ large re-manifesting themselves. The R square of .872 is so high that the model could be subject to the critique of being "over specified." For foreign aid success during the Confrontation Politics Order, the model follows expected patterns as seen in trade and foreign policy. The one exception is that the previously observed chamber differences do not seem to manifest themselves as systematically. The model's strength does decline relative to trade but it is still very robust (see Table 6-12's R square). Now, I will supplement these findings with some tabular analysis of the success rates themselves during this cut of political time.

The Multiple Presidencies of the Confrontation Politics Order, 1973-1989

As indicated in Tables 6-13—6-16, beginning in 1973 there is an overall decline in the rate of presidential success in foreign policy. Further review of these tables indicates that the decline is not felt equally amongst the issue areas of foreign policy. Descriptive analysis indicates that the majority of the decline in foreign policy success occurs in the low politics arena (trade, foreign aid and immigration). This is especially true for foreign aid and immigration, the two issue areas that are in routine practice the "most removed" from the security-driven issue areas of the high politics arena (national security, domestic security and diplomacy). However, closer inspection does show that in diplomacy, especially during the non-unified government presidencies (the others minus Carter) is subject to a lower level of success when seen in comparison to the administrations of the War Power Order (see Tables 5-25—5-28).

Finally, domestic security proves problematic at least for Ford and late Nixon. Also, and quite telling for future developments is that Carter's success rate in trade (particularly in the second half of his term) is not particularly robust given a unified presidency-centered condition with the Congress. This is important because it is telling us that as the intermestic character of the low politics arena increases as corresponding deference to presidential prerogatives (even of the same party) declines.

Summary

This chapter has dealt with a period of political time that can best be summarized as a time of transition in the presidential-congressional foreign policy relationship. From the perspective offered by an issue areas analysis with the multiple presidencies thesis as its guiding frame, we can see that the component core issue areas of foreign policy (national security, trade and foreign aid) were subject to a process of politicization. This process was in turn defined by the increased role of partisanship (though not necessarily) ideology as a decisive factor in dictating presidential success rates on roll call position votes in foreign affairs during the extant timeframe of inquiry—The Confrontation Politics Order, 1973-1989. Both the narrative and the systematic studies found these factors and in turn saw them corroborated in the success rates themselves as derived from tabular analysis. We now turn our attention to how the politicization process relative to executive-legislative foreign policy relations came to fruition in the next act of our drama called—The Imperial Presidency Politicized!

189

Table 6-1. Foreign Policy Success Regression Analysis of Ideological Determinants War Power Order (1953-1972)

| | Un-standardized Coefficients | | Sig. |
	B	Std. Error	
(Constant)	.845	.006	.000
Conservative Coalition For	-.005	.004	.262
Conservative Coalition Against	-.007	.004	.133
Liberal Coalition For	.014	.004	.001
Liberal Coalition Against	.011	.020	.593
ADA Presidential Interest Group Rating	-.013	.007	.083

R Square	Adjusted R Square	Std. Error of the Estimate	Durbin-Watson
.025	.018	.059	.069

Predictors: (Constant), ADA Presidential Interest Group Rating, Liberal Coalition For, Liberal Coalition Against, Conservative Coalition Against, Conservative Coalition For
Dependent Variable: War Power Order Annual Foreign Policy Success Score
N=1157

Table 6-2. National Security Policy Success Regression Analysis of Ideological Determinants War Power Order (1953-1972)

| | Un-standardized Coefficients | | Sig. |
	B	Std. Error	
(Constant)	.841	.014	.000
Conservative Coalition For	-.007	.009	.432
Conservative Coalition Against	-.006	.010	.546
Liberal Coalition For	-.004	.011	.701
Liberal Coalition Against	-.026	.041	.535
ADA Presidential Interest Group Rating	-.024	.016	.147

R Square	Adjusted R Square	Std. Error of the Estimate	Durbin-Watson
.005	-.003	.123	.027

Predictors: (Constant), ADA Presidential Interest Group Rating, Liberal Coalition For, Liberal Coalition Against, Conservative Coalition Against, Conservative Coalition For
Dependent Variable: War Power Order Annual National Security Policy Success Score
N=1157

Table 6-3. Trade Policy Success Regression Analysis of Ideological Determinants War Power Order (1953-1972)

	Un-standardized Coefficients		Sig.
	B	Std. Error	
(Constant)	.743	.012	.000
Conservative Coalition For	-.027	.007	.000
Conservative Coalition Against	-.003	.008	.723
Liberal Coalition For	.030	.008	.000
Liberal Coalition Against	-.026	.037	.482
ADA Presidential Interest Group Rating	.157	.014	.000

R Square	Adjusted R Square	Std. Error of the Estimate	Durbin-Watson
.244	.239	.109	.098

Predictors: (Constant), ADA Presidential Interest Group Rating, Liberal Coalition For, Liberal Coalition Against, Conservative Coalition Against, Conservative Coalition For
Dependent Variable: War Power Order Annual Trade Policy Success Score
N=1157

Table 6-4. Foreign Aid Policy Success Regression Analysis of Ideological Determinants War Power Order (1953-1972)

	Un-standardized Coefficients		Sig.
	B	Std. Error	
(Constant)	.837	.015	.000
Conservative Coalition For	-.005	.009	.567
Conservative Coalition Against	-.015	.010	.151
Liberal Coalition For	.028	.010	.006
Liberal Coalition Against	.041	.046	.379
ADA Presidential Interest Group Rating	-.091	.017	.000

R Square	Adjusted R Square	Std. Error of the Estimate	Durbin-Watson
.059	.053	.137	.053

Predictors: (Constant), ADA Presidential Interest Group Rating, Liberal Coalition For, Liberal Coalition Against, Conservative Coalition Against, Conservative Coalition For
Dependent Variable: War Power Order Annual Foreign Aid Policy Success Score
N=1157

Table 6-5. Foreign Policy Success Regression Analysis of Ideological Determinants
Confrontation Politics Order (1973-1989)

| | Un-standardized Coefficients | | Sig. |
	B	Std. Error	
(Constant)	.664	.003	.000
Conservative Coalition For	.006	.002	.012
Conservative Coalition Against	.006	.005	.207
Liberal Coalition For	.024	.008	.002
Liberal Coalition Against	.013	.013	.317
ADA Presidential Interest Group Rating	.171	.006	.000

R Square	Adjusted R Square	Std. Error of the Estimate	Durbin-Watson
.393	.390	.067	.030

Predictors: (Constant), ADA Presidential Interest Group Rating, Liberal Coalition For, Liberal
Coalition Against, Conservative Coalition For, Conservative Coalition Against
Dependent Variable: Confrontation Politics Order Annual Foreign Policy Success
N=1524

Table 6-6. National Security Success Regression Analysis of Ideological Determinants
Confrontation Politics Order (1973-1989):

| | Un-standardized Coefficients | | Sig. |
	B	Std. Error	
(Constant)	.725	.004	.000
Conservative Coalition For	.006	.003	.058
Conservative Coalition Against	.004	.007	.590
Liberal Coalition For	.018	.011	.102
Liberal Coalition Against	.003	.018	.873
ADA Presidential Interest Group Rating	.114	.009	.000

R Square	Adjusted R Square	Std. Error of the Estimate	Durbin-Watson
.119	.116	.097	.020

Predictors: (Constant), ADA Presidential Interest Group Rating, Liberal Coalition For, Liberal
Coalition Against, Conservative Coalition For, Conservative Coalition Against
Dependent Variable: Confrontation Politics Order Annual National Security Policy Success
N=1524

Table 6-7. Trade Policy Success Regression Analysis of Ideological Determinants Confrontation Politics Order (1973-1989)

	Un-standardized Coefficients		Sig.
	B	Std. Error	
(Constant)	.530	.004	.000
Conservative Coalition For	.003	.004	.361
Conservative Coalition Against	.015	.008	.050
Liberal Coalition For	.004	.012	.744
Liberal Coalition Against	.001	.021	.971
ADA Presidential Interest Group Rating	.309	.010	.000

R Square	Adjusted R Square	Std. Error of the Estimate	Durbin-Watson
.448	.446	.110	.033

Predictors: (Constant), ADA Presidential Interest Group Rating, Liberal Coalition For, Liberal Coalition Against, Conservative Coalition For, Conservative Coalition Against
Dependent Variable: Confrontation Politics Order Annual Trade Policy Success Score
N=1524

Table 6-8. Annual Presidential Foreign Aid Policy Success Regression Analysis of Ideological Determinants Confrontation Politics Order (1973-1989)

	Un-standardized Coefficients		Sig.
	B	Std. Error	
(Constant)	.715	.006	.000
Conservative Coalition For	.003	.005	.627
Conservative Coalition Against	-.004	.011	.733
Liberal Coalition For	-.004	.017	.801
Liberal Coalition Against	-.056	.029	.051
ADA Presidential Interest Group Rating	.060	.014	.000

R Square	Adjusted R Square	Std. Error of the Estimate	Durbin-Watson
.016	.012	.154	.038

Predictors: (Constant), ADA Presidential Interest Group Rating, Liberal Coalition For, Liberal Coalition Against, Conservative Coalition For, Conservative Coalition Against
Dependent Variable: Confrontation Politics Order Annual Foreign Aid Policy Success Score
N=1524

Table 6-9. Foreign Policy Success Regression Analysis of Partisan Determinants Confrontation
Politics Order (1973-1989)

| | Un-standardized Coefficients | | Sig. |
	B	Std. Error	
(Constant)	.597	.033	.000
Senate Partisan Roll Calls	-1.262	.035	.000
House Partisan Roll Calls	.489	.032	.000
House Party Unity (D)	-1.799	.077	.000
Senate Party Unity (D)	.256	.051	.000
House Party Unity (R)	1.509	.077	.000
Senate Party Unity (R)	.555	.023	.000
Unified Government	.080	.002	.000
Mid-Term Election Year	.078	.005	.000
Presidential Election Year	.035	.004	.000

R Square	Adjusted R Square	Std. Error of the Estimate	Durbin-Watson
.834	.833	.036	.026

Predictors: (Constant), Presidential Election Year, House Party Unity (R), Unified Government,
Senate Party Unity (R), Senate Partisan Roll Calls, Mid-Term Election Year,
House
Partisan Roll Calls, Senate Party Unity (D), House Party Unity (D)
Dependent Variable: Confrontation Politics Order Annual Foreign Policy Success
N=1524

Table 6-10. National Security Success Regression Analysis of Partisan Determinants
        Confrontation Politics Order (1973-1989)

	Un-standardized Coefficients		Sig.
	B	Std. Error	
(Constant)	-.926	.061	.000
Unified Government	.022	.010	.036
Mid-Term Election Year	.222	.009	.000
Presidential Election Year	.104	.008	.000
Presidential Party Seat % in House of Representatives	-.963	.092	.000
Presidential Party Seat % in Senate	1.389	.176	.000
Senate Party Unity (R)	-.088	.055	.111
Senate Party Unity (D)	.408	.085	.000
House Party Unity (R)	3.658	.123	.000
House Party Unity (D)	-2.354	.118	.000
Senate Partisan Roll Calls	-.424	.062	.000
House Partisan Roll Calls	.916	.061	.000

R Square	Adjusted R Square	Std. Error of the Estimate	Durbin-Watson
.754	.752	.050	.040

Predictors: (Constant), House Partisan Roll Calls, Senate Partisan Roll Calls, Presidential
        Election Year, Presidential Party Seat % in Senate, House Party Unity (R), Senate
        Party Unity (R), Mid-Term Election Year, Senate Party Unity (D), House Party
Unity
        (D), Unified Government, Presidential Party Seat % in House of Representatives
Dependent Variable: Confrontation Politics Order Annual National Security Policy Success
N=1524

Table 6-11. Trade Policy Success Regression Analysis of Partisan Determinants Confrontation Politics Order (1973-1989)

	Un-standardized Coefficients		Sig.
	B	Std. Error	
(Constant)	-1.531	.068	.000
Unified Government	-.132	.011	.000
Mid-Term Election Year	.333	.010	.000
Presidential Election Year	.082	.008	.000
Presidential Party Seat % in House of Representatives	2.600	.102	.000
Presidential Party Seat % in Senate	-1.787	.195	.000
Senate Party Unity (R)	1.509	.061	.000
Senate Party Unity (D)	-2.616	.095	.000
House Party Unity (R)	7.077	.137	.000
House Party Unity (D)	-2.118	.131	.000
Senate Partisan Roll Calls	-3.215	.069	.000
House Partisan Roll Calls	1.063	.067	.000

R Square	Adjusted R Square	Std. Error of the Estimate	Durbin-Watson
.872	.871	.055	.027

Predictors: (Constant), House Partisan Roll Calls, Senate Partisan Roll Calls, Presidential Election Year, Presidential Party Seat % in Senate, House Party Unity (R), Senate Party Unity (R), Mid-Term Election Year, Senate Party Unity (D), House Party Unity (D), Unified Government, Presidential Party Seat % in House of Representatives

Dependent Variable: Confrontation Politics Order Annual Trade Policy Success Score
N=1524

Table 6-12. Foreign Aid Policy Success Regression Analysis of Partisan Determinants Confrontation Politics Order (1973-1989)

	Un-standardized Coefficients		Sig.
	B	Std. Error	
(Constant)	.299	.102	.003
Unified Government	-.435	.017	.000
Mid-Term Election Year	.242	.015	.000
Presidential Election Year	.224	.013	.000
Presidential Party Seat % in House of Representatives	.208	.154	.177
Presidential Party Seat % in Senate	2.630	.295	.000
Senate Party Unity (R)	2.386	.092	.000
Senate Party Unity (D)	-5.163	.143	.000
House Party Unity (R)	5.218	.206	.000
House Party Unity (D)	-4.742	.197	.000
Senate Partisan Roll Calls	-.550	.104	.000
House Partisan Roll Calls	2.742	.101	.000

R Square	Adjusted R Square	Std. Error of the Estimate	Durbin-Watson
.697	.695	.083	.036

Predictors: (Constant), House Partisan Roll Calls, Senate Partisan Roll Calls, Presidential Election Year, Presidential Party Seat % in Senate, House Party Unity (R), Senate Party Unity (R), Mid-Term Election Year, Senate Party Unity (D), House Party Unity (D), Unified Government, Presidential Party Seat % in House of Representatives
Dependent Variable: Confrontation Politics Order Annual Foreign Aid Policy Success Score
N=1524

Table 6-13. Annual Presidential Success Scores across Issue Areas of Foreign Policy. Nixon Administration (1969-1974) 91st-93rd Congresses*

Year	Foreign Policy	Security	Domestic Security	Diplomacy	Trade	Foreign Aid	Immigration	Totals
1969	C=93 (40:3)	C=91% (20:2)	C=100% (3:0)	C=100% (4:0)	C=100% (5:5)	C=88% (7:1)	C=n/a (0:0)	N=43
	H=89% (8:1)	H=100% (3:0)	H=n/a (0:0)	H=100% (1:0)	H=100% (1:0)	H=75% (3:1)	H=n/a	N=9
	S=94% (32:2)	S=89% (17:2)	S=100% (3:0)	S=100% (3:0)	S=100% (4:0)	S=100% (4:0)	S=n/a	N=34
1970	C=93% (27:2)	C=75% (6:2)	C=100% (1:0)	C=100% (8:0)	C=100% (7:0)	C=100% (4:0)	C=n/a (0:0)	N=29
	H=90% (9:1)	H=0% (0:1)	H=n/a (0:0)	H=100% (3:0)	H=100% (3:0)	H=100% (3:0)	H=n/a (0:0)	N=10
	S=95% (18:1)	S=86% (6:1)	S=100% (1:0)	S=100% (5:0)	S=100% (4:0)	S=100% (1:0)	S=n/a (0:0)	N=19
1971	C=84% (57:11)	C=87% (45:7)	C=n/a (0:0)	C=100% (1:0)	C=60% (3:2)	C=89% (8:1)	C=n/a (0:0)	N=68
	H=95% (19:1)	H=100% (18:0)	H=n/a (0:0)	H=n/a (0:0)	H=0% (0:1)	H=100% (1:0)	H=n/a (0:0)	N=20
	S=79% (38:10)	S=79% (27:7)	S=n/a (0:0)	S=100% (1:0)	S=75% (3:1)	S=88% (7:1)	S=n/a (0:0)	N=48
1972	C=70% (26:11)	C=65% (15:8)	C=n/a (0:0)	C=50% (1:1)	C=66% (2:1)	C=50% (1:1)	C=n/a (0:0)	N=37
	H=92% (12:1)	H=100% (7:0)	H=n/a (0:0)	H=0% (0:1)	H=100% (1:0)	H=n/a (0:0)	H=n/a (0:0)	N=13
	S=58% (14:10)	S=50% (8:8)	S=n/a (0:0)	S=100% (1:0)	S=50% (1:1)	S=50% (1:1)	S=n/a (0:0)	N=24
1973	C=60% (74:49)	C=47% (23:26)	C=50% (1:1)	C=100% (7:0)	C=51% (18:17)	C=75% (9:3)	C=0% (0:1)	N=123
	H=46% (19:22)	H=26% (5:14)	H=100% (1:0)	H=100% (1:0)	H=50% (6:6)	H=86% (6:1)	H=0% (0:1)	N=41
	S=67% (55:27)	S=60% (18:12)	S=0% (0:1)	S=100% (6:0)	S=52% (12:11)	S=60% (3:2)	S=n/a (0:0)	N=82

Table 6-13. Continued

Year	Foreign Policy	Security	Domestic Security	Diplomacy	Trade	Foreign Aid	Immigration	Totals
1974a[1]	C=59% (29:20)	C=71% (12:5)	C=n/a (0:0)	C=100% (2:0)	C=48% (10:11)	C=67% (4:2)	C=n/a (0:0)	N=49
	H=50% (9:9)	H=100% (3:0)	H=n/a (0:0)	H=100% (1:0)	H=38% (3:5)	H=50% (2:2)	H=n/a (0:0)	N=18
	S=65% (20:11)	S=64% (9:5)	S=n/a (0:0)	S=100% (1:0)	S=54% (7:6)	S=100% (2:0)	S=n/a (0:0)	N=31

*Some votes are in mixed categories, which are in a separate table but are included within the aggregate annual foreign policy success scores but not individuated in the issue area scores.

[1] 1974a refers to Nixon's position votes during the year of his resignation from office the rest of the position votes for that year are recorded under the new president Gerald R. Ford and hence, not included in this table.

Table 6-14. Annual Presidential Success Scores across Issue Areas of Foreign Policy. Ford Administration (1974-1977) 93rd-94th Congresses*

Year	Foreign Policy	Security	Domestic Security	Diplomacy	Trade	Foreign Aid	Immigration	Totals
1974b[2]	C=58% (38:28)	C=75% (6:2)	C=40% (2:3)	C=100% (2:0)	C=86% (6:1)	C=75% (18:6)	C=n/a (0:0)	N=66
	H=57% (13:10)	H=60% (3:2)	H=67% (2:1)	H=n/a (0:0)	H=100% (1:0)	H=67% (6:3)	H=n/a (0:0)	N=23
	S=58% (25:18)	S=75% (3:1)	S=0% (0:2)	S=100% (2:0)	S=83% (5:1)	S=80% (12:3)	S=n/a (0:0)	N=43
1975	C=68% (54:25)	C=76% (16:5)	C=100% (2:0)	C=70% (7:3)	C=52% (15:14)	C=88% (7:1)	C=100% (1:0)	N=79
	H=47% (16:18)	H=83% (5:1)	H=n/a (0:0)	H=40% (2:3)	H=39% (7:11)	H=100% (1:0)	H=100% (1:0)	N=34
	S=91% (38:7)	S=73% (11:4)	S=100% (2:0)	S=100% (5:0)	S=73% (8:3)	S=86% (6:1)	S=n/a (0:0)	N=45
1976	C=66% (23:12)	C=79% (15:4)	C=100% (2:0)	C=n/a (0:0)	C=63% (5:3)	C=100% (1:0)	C=n/a (0:0)	N=35
	H=69% (11:5)	H=75% (6:2)	H=100% (2:0)	H=n/a (0:0)	H=67% (2:1)	H=100% (1:0)	H=n/a (0:0)	N=16
	S=63% (12:7)	S=82% (9:2)	S=n/a (0:0)	S=n/a (0:0)	S=60% (3:2)	S=n/a (0:0)	S=n/a (0:0)	N=19

*Some votes are in mixed categories (see separate table); these are included in the aggregate annual foreign policy success scores but are excluded from the individuated issue area success scores.

[2] 1974b refers to President Ford's position votes that he took after assuming power in the wake of Nixon's resignation from office.

Table 6-15. Annual Presidential Success Scores across Issue Areas of Foreign Policy. Carter Administration (1977-1981) 95th-96th Congresses*

Year	Foreign Policy	Security	Domestic Security	Diplomacy	Trade	Foreign Aid	Immigration	Totals
1977	C=82% (47:10)	C=75% (15:5)	C=n/a (0:0)	C=100% (4:0)	C=100% (13:0)	C=71% (10:4)	C=100% (1:0)	N=57
	H=74% (23:8)	H=80% (12:3)	H=n/a (0:0)	H=100% (1:0)	H=100% (7:0)	H=67% (4:2)	H=n/a (0:0)	N=31
	S=92% (24:2)	S=60% (3:2)	S=n/a (0:0)	S=100% (3:0)	S=100% (6:0)	S=75% (6:2)	S=100% (1:0)	N=26
1978	C=85% (109:19)	C=91% (31:3)	C=92% (12:1)	C=100% (14:0)	C=79% (31:8)	C=72% (18:7)	C=n/a (0:0)	N=128
	H=70% (35:15)	H=63% (5:3)	H=83% (5:1)	H=100% (1:0)	H=61% (11:7)	H=65% (11:6)	H=n/a (0:0)	N=50
	S=95% (74:4)	S=100% (26:0)	S=100% (7:0)	S=100% (13:0)	S=95% (20:1)	S=88% (7:1)	S=n/a (0:0)	N=78
1979	C=79% (121:33)	C=80% (16:4)	C=n/a (0:0)	C=83% (20:4)	C=78% (46:13)	C=75% (33:11)	C=100% (1:0)	N=154
	H=72% (54:21)	H=75% (9:3)	H=n/a (0:0)	H=89% (8:1)	H=70% (21:9)	H=67% (16:8)	H=n/a (0:0)	N=75
	S=85% (67:12)	S=88% (7:1)	S=n/a (0:0)	S=80% (12:3)	S=86% (25:4)	S=85% (17:3)	S=100% (1:0)	N=79
1980	C=71% (60:24)	C=76% (19:6)	C=n/a (0:0)	C=67% (4:2)	C=61% (14:9)	C=83% (20:4)	C=n/a (0:0)	N=84
	H=69% (29:13)	H=77% (10:3)	H=n/a (1:0)	H=100% (1:0)	H=60% (6:4)	H=77% (10:3)	H=n/a (0:0)	N=42
	S=74% (31:11)	S=75% (9:3)	S=n/a (0:0)	S=60% (3:2)	S=62% (8:5)	S=91% (10:1)	S=n/a (0:0)	N=42

*Some votes contain mixed categories (see separate table); these are included in the aggregate annual foreign policy success scores but are excluded from the individuated issue area success scores.

201

Table 6-16. Annual Presidential Success Scores across Issue Areas of Foreign Policy. Reagan Administration (1981-1989) 97th-100th Congresses*+

Year	Foreign Policy	Security	Domestic Security	Diplomacy	Trade	Foreign Aid	Immigration	Totals
1981	C=75% (51:17)	C=77% (23:7)	C=100% (2:0)	C=89% (8:1)	C=63% (12:7)	C=86% (6:1)	C=n/a (0:0)	N=68
	H=67% (16:8)	H=69% (9:4)	H=100% (2:0)	H=100% (1:0)	H=50% (4:4)	H=n/a (0:0)	H=n/a (0:0)	N=24
	S=80% (35:9)	S=82% (14:3)	S=n/a (0:0)	S=88% (7:1)	S=73% (8:3)	S=86% (6:1)	S=n/a (0:0)	N=44
1982	C=79% (66:18)	C=77% (23:7)	C=90% (9:1)	C=0% (0:1)	C=67% (12:6)	C=33% (1:2)	C=93% (14:1)	N=84
	H=63% (22:13)	H=63% (12:7)	H=67% (2:1)	H=n/a (0:0)	H=73% (8:3)	H=0% (0:2)	H=n/a (0:0)	N=35
	S=88% (38:5)	S=100% (11:0)	S=100% (7:0)	S=0% (0:1)	S=57% (4:3)	S=100% (1:0)	S=93% (14:1)	N=43
1983	C=76% (78:24)	C=80% (37:9)	C=100% (1:0)	C=89% (16:2)	C=47% (9:10)	C=88% (7:1)	C=78% (7:2)	N=102
	H=59% (26:18)	H=75% (18:6)	H=100% (1:0)	H=33% (1:2)	H=11% (1:8)	H=83% (5:1)	H=0% (0:1)	N=44
	S=90% (52:6)	S=86% (19:3)	S=n/a (0:0)	S=100% (15:0)	S=80% (8:2)	S=100% (2:0)	S=88% (7:1)	N=58
1984	C=78% (58:16)	C=73% (16:6)	C=50% (2:2)	C=75% (6:2)	C=70% (7:3)	C=92% (11:1)	C=82% (9:2)	N=74
	H=71% (29:12)	H=58% (7:5)	H=33% (1:2)	H=100% (2:0)	H=60% (3:2)	H=75% (3:1)	H=82% (9:2)	N=41
	S=88% (29:4)	S=90% (9:1)	S=100% (1:0)	S=67% (4:2)	S=80% (4:1)	S=100% (8:0)	S=n/a (0:0)	N=33
1985	C=66% (52:27)	C=86% (24:4)	C=60% (3:2)	C=83% (10:2)	C=50% (6:6)	C=50% (7:7)	C=0% (0:3)	N=79
	H=54% (20:17)	H=71% (10:4)	H=60% (3:2)	H=67% (2:1)	H=25% (1:3)	H=50% (3:3)	H=0% (0:1)	N=37
	S=76% (32:10)	S=100% (14:0)	S=n/a (0:0)	S=89% (8:1)	S=63% (5:3)	S=50% (4:4)	S=0% (0:2)	N=42

202

Table 6-16. Continued

Year	Foreign Policy	Security	Domestic Security	Diplomacy	Trade	Foreign Aid	Immigration	Totals
1986	C=59% (57:40)	C=75% (18:6)	C=58% (7:5)	C=18% (2:9)	C=36% (8:14)	C=79% (15:4)	C=0% (0:1)	N=97
	H=29% (13:32)	H=60% (6:4)	H=29% (2:5)	H=0% (0:7)	H=15% (2:11)	H=40% (2:3)	H=0% (0:1)	N=45
	S=85% (44:8)	S=86% (12:2)	S=100% (5:0)	S=50% (2:2)	S=67% (6:3)	S=93% (13:1)	S=n/a (0:0)	N=52
1987	C=61% (50:32)	C=83% (20:4)	C=56% (5:4)	C=45% (5:6)	C=60% (12:8)	C=63% (5:3)	C=33% (1:2)	N=82
	H=53% (24:21)	H=79% (15:4)	H=40% (2:3)	H=17% (1:5)	H=38% (3:5)	H=50% (3:3)	H=0% (0:1)	N=45
	S=70% (26:11)	S=100% (5:0)	S=75% (3:1)	S=80% (4:1)	S=75% (9:3)	S=100% (2:0)	S=50% (1:1)	N=37
1988	C=62% (60:37)	C=73% (19:7)	C=30% (3:7)	C=100% (4:0)	C=48% (10:11)	C=50% (3:3)	C=50% (1:1)	N=97
	H=48% (24:26)	H=61% (11:7)	H=13% (1:7)	H=100% (1:0)	H=25% (2:6)	H=50% (2:2)	H=50% (1:1)	N=50
	S=79% (37:10)	S=100% (8:0)	S=100% (2:0)	S=100% (3:0)	S=62% (8:5)	S=50% (1:1)	S=n/a (0:0)	N=47

*Some votes contain mixed categories, these are included in the aggregate annual foreign policy success scores but are excluded (and included on a separate table) from the individuated issue area success scores.

+Win-Loss Ratios of votes in specific issue areas are contained in the parentheses.

CHAPTER 7

THE IMPERIAL PRESIDENCY POLITICIZED: PRESIDENTIAL RE-EMPOWERMENT AGAINST AN UNENCUMBERED CONGRESS' IDEOLOGICAL PARTY GOVERNMENT, 1990-2000

Introduction

This chapter brings us right up to the edge of political time that we currently occupy. Like previous empirical chapters, we will follow the now set pattern of setting the context, analyzing it, interpreting it and finally, summarizing the big story of our presidential-congressional drama regarding foreign policy relations. The Imperial Presidency Politicized covers the extant period of political time during the tumultuous decade of the 1990's. A time in US foreign affairs that began with the promise of a Post-Cold War "peace dividend" but saw that promise eroded, compromised and ultimately shattered on the shores of a fully politicized, partisan driven and ideologically codified executive-legislative conflict. First a Republican president facing a fully liberal Democratic Congress and was impeded every step of the way. Then, after a brief return to unified government a Democratic president faced ultimate censure from an unapologetically conservative Republican Congress.

What changed during this time was not the quality of the personnel involved. Both sides were well meaning in their efforts to construct a foreign policy that spoke with a unanimous voice in world affairs. Instead, it was the nature of the relationship itself, the age of bi-partisan support for presidential initiatives and/or positions in foreign policy during the War Power Order (1953-1972) had given way to a more partisan atmosphere offset by the lack of ideological unity within the two major parties in the Congress during the Confrontation Politics Order (1973-1989). The persistence of the cross-partisan coalitions, albeit in a much muted form offset partisanship's role in such a way that presidents were still able to construct coalitions of support within (and to a lesser extent) across congressional party lines for their preferred positions and initiatives in foreign policy. However, by the end of this period of political time the liberal coalition was a distant memory and the conservative coalition was in such severe decline that its strength as an influencer on presidential success had been reduced to near negligibility (see Bond and Fleisher 1990 for corroborating evidence).

As a series of recent articles have shown that by the 1990's, "the dynamics of party government in the Congress have changed." (Smith and Gamm in Dodd and Oppenheimer 2005). Ideological polarization had taken hold, influencing the appointment process on committees, prescribing procedural maneuvering in the Senate, defining electoral districting for the House, and establishing a new type of partisan leadership in the House of Representatives.[1] Basically, as the parties-in-Congress became ideologically coherent executive-legislative relations completed a process of politicization during the Imperial Presidency Politicized Order that had begun in the previous order. In other words, "with great power comes great responsibility" and an ideological party government in the Congress began to hold the president to the same level of accountability long seen in domestic affairs.[2]

Likewise, the presidency itself had attained a level of restoration, particularly through the results of the Reagan administration.[3] This was especially true in foreign policy as Reagan had re-asserted US free world leadership in the struggle with the USSR in the late Cold War and had passed on a perceived victory to his successor (Milkis and Nelson 2003). Reagan had set a precedent for coalition building regarding defense policies in particular, so it is reasonable to think that his successors would have similar such opportunities (Jones 1988 and Smith 1982). The fact that they did not is instructive in itself as regards the extreme congressionalized limitations which would now face the foreign policy presidencies of Bush and Clinton. We now turn to the employment of this phenomenon through the "eyes" of the unit level foreign policy relationship between the presidency and the Congress in the Order of the Imperial Presidency Politicized!

Issue Areas of Foreign Policy across the Order of the Imperial Presidency Politicized, 1990-2000

When examining the Order of the Imperial Presidency Politicized, we must first look at why I have given such a name to this period of executive-legislative foreign policy history. The historian and political scientist Arthur M. Schlesinger, Jr. first coined the term "the imperial presidency," in a normative critique of the expansion of presidential power, especially in foreign affairs during the Cold War (Schlesinger 1973). Schlesinger had argued that the Johnson-Nixon

---

[1] See Aldrich and Rohde 2005, Evans and Lipinski 2005, Oppenheimer 2005 and Schickler and Pearson 2005 all in Dodd and Oppenheimer's (2005) *Congress Reconsidered*.

[2] The comment, "with great power comes great responsibility," originated with Stan Lee and Steve Ditko's (1962) "Amazing Fantasy #15"—the comic book where the superhero character Spiderman was first introduced.

[3] See Jones (in Jones 1988), Tullis 1987 and Smith (in Cronin 1982) for explicit scholarly examples of the concept of the Reagan "Restoration Presidency."

presidencies were something of a "tipping point" in presidential-polity relations and an inevitable "backlash" to executive prerogatives was at that very point in time underway (Schlesinger 1973). Years later he would look back at that prediction and claim that it was largely successful, however, in recent times he has suggested that we are once again in a time of presidential "excess," regarding foreign relations (Schlesinger 1989, 2005). Of course, Schlesinger's reassessment is actually based on security policy making and not foreign affairs writ-large, thus while instructive it should not be thought of as axiomatic, especially regarding an issue areas perspective to understanding foreign policy.

Nevertheless, the security initiatives undertaken by the Reagan administration including placing US forces in "harms way" in small scale military operations like Urgent Fury (the invasion of Grenada in 1983) were subject to considerable exponentiation under Bush and Clinton. The first Bush built his security policy profile off a "War on Drugs" which included Operation Just Cause (the invasion of Panama) among others involving militarized drug interdiction exercises in Latin America. Of course, Bush is best remembered for his international as well as national security leadership in the build up for, execution of and follows through to the Persian Gulf War of 1991.

Clinton, while never as fully aggressive in his employment of military power as the first Bush, did show a proclivity toward "pulling out the Big Stick" of US military might as a credible instrument of foreign policy. As Michael Mandelbaum (1996) has detailed and subsequent real world empirics have shown, Clinton deployed troops abroad in more places and in higher numbers with more direct "action potential" than any of his "peacetime" presidential predecessors did in combination. This led to within and without security critiques around the Pentagon Establishment about "mission creep" and "operational overstep" (Mandlebaum 1996). Therefore, on a cursory review of the Bush and Clinton security policy presidencies we can suggest that any notion of a congressional resurgence is certainly questionable. However, as this project has demonstrated again and again, not all foreign policy is security. And, the main thing to remember from the last "order" of executive-legislative foreign relations is that security may not even be the "main thing" in foreign policy anymore.

Even a cursory review of the legislative histories during this period of political time is revealing as far as presidential-congressional *conflict* in foreign policy is concerned. For instance, the divisive abortion debate long a hallmark of social policy in the domestic sphere

206

became a place of "congressionalization/domestication" in the security realm itself. Entrenched battles over defense authorization and appropriations bills were fought as Bush attempted to restrict abortion access at military hospitals both at home and abroad and a liberal Democratic Congress tried to expand such access (CQ Almanacs 1990 and 1992, legislative histories). The fight would begin again in the 104th Congress as the protagonists changed chambers of power with a Democratic president facing off against a conservative Republican Congress (CQ Almanac 1995, legislative history). This fight would continue throughout the rest of the Clinton presidency and only be resolved by the return of unified government with the second Bush (CQ Almanac 2001, special study on abortion in military hospitals). While, this conflict was new to the foreign policy relationship between the presidency and the Congress it was in keeping with a tradition of congressionalized attempts to "take over" the foreign policy prerogatives of presidents (regardless of party) by "domesticating the issue involved."

More generally, trade was now open to full dispute between the executive and legislative branches as the battles over NAFTA, FTAA and the results of the Uruguay Round (the creation of the WTO in 1994). While, on the surface both Bush and later Clinton won these insurgent challenges to their respective roles as "chief trade negotiators," these challenges are emblematic of the fact that the Congress no longer recognized that role as a "single claim to power" but rather as a place for congressionalized "advice and consent." (see the special report on NAFTA ratification in the 1993 CQ Almanac). It also suggests the potential for new issue area cross-partisan coalition formation, which despite their more amorphous nature relative to the liberal and conservative coalitions of old; they can still exert a largely unpredictable dynamic on the already politicized executive-legislative international affairs relationship. The fair trade movement within the Congress unites populist forces within both the Republican and Democratic parties-in-Congress as social conservatives and economic liberals united in opposition to free trading forces led by both Bush and Clinton (Lindsay 1994 and CQ Almanac 1993, legislative history). Clearly, more study is needed in this area but due to time considerations it must remain beyond the scope of this inquiry.

Foreign operations funding, long a kind of "mixed category" containing trade, foreign aid and security elements within it was for the first time in its existence (these specific funding devices date back to the 1960's) a place for prolonged political conflict between the presidency and the Congress. Why, is instrumental to a multiple presidencies understanding of the executive-legislative dynamic in foreign relations. For starters, since these votes have combinations of issue areas within them, they tend to be subject to certain disarray in how the president and Congress come to agreement during this timeframe. The fact that they did *not* follow such a diffuse pattern even as early as the Confrontation Politics Order is telling as far as the extent to which the politicization of the foreign policy process across these issue areas has become. In the past, such mixed aggregations got "swallowed up" in the broader politics of the day. Now, foreign policy itself has developed into such a nuanced process that it is possible that there has been a "multiplication of issue areas" (see CQ Almanacs 1995-2000, foreign operations section summaries) We can see that by looking at the fights over foreign operations authorizations and appropriations as this mix of issue areas means that no single one like security (and hence presidentialization) or foreign aid (and hence congressionalization) can take place. In fact, these may represent something of an excellent case study for predicting the future of presidential-congressional relations in foreign policy though of course that will have to wait for another time.

Base closings are another interesting case for future study during this time, as members of Congress regardless of partisanship or stated ideology try to "hold" on to bases recommended by the military and outside groups for closing due to the restructuring needs of a "military in post-Cold War transition" (from CQ Almanac 1990, report from Base Closure Commission). Immigration becomes subject to a push and pull effect as presidents push domestic security in the War on Drugs and the Congress emphasizes the free flow of goods and services in "trade commodity relations" (CQ Almanac 1990, legislative history).

Finally, in the vaunted realm of national security policy congressional deference to presidential agency is no longer even thought of as anything other than a "rhetorical statement." With great power, Bush and Clinton deployed troops abroad to East Africa, Southeastern Europe, Southwestern Asia and the Caribbean but with great responsibility the Congress questioned, placed limits on activities and often threatened (though never actually did) to cut funding (CQ Almanacs 1992-1999, various legislative histories). One could suggest that this is maintenance of "security power" within the executive. However, a closer inspection reveals that all is not quite what it seems on the surface because previous operations were not even questioned as recently as the Grenada invasion the Congress was openly "snubbed" by President Reagan who told the leadership about Urgent Fury after it was already under way (from Fisher 2000). Bush and

Clinton did not, nor could they ignore the Congress's role both real and imagined in security policy execution. Despite his protestations otherwise, the first Bush did actively seek (and eventually won) congressional authorization to wage war on Iraq in early 1991 before he ordered the start of Operation Desert Storm (CQ Almanac 1991, special report on the Persian Gulf War). And, Clinton's "Air War" over Kosovo was accompanied by another "air war" as a campaign strategy where he maintained congressional support by a combination of a "media blitz" over the heads of the Congress and a self-limitation as to ends and means (Holbrooke 2005, PBS 2000, documentary). The Imperial Presidency Politicized, 1990-2000 is our most recent period of political time relative to the executive-legislative divide in foreign relations. But, in order to develop the kind of understanding needed for generalizable findings from this period of political time we must engage in more systematic unit level study and to that we now turn.

Empirical Results

Harkening back to established patterns, we will begin our systematic examination by way of comparison regarding "time order effects" on the foreign affairs relationship between our institutions of interests and in this case "mixed issue area success." Comparing the results of the two regressions is revealing in the extent of the environmental change in the role of partisanship as a determinant of presidential mixed issue area success with the Congress. The greatest change is in the role of the constitution of government itself. Unified government, which has a relatively strong and positive correlation with presidential success in mixed issue areas of foreign policy during the Confrontation Politics Order (1973-1989) (r=.689), actually reverses direction in the Imperial Presidency Politicized Order (1990-2000) with a perfect negative partial correlation of (partial r=-1.0). However, this is offset by the failure of a collinerarity tolerance test, so the variable was actually purged from the model in order to maintain inter-variable co-relational stability (Agresti and Finlay 2001). The interpretation that is most telling deriving out of this relationship is that unified government is now the overwhelming *aberration* from the norm of national level executive-legislative relations and cannot be routinely counted upon as a factor in dictating presidential success. In fact, during this entire decade, only two years (under Bill Clinton 1993-1995) were actually subject to unified governmental conditions. Thus, the pattern we saw in the Confrontation Politics period of a *declining* influence for unified government as a presidency-centered condition is now completed as the partisan reality of the more congress-centered divided government condition has taken over as the determinative factor in foreign policy interactions.

Regarding other partisan political factors revealed by comparing these two models' results, include a general trend toward increasing influence of the variables from one period to the next. Both the measures of overall robustness (the R squares) and the influence measures (the individual correlation coefficients) increase exponentially (see Tables 7-1 — 7-2). Also, previously discerned patterns regarding chamber and party differences continue with party mattering more in the House than in the Senate with Democratic unity this time supporting and Republican unity standing in opposition to presidential success. This is to be expected given the fact that for much of this time it is a Democratic president juxtaposed against a Republican Congress. What is important here is that the *institutional relationship* is now determined more by *partisan composition of government*. A final observation garnered from comparing these two tables is that unlike the War Power Order, mixed issue areas are now numerous enough that they matter as units of analysis unto themselves. This supports one of the more general hypotheses coming out of the multiple presidencies thesis which is that as time goes by there is in fact a multiplication of issue areas in foreign policy as the presidential-congressional relationship in that domain becomes more and more nuanced. This is supporting evidence for notions about the general decline of presidential success in foreign policy, its increased politicization as a partisan (and even ideological entity) and its increased likelihood for congressionalization/domestication. This last phenomenon is due to the fact that the mere notion of a "mixed issue area of foreign policy" is itself an invitation for the inclusion of greater degrees of "intermestic composition" amidst the extant body of issue areas.

Looking specifically at the foreign policy success during the Imperial Presidency Politicized Order we find supporting evidence for the claims emanating out of the previous analysis. In fact, partisanship seems now to be about an equal factor in dictating both the House and the Senate's relationship with the president in foreign policy writ large. However, there is some residual bi-partisanship within the Senate as the Republican Party unity variable is indicating (see Table 7-3). However, the relatively robust ($r=-.556$) negative relationship between the percentage of partisan roll calls in the Senate and the proportion of presidential position vote success tends to serve as an offsetting (in this case a re-politicizing) factor in presidential-senatorial foreign affairs. Within the House, the strongly negative relationship

210

between presidential success and within chamber party unity is perhaps the single most telling systematic representation of the highly politicized relationship. Remember that since the Democrats held the White House during much of this decade (seven of the 10 years), strong Democratic *positive* correlation with presidential success as well as strong Republican *negative* association is indicative of a highly partisan (read politicized) unit level environment for foreign policy construction. Likewise, the unified government variable is once again falling out of the model for the same reasons as the mixed issue areas model. This is to be expected, especially when looking at foreign policy as a *totality* during this period of political time.

Taking a more nuanced perspective, we see in Table 7-4 that national security success has suffered severe decline at least as far as its partisan determinants are concerned. In general, the co-relational strength has declined in a number of the variables in comparison to foreign policy success. This is indicative of the more amorphous nature that foreign policy has taken during this order relative to previous ones. However, the strength of the model overall as measured by the R square (.993) is still very robust so we cannot say that national security has been "reduced to the dustbin of foreign policy history" in the executive-legislative relationship. But, we can say that it has been reduced to one among many components of foreign policy and not necessarily the dominant component issue area, especially in peacetime as this is the condition which defines most of this period.

In the areas of trade and foreign aid (see Tables 7-5 — 7-6), the models have corroborating results with an extreme qualification. The model for foreign aid (Table 7-6) is over specified as given by its perfect R square (1.0). This makes it problematic as an inferential device. This is a problem with population data at times, so any interpretations made from this model are questionable at best, for instance the "return" of unified government as an accurate predictor of the presidential-congressional foreign policy relationship. Therefore, we will spend our time on the less problematic outcomes associated with the trade success model for the Imperial Presidency Politicized Order. First of all, the role of partisanship as a strong indicator is supported overall regarding significance tests and co-relational coefficients (see Table 7-5). Secondly, there has been some "issue specific" movement among the indicators with trade success now being associated with the Senate more so than the House as measured by the percentage of the president's party seats, the percentage of partisan roll calls and Republican party unity within the Senate (remember, this is a time defined mostly by divided government).

What this supports is the notion that much of the intensity of the "partisan" heat between the presidency and the Congress over trade relations is located in the presidential-House relationship. And, trade is therefore still subject to a degree of "traditional deference" in the presidential-senatorial relationship well into this otherwise politicized order. Now, let us try to pull things together by looking at these issue areas form the perspective offered by the multiple presidencies.

The Multiple Presidencies of the Imperial Presidency Politicized Order, 1990-2000

Perhaps there is no stronger indicator of the alteration in the unit level foreign policy relationship between the presidency and the Congress than to indicate the "within case variance" by comparing Bush and Clinton's success rates in the "vaunted" realm of national security policy making. Excepting the first two years of Clinton from study because of the unified government condition, we see that Clinton's success rate in national security was 58.3% v. Bush's 65.5% on average (Tables 7-7—7-8). Taking a closer look at Bush we see that in the presidential election year of 1992 his success rate in national security policies was a paltry 42%. Clinton drops to a 30% success rate in national security in 1995, the first year of the "Republican Revolution" in the 104th Congress. In fact, despite reelection in 1996 Clinton's national security rates are below 60% throughout every year of his second term with the exception of 1999 (73% success in national security). Of course, that was the year of the "Kosovo Air War," as well as the senatorial failure to convict in Clinton's impeachment trial (CQ Almanac 1999, special reports Kosovo Air War and Clinton Impeachment). More than anything else, what this tabular analysis is suggesting is that we can draw a descriptive inference relative to the degree of presidential empowerment in foreign policy. That inference is simply this, "things are not what they once were." The ability of presidents to dominate the foreign policy construction process relative to the Congress has been impeded to the point that even the once "secure" category of national security is no longer the exclusive domain of presidentialized foreign affairs. The fact of the matter is that security itself has become subject to the congressionalization/domestication process and this is largely a function of the politicization (read partisan driven) development which has now coalesced in inter-institutional foreign policy making.

Of course, this inference is subject to the critique that national security was *not* an overarching arena of power for presidents Bush and Clinton because of the declined role of security in world affairs during this time. The Cold War was over, the Persian Gulf War was short and Kosovo, Bosnia, Somalia, Haiti, etc... were just not much of anything! So, what would happen if there really was a new systemic level threat, for starters the president would be re-empowered relative to the Congress as he could once again "securitize/presidentialize" the various issue areas of foreign policy. However, the 1990's and to a lesser extent the two preceding decades showed that War Power Order style deference by the Congress to presidential leadership was a thing of the now distant past. After, a short time of adjustment the Congress would routinely re-assert itself in mini-confrontation politics, possibly playing out across the by now "well differentiated issue areas of foreign policy." Unfortunately, for us we do not need to run some counterfactual simulation in order to find these conditions and test them. The real world attack on the World Trade Center in New York City on September 11, 2001 provided us with such a place to visage the responses of our two proactive institutions of national government (the presidency and the Congress). And, in the conclusion to this project we will examine these events and the role, if any of the political determinants of interest (the partisan factors) governing the foreign policy relationship between the president and the Congress across the component issue areas and their attendant "multiple presidencies."

Summary

This chapter has assessed the extant executive-legislative relationship across the issue areas of foreign policy during the Imperial Presidency Politicized Order of 1990-2000. In this effort, we have seen the completion of the "politicization" process driven by increasing within as well as across chamber partisanship in the Congress. "The politics that the foreign policy presidencies make" are now subject to intense scrutiny and opposition by the ideological partisans of the Congress. While, there were some differences in the patterns, like a House that tended to be more partisan driven generally in foreign policy. Or, a Senate that still tended toward some bi-partisanship across its issue area relationship with the president.

But, the "big story" is still that presidential success in foreign policy is no longer as driven as it once was by the security dynamic. Hence, there has been a successful "congressionalization/domestication" of foreign policy. This has been facilitated by the multiplication of issue areas in foreign policy as revealed in the mixed issue area analysis. And, also in the narrative where even security policy making is now subject to a phenomenon of

213

intermestic politics, as suggested in the struggles over abortion policy in military hospitals and base closures that helped to define the presidential-congressional foreign affairs of the 1990's.

The conclusion to this overall study will come in three parts, with the first two following previously established patterns and the third diverging from the rest of the analysis. We will engage in a narrative analysis of the current context of presidential-congressional foreign and issue area relations in the early Extra-Systemic Dilemma Order of the 2000's. Next, we will look at cross-sectional analysis of the partisan determinants, if any of the before-mentioned relationship. Finally, this project will close with a review of the study overall, an assessment of implications deriving from it and a prescription for future research.

Table 7-1. Mixed Issue Area Success Regression Analysis of Partisan Determinants
Confrontation Politics Order (1973-1989)

| | Un-standardized Coefficients | | Sig. |
	B	Std. Error	
(Constant)	5.652	.176	.000
Mid-Term Election Year	.181	.025	.000
Presidential Election Year	-.170	.022	.000
Presidential Party Seat % in House of Representatives	-3.645	.267	.000
Presidential Party Seat % in Senate	-.769	.510	.132
Unified Government	.689	.030	.000
House Partisan Roll Calls	-.385	.176	.028
Senate Partisan Roll Calls	-3.823	.181	.000
House Party Unity (D)	3.034	.341	.000
House Party Unity (R)	-2.097	.357	.000
Senate Party Unity (D)	1.503	.247	.000
Senate Party Unity (R)	-4.804	.160	.000

R Square	Adjusted R Square	Std. Error of the Estimate	Durbin-Watson
.650	.648	.144	.049

Predictors: (Constant), Senate Party Unity (R), Senate Partisan Roll Calls, Presidential Election Year, Presidential Party Seat % in Senate, Mid-Term Election Year, Senate Party Unity (D) House Partisan Roll Calls, House Party Unity (R), House Party Unity (D),

Unified Government, Presidential Party Seat % in House of Representatives
Dependent Variable: Confrontation Politics Order Annual Presidential Success Score in Mixed Issue Areas

N=544

Table 7-2. Mixed Issue Area Success Regression Analysis of Partisan Determinants Imperial
         Presidency Politicized Order (1990-2000)

	Un-standardized Coefficients		Sig.
	B	Std. Error	
(Constant)	-22.817	.545	.000
Mid-Term Election Year	.095	.013	.000
Presidential Election Year	.779	.008	.000
Presidential Party Seat % in House of Representatives	-3.442	.345	.000
Presidential Party Seat % in Senate	-1.238	.353	.000
House Partisan Roll Calls	6.846	.065	.000
Senate Partisan Roll Calls	-2.557	.034	.000
House Party Unity (D)	18.222	.648	.000
House Party Unity (R)	-3.533	.260	.000
Senate Party Unity (D)	13.968	.314	.000
Senate Party Unity (R)	-.679	.202	.001

R Square	Adjusted R Square	Std. Error of the Estimate	Durbin-Watson
.988	.988	.033	1.894

Predictors: (Constant), Senate Party Unity (R), House Party Unity (D), House Partisan Roll
         Calls, Presidential Election Year, Mid-Term Election Year, Senate Partisan Roll
         Calls, Presidential Party Seat % in Senate, House Party Unity (R), Senate Party
         Unity (D), Presidential Party Seat % in House of Representatives
Dependent Variable: Imperial Presidency Politicized Order Annual Presidential Success Score
         in Mixed Issue Areas
N=544

216

Table 7-3. Foreign Policy Success Regression Analysis of Partisan Determinants Imperial
Presidency Politicized Order (1990-2000)

	Un-standardized Coefficients		Sig.
	B	Std. Error	
(Constant)	-7.296	.092	.000
Mid-Term Election Year	.229	.002	.000
Presidential Election Year	.069	.001	.000
Presidential Party Seat % in House of Representatives	-4.200	.058	.000
Presidential Party Seat % in Senate	7.718	.059	.000
House Partisan Roll Calls	-.109	.011	.000
Senate Partisan Roll Calls	-.556	.006	.000
House Party Unity (D)	4.033	.109	.000
House Party Unity (R)	-1.648	.044	.000
Senate Party Unity (D)	.309	.053	.000
Senate Party Unity (R)	5.152	.034	.000

R Square	Adjusted R Square	Std. Error of the Estimate	Durbin-Watson
.999	.999	.005	1.894

Predictors: (Constant), Senate Party Unity (R), House Party Unity (D), House Partisan Roll
Calls, Presidential Election Year, Mid-Term Election Year, Senate Partisan Roll
Calls, Presidential Party Seat % in Senate, House Party Unity (R), Senate Party
Unity (D), Presidential Party Seat % in House of Representatives
Dependent Variable: Imperial Presidency Order Annual Success Score in Foreign Policy
N=544

Table 7-4. National Security Policy Success Regression Analysis of Partisan Determinants Imperial Presidency Politicized Order (1990-2000)

	Un-standardized Coefficients		Sig.
	B	Std. Error	
(Constant)	2.949	.271	.000
Mid-Term Election Year	-.017	.006	.008
Presidential Election Year	-.157	.004	.000
Presidential Party Seat % in House of Representatives	-1.885	.171	.000
Presidential Party Seat % in Senate	6.497	.175	.000
House Partisan Roll Calls	-.121	.032	.000
Senate Partisan Roll Calls	.066	.017	.000
House Party Unity (D)	-8.191	.322	.000
House Party Unity (R)	-5.135	.129	.000
Senate Party Unity (D)	5.299	.156	.000
Senate Party Unity (R)	2.506	.100	.000

R Square	Adjusted R Square	Std. Error of the Estimate	Durbin-Watson
.993	.993	.016	1.894

Predictors: (Constant), Senate Party Unity (R), House Party Unity (D), House Partisan Roll Calls,
Presidential Election Year, Mid-Term Election Year, Senate Partisan Roll Calls, Presidential Party Seat % in Senate, House Party Unity (R), Senate Party Unity (D), Presidential Party Seat % in House of Representatives
Dependent Variable: Imperial Presidency Politicized Order Annual National Security Success Score
N=544

Table 7-5. Trade Policy Success Regression Analysis of Partisan Determinants Imperial Presidency Politicized Order (1990-2000)

	Un-standardized Coefficients		Sig.
	B	Std. Error	
(Constant)	-1.323	.243	.000
Mid-Term Election Year	.156	.006	.000
Presidential Election Year	.082	.003	.000
Presidential Party Seat % in House of Representatives	-6.013	.154	.000
Presidential Party Seat % in Senate	15.820	.158	.000
House Partisan Roll Calls	-3.509	.029	.000
Senate Partisan Roll Calls	1.169	.015	.000
House Party Unity (D)	-7.569	.290	.000
House Party Unity (R)	2.397	.116	.000
Senate Party Unity (D)	-2.551	.140	.000
Senate Party Unity (R)	5.787	.090	.000

R Square	Adjusted R Square	Std. Error of the Estimate	Durbin-Watson
.997	.997	.014	1.894

Predictors: (Constant), Senate Party Unity (R), House Party Unity (D), House Partisan Roll Calls, Presidential Election Year, Mid-Term Election Year, Senate Partisan Roll Calls, Presidential Party Seat % in Senate, House Party Unity (R), Senate Party Unity (D), Presidential Party Seat % in House of Representatives

Dependent Variable: Imperial Presidency Politicized Order Annual Trade Policy Success Score
N=544

Table 7-6. Foreign Aid Policy Success Regression Analysis of Partisan Determinants Imperial Presidency Politicized Order (1990-2000)

| | Un-standardized Coefficients | | Sig. |
	B	Std. Error	
(Constant)	17.175	.000	.
Mid-Term Election Year	-1.489	.000	.
Presidential Election Year	.180	.000	.
Unified Government	.461	.000	.
House Partisan Roll Calls	-15.805	.000	.
Senate Partisan Roll Calls	8.721	.000	.
House Party Unity (D)	19.442	.000	.
House Party Unity (R)	19.671	.000	.
Senate Party Unity (D)	-43.676	.000	.
Senate Party Unity (R)	-10.408	.000	.

R Square	Adjusted R Square	Std. Error of the Estimate	Durbin-Watson
1.000	1.000	.000	.509

Predictors: (Constant), Senate Party Unity (R), Unified Government, Presidential Election Year, House Partisan Roll Calls, Mid-Term Election Year, Senate Partisan Roll Calls, House Party Unity (R), House Party Unity (D), Senate Party Unity (D)

Dependent Variable: Imperial Presidency Politicized Order Annual Foreign Aid Policy Success Score

N=544

Table 7-7. Annual Presidential Success Scores across Issue Areas of Foreign Policy. Bush Administration (1989-1993) 101st-102nd Congresses*+

Year	Foreign Policy	Security	Domestic Security	Diplomacy	Trade	Foreign Aid	Immigration	Totals
1989	C=72% (52:20)	C=70% (16:7)	C=33% (2:4)	C=88% (7:1)	C=67% (2:1)	C=80% (20:5)	C=n/a (0:0)	N=72
	H=55% (16:13)	H=38% (3:5)	H=25% (1:3)	H=n/a (0:0)	H=50% (1:1)	H=83% (10:2)	H=n/a (0:0)	N=29
	S=84% (36:7)	S=87% (13:2)	S=50% (1:1)	S=88% (7:1)	S=100% (1:0)	S=77% (10:3)	S=n/a (0:0)	N=43
1990	C=53% (33:29)	C=76% (16:5)	C=60% (3:2)	C=0% (0:1)	C=40% (6:9)	C=22% (2:7)	C=50% (3:3)	N=62
	H=37% (13:22)	H=70% (7:3)	H=100% (1:0)	H=n/a (0:0)	H=10% (1:9)	H=20% (1:4)	H=40% (2:3)	N=35
	S=74% (20:7)	S=82% (9:2)	S=50% (2:2)	S=0% (0:1)	S=100% (5:0)	S=25% (1:3)	S=100% (1:0)	N=27
1991	C=59% (45:31)	C=74% (25:9)	C=100% (7:0)	C=100% (3:0)	C=36% (4:7)	C=29% (5:12)	C=n/a (0:0)	N=76
	H=47% (21:24)	H=57% (12:9)	H=n/a (0:0)	H=n/a (0:0)	H=38% (3:5)	H=31% (4:9)	H=n/a (0:0)	N=45
	S=78% (25:7)	S=100% (13:0)	S=100% (7:0)	S=100% (3:0)	S=33% (1:2)	S=25% (1:3)	S=n/a (0:0)	N=32
1992	C=40% (21:32)	C=42% (5:12)	C=80% (4:1)	C=29% (2:5)	C=31% (5:11)	C=83% (5:1)	C=n/a (0:0)	N=53
	H=31% (11:24)	H=23% (3:10)	H=100% (3:0)	H=0% (0:4)	H=9% (1:10)	H=100% (3:0)	H=n/a (0:0)	N=35
	S=56% (10:8)	S=50% (2:2)	S=50% (1:1)	S=67% (2:1)	S=80% (4:1)	S=67% (2:1)	S=n/a (0:0)	N=18

*Some votes contain mixed categories (which are included on a separate table) those votes are included in the aggregate annual foreign policy success scores but excluded in the issue area success scores.

+Win-Loss Ratios in parentheses.

221

Table 7-8. Annual Presidential Success Scores across Issue Areas of Foreign Policy. Clinton Administration 103rd -106th Congresses*+

Year	Foreign Policy	Security	Domestic Security	Diplomacy	Trade	Foreign Aid	Immigration	Totals
1993	C=85% (39:7)	C=88% (23:3)	C=50% (1:1)	C=100% (1:0)	C=100% (6:0)	C=78% (7:2)	C=0% (0:1)	N=46
	H=83% (25:5)	H=83% (15:3)	H=n/a (0:0)	H=n/a (0:0)	H=100% (4:0)	H=67% (4:2)	H=n/a (0:0)	N=30
	S=88% (14:2)	S=100% (8:0)	S=50% (1:1)	S=100% (1:0)	S=100% (2:0)	S=100% (3:0)	S=0% (0:1)	N=16
1994	C=83% (43:9)	C=85% (28:5)	C=n/a (0:0)	C=67% (2:1)	C=100% (7:0)	C=n/a (0:0)	C=n/a (0:0)	N=52
	H=83% (25:5)	H=81% (17:4)	H=n/a (0:0)	H=n/a (0:0)	H=100% (5:0)	H=n/a (0:0)	H=n/a (0:0)	N=30
	S=82% (18:4)	S=92% (11:1)	S=n/a (0:0)	S=67% (2:1)	S=100% (2:0)	S=n/a (0:0)	S=n/a (0:0)	N=22
1995	C=38% (28:45)	C=30% (10:20)	C=67% (4:2)	C=14% (1:6)	C=57% (4:3)	C=42% (8:11)	C=n/a (0:0)	N=73
	H=32% (14:30)	H=29% (5:12)	H=100% (1:0)	H=0% (0:4)	H=40% (2:3)	H=23% (3:10)	H=n/a (0:0)	N=44
	S=53% (16:14)	S=38% (5:8)	S=60% (3:2)	S=33% (1:2)	S=100% (2:0)	S=83% (5:1)	S=n/a (0:0)	N=30
1996	C=58% (26:19)	C=53% (10:9)	C=25% (1:3)	C=50% (1:1)	C=100% (1:0)	C=60% (3:2)	C=71% (5:2)	N=45
	H=52% (15:14)	H=45% (5:6)	H=0% (0:1)	H=100% (1:0)	H=100% (1:0)	H=60% (3:2)	H=60% (3:2)	N=29
	S=69% (11:5)	S=63% (5:3)	S=33% (1:2)	S=0% (0:1)	S=n/a (0:0)	S=n/a (0:0)	S=100% (2:0)	N=16
1997	C=43% (24:29)	C=39% (10:18)	C=n/a (0:0)	C=100% (4:0)	C=50% (4:4)	C=67% (4:2)	C=100% (1:0)	N=53
	H=29% (8:20)	H=27% (4:11)	H=n/a (0:0)	H=n/a (0:0)	H=20% (1:4)	H=50% (2:2)	H=100% (1:0)	N=28
	S=68% (17:8)	S=54% (7:6)	S=n/a (0:0)	S=100% (4:0)	S=100% (3:0)	S=100% (2:0)	S=n/a (0:0)	N=25

Table 7-8. Continued

Year	Foreign Policy	Security	Domestic Security	Diplomacy	Trade	Foreign Aid	Immigration	Totals
1998	C=61% (23:15)	C=55% (5:4)	C=100% (2:0)	C=100% (1:0)	C=38% (3:5)	C=n/a (0:0)	C=40% (2:3)	N=38
	H=47% (7:8)	H=25% (1:3)	H=n/a (0:0)	H=100% (1:0)	H=38% (3:5)	H=n/a (0:0)	H=n/a (0:0)	N=15
	S=70% (16:7)	S=80% (4:1)	S=100% (2:0)	S=n/a (0:0)	S=n/a (0:0)	S=n/a (0:0)	S=40% (2:3)	N=23
1999	C=58% (15:11)	C=73% (5:3)	C=n/a (0:0)	C=50% (1:1)	C=75% (6:2)	C=20% (1:4)	C=100% (1:0)	N=27
	H=53% (9:8)	H=60% (3:2)	H=n/a (0:0)	H=0% (0:1)	H=67% (4:2)	H=25% (1:3)	H=100% (1:0)	N=17
	S=67% (6:3)	S=67% (2:1)	S=n/a (0:0)	S=100% (1:0)	S=100% (2:0)	S=0% (0:1)	S=n/a (0:0)	N=10
2000	C=70% (14:6)	C=50% (3:3)	C=100% (1:0)	C=n/a (0:0)	C=100% (8:0)	C=33% (1:2)	C=0% (0:1)	N=20
	H=67% (10:5)	H=60% (3:2)	H=100% (1:0)	H=n/a (0:0)	H=100% (6:0)	H=0% (0:2)	H=0% (0:1)	N=15
	S=80% (4:1)	S=0% (0:1)	S=n/a (0:0)	S=n/a (0:0)	S=100% (2:0)	S=100% (1:0)	S=n/a (0:0)	N=5

*Some votes contain mixed categories (these are on a separate table); they are included in the aggregate annual foreign policy success scores but excluded from the individuated issue area success scores.

+Win-Loss Ratios are in parentheses.

223

CHAPTER 8
CONCULSION/IMPLICATIONS: THE EXTRA-SYSTEMIC DILEMMA OF EXECUTIVE-LEGISLATIVE RELATIONS IN A POST-9/11 WORLD

Introduction

The reader(s) of this document can probably tell where they were, what they were doing and even the minutest details of their immediate responses to the tragic events of the fateful day in not quite mid-September, when as President W. Bush has repeatedly stated "everything changed." Certainly, the largest most intrusive as well as pervasive attack on the United States since Pearl Harbor had altered foreign policy relations not only between the executive and the legislature but between both and the polity writ large as well. Or, had it? There were major "historical" differences between the Japanese attack on Pearl Harbor and Al Qaeda's attacks on the twin towers of the World Trade Center, the Pentagon and their failed attempt at the White House itself. For our perspective, that major difference was in the mere recognition by the enemy about the disparate issue areas of foreign policy, the Japanese attacked the "strategic center" of foreign policy "power" for the US in the Pacific on December 7, 1941. Al Qaeda struck nearly simultaneously at the centers of US economic power in world affairs (the World Trade Center), deployable security power (the Pentagon) and finally, the center of diplomatic power in the form of the White House.

Also, the Japanese were a great power empire challenging the US for regional hegemony over the Pacific Rim in the balance of power politics of global multipolarity. But, Al Qaeda was a non-state actor challenging what it felt to be the "Great Satan" of global socio-cultural debasement, politico-religious corruption, globalized capitalist exploitation and imperialist military-centric hegemony. Japan was not only a state but an empire standing within the game of great power politics while Al Qaeda is a terrorist organization of self-proclaimed Islamic revolutionaries operating outside the international system in the only way they can with the weapons of the weak deployed against the strong. President W. Bush was correct, everything had changed but Al Qaeda had nothing to do with it. The change had been ongoing since the Cold War started its retreat after Vietnam and during détente (the Confrontation Politics Order, 1973-1989). With the decline of superpower driven conflict, the bipolarity of the international system began to give way to the forces of interdependence first in economics and then in socio-cultural matters. Toward the middle and end of the Cold War John Spanier (1975) had suggested that the

224

new international order would remain bipolar only in politics as in economics (and presumably) other areas it had already developed multipolarity. Still others, like Fukayama (1989) declared an "end to history," as inter-state conflict had reached its apex with the super power struggles of the Cold War but would not be displaced by other concerns previously deemed "low politics." W. Bush's own father had suggested a "New World Order," driven by democratic-capitalism something still prescient in the Clinton doctrine's notion of the selective engagement principle. Finally, the notion of "new security" had taken hold within the foreign policy research community analyzing the growing internecine conflicts over ethno-religious divides and resource access/control as the fortunes of globalization tended to help the "already there" (read the Global North) at the expense of the "still trying" (read the Global South) (Matthews 1989, Kegley and Wittkopf 2001).

In fact, all religious rhetoric (from both protagonists and antagonists) aside much of what probably lies behind the machinations of Al Qaeda is that it as an organization purports to represent the many (the Global South masses) in the face of the few (the Global North elites). Nonetheless, by taking a closer look at the legislative history of the presidential-congressional relationship can we find evidence supporting our president's now regularized claim "that everything changed on September the eleventh of 2001" (Bush 2002, inauguration speech excerpt)?

The Issue Areas of the Extra-Systemic Dilemma in Executive-Legislative Foreign Policy

Regarding the *sine qua non* of security, presidential dominance was so high that even domestic politics seemed to follow the dictates of this presidentialized/securitized "sphere of authority." For instance, air, sea and to some extent ground transportation was "federalized" at least as far as cargo and personnel inspections were concerned. The creation of the Transport Security Administration as well as the increase in the domestic inspection authority of the US Coast Guard, Customs Office and even the Postal Service were clear examples of this phenomenon. Another interesting note, emanating out of this condition is that much of it was done through administrative rule changes and executive orders, thus by-passing the normal legislative route (Sinclair in Conley 2005).

However, it was in the realm of national security itself where presidential power seemed to re-assert itself fully. Operation Enduring Freedom and Operation Iraqi Freedom both agitated for by President W. Bush and overwhelmingly supported by the members of Congress (CQ

Almanacs 2001 and 2003, special reports on Afghanistan and Iraq Wars). But, it is interesting to note that in both cases (especially for Iraq where a direct link with 9/11 could only be inferred) the president engaged in a "public relations campaign" reminiscent of his father's for Desert Shield/Storm and even Clinton's varied "overseas military adventures." Despite Vice-President Cheney's articulation of the "unitary executive theory," whereby executive authority was unquestionable in security matters (Cheney 2002, Russert interview on *Meet the Press*) because only the president could determine the level and type of "threat" faced by the American people, President W. Bush still felt the need to garner popular and congressional support for his two major security initiatives. Additionally, recent research has shown that the Congress in particular was directly involved in *all* of the security activities loosely grouped under the rather innocuous term the "War on Terror" (Wolfensberger in Dodd and Oppenheimer 2005). Major concessions over funding, time durations, limits of authority, oversight guarantees and extended hearings over the "merits" of such procedures were imposed by the Congress under unified government conditions (Wolfsenberger in Dodd and Oppenheimer 2005). Of course these concessions were set against a president who was seen as the ideological heir to the conservative movement that so dominated Republican Party congressional politics at that time (Wolfsenberger in Dodd and Oppenheimer 2005).

Moving away from national security policy making into the realm of domestic security policy construction we find even more examples of presidential prerogative execution juxtaposed to congressional re-assertions of will. The most famous case of course is the Anti-Terrorism Act of 2001 and 2003 (collectively referred to as the "Patriot Act") which increased the level of allowance for internal domestic intelligence gathering to its highest levels since the largely unregulated days of the red scares. While, initially supported with relatively high levels of bipartisanship in both houses of the Congress in 2001 by 2003 it had become a "hot button" election issue which tore the Republican Party apart from within and moved it ideologically distal from the Democratic Party at least as far as the Congress was concerned. The next time the "Patriot Act" came through the halls of Congress it was subject to intense "domestication/congressionalization" as members became more responsive to their constituent interests than to the "security prerogatives" of the current administration (Wolfensberger 2005 in Dodd and Oppenheimer 2005). Another place for the ebb and flow of power between the president and the Congress is to be found in the creation of the Department of Homeland

Security. DHS was constructed out of the immediate post-9/11 needs for internal coordination between the disparate apparatuses of domestic security (22 separate agencies in all) and began as an entity within the White House Staff. As Conley (2005 in Conley 2005) makes clear this was about as far as the "limited government" Republican George W. Bush wanted to go but the Congress with certain allied clientele groups wanted something more. The end result was a president "pushed" into endorsing the largest reorganization of the federal government since the Truman era National Security Act of 1947 which established the "National Military Establishment" that shortly evolved into the Department of Defense. Any one of these cases, either as discrete entities or in comparison would make excellent analyses of the ebb and flow of issue area specific power between the executive and legislative branches of national government but that will have to wait for further study later on. For now let us close out this section by looking at a couple of cases of presidential empowerment outside of national or domestic security which can be directly linked to the aftermath of 9/11.

Fast-track trade negotiating authority has been a sore point for presidents and congresses of both parties since the late 1980's. The bipartisan consensus on deference to the president as "chief trade negotiator" has been discussed earlier but what is important to remember is that it was clearly in jeopardy as early as the 1970's and gone by the 1990's. From the last two years of the Reagan presidency through most of the Clinton administration, fully divided government forced presidents to lose valuable political capital in largely unsuccessful battles with the Congress in order to regain what from FDR to Reagan's first six years had largely been seen as a "rubber stamp" for executive fiat in trade relations. But, the foreign relations crises of the Great Depression, World War and Cold War had given way to intermestic crises of job outsourcing, windfall profiteering, overseas black marketeering, accusations of foreign neo-mercantile trade activities and generally a "fair trade Congress" v. a "free trade presidency" (Lindsay 1994, Ripley & Lindsay 1993 and McCormack 1999). It took a securitized argument *with* unified (and not coincidentally largely conservative) Republican Party congressional government by President George W. Bush to win fast track reauthorization in late 2001 (from CQ Almanac 2001, vote summary).

Lastly, we can examine the foreign funding of the Extra-Systemic Order (2001-present) and see that presidential initiatives regarding the allocation of funding took on a particularistic tone as funding was tied to alliance in the War on Terror. Of course it led to some strange bedfellows like Pakistan which had just recently been under sanctions for its "unlawful" entry into the "nuclear club" in 1998. But on the whole, we can suggest that W. Bush "got his way" in this effort, except that there is considerable evidence to show that a lot of "domestic pork" was allowed into various appropriations bills in order to get the kinds of military foreign aid (and to a lesser extent humanitarian) that the president wanted (CQ Almanacs 2002-2003, vote summaries). This hardly seems like a "wartime president" in complete control of the foreign policy process when he has to "bargain" with a Congress even if it was subject to split control conditions (the Democrats had the Senate at the time). Nevertheless, it is time now to take a more systematic look at the presidential success rates in foreign and issue area policies.

Empirical Results

One way of testing notions about the "multiplication effect" of mixed issue areas in the Extra-Systemic Dilemma (2001-2004 in this case) is to repeat the regression relating to success in these areas relative to the partisan indicators that have served us so well in the past. As Table 8-1 indicates, only descriptive indicators are possible as the dependent variable is "purged" from the model due to the lack of any systematically present co-relational effect when the explanatory variables (the various partisan indicators) are regressed on it. Supporting notions for the multiple presidencies thesis are to be found amidst the descriptive variables when you observe the high rate of occurrence regarding the mixed issue indicator itself (n=60). It is also interesting to note that all sixty votes that appear as "mixed issues" are found in only two of the four years examined in this table. However, the fact that no systematic relationships were uncovered is troubling, though it is possible that the limited nature of the size of the relevant portion of the data set in this analysis is reducing the relationships or in fact imposing a non-linearity condition amongst them. Further study is needed on this question as well as additional data collection and operationalization but that will have to wait for another day. Regarding the issue of "the multiplication effect" for issue areas, we can assert that it is upheld but its true systematic impact on presidential foreign policy success if any is not at this time known.

Looking ahead a bit, if we engage in a tabular study of the various mixed issue area success scores across the presidential administrations of the Post-War Era (see Tables 8-7 — 8-10) we can make some descriptive inferences that speak to the idea of a multiplication effect among the issue areas in general and the mixed issue areas specifically. There are two striking patterns that appear and in general support the contentions of a multiple presidencies theory for inter-institutional foreign policy making. First, there is a multiplication regarding the sheer presence of "mixed issue areas of foreign policy," this is especially true regarding comparing the War Power Order (1953-1972) (Table 8-7 and early Nixon in Table 8-8) with the Confrontation Politics Order (1973-1989) (Table 8-8 and 8-9). Second, there is a corresponding observable decline in the presidential success rate among the individual mixed issue areas across those first two orders of political time (again see tables 8-7 — 8-9). This also supports conceptions of the multiple presidencies because as foreign policy gets more nuanced, it becomes less subject to single-issue concerns. Where this regards that component of foreign affairs devoted to security, the president will be correspondingly constrained in his ability to persuade the Congress to support his efforts to dominate the construction of foreign policy.

Offsetting these two above trends but supporting the notion that there was some "restoration" of presidential power in foreign policy during the Imperial Presidency Politicized Order and in the current Extra-Systemic Dilemma Order (if there can be said to be one that is?) we actually see a decline in the number of mixed issue area votes and a corresponding increase in the president's success rate. This of course supports that portion of the multiple presidencies which suggests that as much as things change at the structural level (i.e. the rise and fall of "orders" of political time), at the unit level much remains the same where a securitizing president can and still does get his way when political time allows him to. Of course, further inquiry is necessary, especially that of a more systematic fashion but for right now let us return to the core issue areas of foreign policy for a stronger analysis of the impacts of partisan determinants on the executive-legislative association in this regard.

As done in previous portions of this project, we will first look at foreign policy success writ large during the Extra-Systemic Dilemma Order (2001-2004) and see if we can find any differences with the previous order. Because, if we cannot find such differences then the notion that 9/11 "changed everything," in foreign policy relations may exist more in the mind of President W. Bush than anywhere else, especially the Congress. Table 8-2 is revealing in that there is a significant change in the extant presidential-congressional relationship in foreign affairs but perhaps *not* in the ways one would expect. For instance, many of the partisan factors drop out of the model due to a *lack of co-relational association*. On the one hand, this could be used as evidence for the notion of a *de-politicization*, however independent correlation analysis (Table 8-1) does indicate a significant relationship. It just does not seem to maintain in systematized regression. This, of course, could be explained as an unintended consequence of the relatively small N but remember I am utilizing population not sample data. Probably there is some type of non-linear relationship here but it is probably better to wait for more data points (derived from future years) and see if this inconsistency does not just wash out as we move forward in this period of political time. A final observation which places further doubt on the alternative hypothesis's contention that since 9/11 there has been a de-politicization of executive-legislative relations in foreign policy is found in the fact that certain political variables like unified government are portraying directional correlations in *counterintuitive* manners (in this case its negative association with foreign policy success). Again, this may be due to the limited nature of the data since almost *half* the time the president faced a split control governmental condition which if anything would have a *neutral* or even *negative* impact on presidential success. Read from that perspective then the findings may not be as counterintuitive as first viewed.

Looking at the first of the "core" issue areas—national security—we see that it generally follows the predicted pattern of "matching well" with the observed relationships in foreign policy success. In this case, that even includes the number and type of variables that drop out of the model due to non-correlation. Interesting, though is that in both foreign as well as national security success we see that Senate Democratic Party Unity is associated with presidential success (Tables 8-2—8-3). Remember that the form split control government took during this timeframe was with a Democratic majority Senate juxtaposed against both a Republican House and presidency. Therefore, senatorial bi-partisanship was a source of continued strength for the president in the immediate years after 9/11. This is evidence for notions of a de-politicization and it will be interesting in the future work to see if it continues as a systematic phenomenon long after 9/11 has been displaced as the central US foreign policy issue of the 21st century (which many might suggest that the Iraq War has done just that during Mr. Bush's second term).

Comparing the results for the models dealing with presidential success in trade and foreign aid relative to the Congress (Tables 8-4 and 8-5), we can discern that trade success tends to follow predicted *partisan* patterns (with the exception of the role of the presidential election variable but that could be due to "compounding effects" brought on by the high role of national and domestic security politics in the 2004 election). Nevertheless, this output looks more like a continuance of the Imperial Presidency Politicized than any notions of a "new order" in the

230

aftermath of 9/11. Meanwhile, foreign aid policy also seems to follow a somewhat deviating pattern that might suggest a new order of presidential-congressional foreign policy relations as a review of the Senate Democratic party unity variable indicates but the Senate partisanship indicator offsets this, so we are left largely unknowing on this particular question.

So what, if anything can we conclude from this statistical analysis of presidential success in foreign and core issue areas? Well, unfortunately not much at least as far as anything conclusive regarding the extant executive-legislative relationship is concerned. The data is too limited overall and has severe problems regarding asymptotic properties but as far as we can make inferences from it, it tends to *not* support the president's statement that "everything changed" in the wake of the 9/11 tragedy. This tends to support the narrative's assessment that presidential-congressional relations across the component issue areas of foreign policy remain *politicized* and hence more governed by partisan relations rather than some re-institutionalization of a *presidentialized/securitized* foreign policy.

President Bush utilized his "restored" power in security to push a national security and domestic security agenda but the impetus for this was *not* 9/11 but rather an ongoing employment of his base "opportunity structure" in national security that was re-emboldened during the *first* Bush administration. Likewise, the fact that such activities have been subject to congressional scrutiny has been a characteristic *norm* of the executive-legislative foreign affairs relationship since the Confrontation Politics of the early 1970's. They have been able to do this because absent a new credible *systemic* dilemma, the opportunity structure that president's enjoy in national security is weakened and therefore their own opportunity structure in domestic affairs is emboldened. Helping this process out is the fact that issue areas outside of security which have always been more *intermestic* by nature have come into their own as nexus points for presidential-congressional interaction. Thus, the world of international relations policy construction is still defined by a securitizing president versus a domesticating Congress under the conditions begun in the Confrontation period and coalesced in the Imperial Presidency Order.

Lastly, as tabular study of the current administration's success rates across foreign policy reveals, outcomes are not always what they seem. President W. Bush was overwhelmingly successful across the seemingly not so disparate issue areas of foreign policy (Table 8-6). On the surface, this clearly supports hypotheses regarding the de-political nature of the Post-9/11 re-presidentialized foreign policy frame. But, does that not countermand the previous studies in this chapter? This re-presidentialization process is well supported by an examination of the specific issue area as well as overall foreign policy success rates the president enjoyed with the Congress during his first term, however, this fact remains true only as long as you avoid looking too closely at Table 8-6.

For starters President W. Bush takes very few positions in foreign (or any other) type of policy; in his most prolific year (2002 — the mid-term election year where his party regained control over the Congress) he took a mere *thirty-five* positions across both chambers of the Congress. Presidential position taking has been in decline since the late Reagan presidency but W. Bush is known as the *least* prone to take roll call positions (Leloup and Shull 2003). It is also true that in general more positions are taken in domestic policy votes by presidents than in foreign policy ones but it is also true that the president "wins" more in foreign policy (Shull and Shaw 1999). Nevertheless, these two facts together means that to some extent our current president stacked the deck regarding which foreign policy votes he took positions on and which ones he did not in order to guide the outcomes in his favor. LBJ was known for his "strategic" position taking on roll calls and Carter for his propensity to do it. But, W. Bush may be known for combining strategic with a *lack* of propensity. Thus a kind of negative power seems to be in play here (from Shull and Shaw 1999). This concludes our last act in the drama of presidential-congressional foreign policy relations but before the movie concludes we will take a "look back" at the main highlights. We do this to get the "allegorical message" out of the movie by achieving a sense of overall continuity and to foreshadow some natural implications/prescriptions which emanate out of the film as we leave the metaphorical theater and go home for the evening.

Summary of the Project: The Multiple Presidencies Thesis across the Issue Areas of Foreign Policy throughout the Political Time of the Post-War Era, 1953-2004

This summation will involve three principle elements, a review of the basic argument relative to the multiple presidencies and issue areas of foreign policy, a re-articulation of the general as well as some of the specific findings across political time. And, it will close with a discussion of the implications and prescriptions which attend the theory and its findings for the future of executive-legislative relations in this policy domain. Finally, I will close this section by offering up additional opportunities for further study and make some final remarks on the importance of this piece as a contribution to the extant body of knowledge regarding its component elements including presidential-congressional relations, foreign policy research and the employment of the "historical construction of politics."[1] This last point will be driven by both *empirical* as well as *normative* concerns and serve as a general invitation for more scholarly study in these two often though not exclusively divergent research trajectories.

This project began by asking a relatively simple question, "Whither the two presidencies?" And, what I meant by that was that since the two presidencies scholarship which purported to suggest that presidents dominated the general and specific construction of foreign policy vis-à-vis the Congress, why was there such an empirical gap in demonstrating the phenomenon? Furthermore, then a specific research question arose like a phoenix out of the ashes of a failed two presidencies, *"What is the exact inter-institutional relationship between the national executive and legislature in the construction of foreign policy?"* This larger question actually contained two component questions of mutual significance within it, first "what was the governing principle for the unit level relationship between the president and the Congress?" and "what was the structuring principle for that same relationship within a larger foreign policy environment seen as part and parcel of "political time?" My answer given to these questions has been two-fold and has served as the operational principle for this entire project.

From an analytical perspective I have offered up a new theory of executive-legislative relations and applied it specifically to the case of US foreign policy construction during the extant Post-War Era of 1953-2004. I called this theory *the Multiple Presidencies Thesis* which states that presidential-congressional relations is best viewed as a struggle for power in foreign policy by a *securitizing* presidency versus a *domesticating* Congress across component issue areas including national security, domestic security, diplomacy, trade, foreign aid and immigration policies. Each institution has "reservoirs of power" known as "opportunity structures" and utilizes them to impose their will on the competing institution. For the presidency, that opportunity structure lies with national security as the historical and constitutional "locus" of national executive authority. Issue areas most proximate to national security are the ones best emplaced for a process of *presidentialization*. For the Congress its historical and constitutional placement of prerogatives is found outside of foreign policy itself in the realm of domestic politics. Therefore, issue areas which are further removed from security

---

[1] From Orren and Skowronek (2004) *The Search for American Political Development*, wherein they offer the notion of the "historical construction of politics," as the unifying "theme" of American Political Development (APD) research.

and thus contain a higher level of "confluence" regarding the mix of foreign and domestic politics, called intermestic policies have a greater likelihood of being *congressionalized*.

The above describes an ongoing static unit level relationship between the presidency and the Congress which was codified by constitutional doctrine, institutionalized by historical practice and upheld by the traditions of the political culture itself. However, it is only half the "analytical story," as the "setting" of the political environment provides the structural impulses to either uphold or impede the interplay of the executive-legislative foreign affairs relationship. Accordingly, certain "orders" of time cause a "push or pull" phenomenon relative to the various "sets" of executive-legislative relations amidst the component issue areas of foreign policy. In the early days of the Post War Era, what I call the War Power Order (1953-1972), the president was able to fully (or at least nearly so) "securitize" hence "presidentialize" foreign policy. Then, during the aftermath of the Vietnam War and the height of détente between the superpowers the Congress conducted a relatively successful "confrontation politics" against presidential prerogatives in foreign policy construction—I call this timeframe the Confrontation Politics Order (1973-1989). Finally, the process of foreign policy politicization which began in the previous order as more and more issue areas of foreign policy became subject to "domestication" and hence "congressionalization" came to fruition with an attendant yet incomplete "restoration" of presidential power through the revitalization of the security apparatus of foreign affairs. I call this last period the Imperial Presidency Politicized (1990-2000) and concluded it with an examination of the current Extra-Systemic Dilemma Order (2001-2004). In this last effort, I found little real evidence that the now highly politicized and even ideological nature of presidential-congressional international relations in the aftermath of 9/11 has actually been systematically altered.

In addition to the analytical perspective offered by this account, I have also endeavored to suggest a new way of looking at foreign policy from a methodological perspective. In this project, I called for the employment of an "issue areas" alternative to the dominant domain-specific approaches associated with both the statist and the domestic variables studies in American foreign policy research. I have suggested that by looking at foreign policy as a polyglot of *component issue areas* we can "see the forest for the trees as well as the trees for the forest." From the perspective of the multiple presidencies thesis, I envisioned six inter-related yet distinct issue areas of foreign policy and arranged them along two interconnected dimensions.

234

First, I placed them along a frontier defined by their proximity to the opportunity structures of power for the presidency and the Congress in order to conceptualize the unit level relationship. Beginning with national security affairs, we see a "movement" of issue areas in descending proximity to the source of presidential "power" in foreign affairs—national security itself. The movement continues from domestic security to diplomacy, to trade, through foreign aid and ends at immigration; the place with the greatest level of intermestic quality and hence highest potential for subsequent domestication by the Congress.

Second, I accounted for the structural level determinants of the issue areas of foreign affairs by conceptualizing these disparate entities as co-existing within larger *arenas of issue areas*. I based the issue areas placement on their proximity to the high (the politics of war and peace) versus low (the politics of everything else, especially economics) politics framework so common in classical depictions of the US foreign policy process. I did this because these larger *issue arenas* capture in aggregate the influences of the macro-level historical and economic factors in the political time of American foreign policy, in other words they record the systemic changes to the background setting for the unit level executive-legislative relationship. Finally, I proposed that the unit level relationship would be tested by the relevant political factors involved measured along popular, electoral and partisan/ideological factors. And, I also suggested that a related phenomenon needed to be examined which was central to the selected unit of analysis (that being presidential position roll call votes in foreign and issue area policies) which was the role of the type of vote as well as the presence (or lack thereof) regarding the employment of securitization-domestication and mixed issue areas as influencers of the presidential-congressional foreign policy dynamic.

So what were the results of all of this? Each one of the empirical chapters (4-7) followed a moderately similar pattern by first setting the context with historical analysis of the structure and unit level factors. Then, we looked at the systematic results deriving out of longitudinal and later cross-sectional examinations of the impacts of various historical, economic and political indicators on our dependent variables of interest—the presidential success rates in foreign and component issue area policies. Finally, we closed out each empirical chapter by synthesizing the narrative and statistical components through the lens provided by the multiple presidencies thesis. This process was done with analogy and tabular analysis of the various success rates in order to draw some descriptive inferences about the executive-legislative relationship from

235

within and across time perspectives. In all of these efforts, I tried to operationalize the variables involved in such a way as to test hypotheses in the direction of supporting/refuting presidency-centered versus Congress-centered conditions.

The cross-time findings were developed from three types of statistical methods aimed at the success rates themselves including percent differencing with significance tests, time-series analysis and longitudinally applied simple multivariate regression. The explanatory factors involved included macro-historical, macro-economic and to a lesser extent macro-political. Additionally, internal factors including type of vote, the role of mixed issue areas and the extent of securitization or domestication were also examined in a longitudinal manner. The initial set of findings largely supported the views of the multiple presidencies thesis, in that, generally speaking differential success rates exist, persist over time and follow expected patterns as to the level of success enjoyed by presidents in their relationship with the Congress. These findings further suggested that within foreign policy there exists a *core set of issue areas including national security, trade and foreign aid*. All issue area regression on foreign policy presidential success indicates that the core issue areas, especially national security are in fact driving the president's success rate vis-à-vis the Congress in foreign affairs. Also, the time series and later the longitudinal regressions support basic notions with some modest deviations about the role of political time as well as economic indicators in pushing presidential success in either positive (presidency centered conditionality) or negative (Congress-centered conditionality) directions.

Regarding the cross-sectional analyses, these were all accomplished by a qualitative overview of legislative histories built around the various issue areas of foreign policy. Then, this was followed up with more systematic study based on employing simple multivariate regressions of the various political factors on the success rates in foreign and core issue areas—national security, trade and foreign aid. In general, amidst the various political factors only partisan determinants seemed to have an ongoing systematic relationship with the president's foreign and core issue area roll call success rate. This is probably because popular and electoral determinants are more behavioral in both their design and their impact; they do *not* tend to have ongoing relational impacts on the inter-institutional relationship shared by the presidency and the Congress in foreign policy. Hence, one of the most profound lessons to be learned from this study is the *inter-institutional analysis* should utilize *institutional* determinants like partisanship and ideology (though ideology by itself in this study was not found to be a decisive indicator).

Partisanship within the Congress as an organizing force, a programmatic instrument, a locus of ideology (or lack thereof) has been found to be central to understanding the unit level executive-legislative relationship in international affairs. During the War Power Order (1953-1972) a bi-partisan Cold War Consensus that was non-ideological and de-politicized characterized presidential-congressional relations in foreign policy. During the Confrontation Politics Order (1973-1989), the Cold War Consensus broke down and the inter-institutional policy making relationship *began* a process of politicization, where the old cross-partisan coalitional formation of old began to take on a decidedly *ideological* cast. We can say that during the Confrontation Politics Order, presidential-congressional relations in foreign policy began to be congressionalized/domesticated. Or, in other words, that the Congress has increasingly approached foreign policy issues as domestic policy matters. In the Imperial Presidency Politicized Order (1990-2000), executive-legislative relations in foreign policy became fully politicized as the parties divided along strictly ideological grounds sounding the final death knell of the Conservative Coalition along with the already dead Liberal Coalition. Despite, a restoration of presidential prerogatives in the security realm as witnessed by the first Bush's statement after the Persian Gulf War that, "the ghost of the Vietnam syndrome has been laid to rest!"[2] The results indicate that despite initially hypothesized claims we are probably still in this last period of political time as the Extra-Systemic Dilemma Order (2001-present) is probably not a decisive break with the immediate past and some "reinvigoration" of the presidentialized/securitized War Power Order. In fact, the time we live in today is probably a "continuance of more of the same," where to whom great power is given (the presidency), great responsibility is required (the Congress).

Implications and prescriptions which come out of the above findings suggest two basic conclusions about the future of executive-legislative relations in the sphere of foreign politics. First, they contend that absent a true *systemic level dilemma* the presidential-congressional relationship will remain a *politicized and hence partisan* phenomenon. The president has largely *lost* the battle that the War on Terror represents some new Cold War and without such a structural securitizing force the Congress will *not* routinely acquiesce to the will of presidential government in foreign policy. Unified government is now more important than ever for

---

[2] George Bush said this in an "off the record" statement to reporters after the advance of US forces into Iraq was halted on February 28, 1991.

presidents to push their foreign policy agenda through the Congress but offsetting this is the inherent inconsistencies caused by the fact that foreign policy is not "one thing" but "many things."

This brings us to our second basic implication, that the divide among issue areas of foreign policy is becoming thinner and thinner. The ever increasing intermestic content of issue areas in foreign policy allows for interesting mixes of the two institution's opportunity structures, however, they now require a degree of nuanced strategizing by both actors that was unheard of as early as Reagan's last term. This is because the extra security dilemma represented by the War on Terror and to a lesser extent by other phenomena like the War on Drugs, etcetera is in itself intermestic in its very nature. Thus, securitization may not even be a privileged activity within the national security (and definitely not in the domestic security) areas of foreign policy anymore. Complicating this is the fact that these are still "dilemmas," therefore the Congress will never be likely to be able to actually displace the inherent opportunity structure of power so jealously held by every president Republican or Democratic. Therefore, we are in a cycle of granting and then rescinding power in ever more nuanced and complicated fashions as foreign policy both explodes and implodes with issue areas within and across spans of political time.

So what can future presidents and Congresses learn from this project? Well, for one thing they can learn to appreciate the others' stake in foreign policy. Too often presidents (and want to be presidents) think that any encroachment on their "prerogatives" in foreign policy by the Congress (or anyone else for that matter) is an attack on their fundamental roles as Chief Diplomat, Commander-in-Chief, Chief Executive of foreign aid provision as well as immigration and finally, Chief Trade Negotiator for the country as a whole. This is not true because a separation of powers system like ours with its attendant checks and balances requires shared governance even in the vaunted realm of national security affairs. The Congress needs to recognize that the Founding Fathers were on to something in their call for "energy in the executive," especially in foreign and *defense* affairs. The Congress needs to recognize presidential "rights" as the national executive in international affairs elected by the people and held accountable ultimately to them, not the Congress. Presidents should be given their due with congressional support on issues of national importance in the foreign affairs realm but that support should be qualified with aggressive oversight. In our most recent presidential-congressional "conflict" over the Iraq War it should be remembered that many who now oppose the president "signed away" massive amounts of policy making discretion without so much as an afterthought, until it was too late. With great power, comes great responsibility; *both* the presidency and the Congress need to remember that as national security frequently costs lives, trade often costs jobs and foreign aid while small overall may cost our very values. Especially, given the tendencies for this country to make deals with the devil in order to achieve some, often short sighted diplomatic/security goal—like supporting Iraq in the Iraq-Iran War and then having to fight our one time ally within a handful of years.

Future Research

On the issue of suggestions for further research, I would like to make some basic contentions as to "places to go from here." In the first place, a more rigorous qualitative empirical study is needed of these issue areas within foreign policy. A natural outcrop of this inquiry is found in the event and legislative histories utilized in the empirical portions of this analysis. However, these studies were rudimentary and excessively tertiary in their employment. A full blown comparative historical analysis of specific exemplifying and deviating case studies and legislative histories is called for. One technique could be to compare and contrast different legislative histories across issue areas within the same period of political time. Or another way of comparing/contrasting through the study of legislative histories is to do the same thing only in a single issue area across different periods of political time in order to get a sense of how the foreign policy production process has altered across history. Another technique could involve employing larger event histories to showcase elements of presidential-congressional relations in foreign policy by engaging in a "deep description," of those activities across issue areas and even across periods of political time.

Also, more specifically normative study is needed as the search for the locus of inter-institutional power in foreign affairs construction has fundamentally normative implications; it is not solely an empirical question. While normative study was not openly addressed in this research it could serve as the starting point for such a constituted study in the future. For instance one could follow the prescriptions above by tracing the historical development of executive versus legislative power both as theories in practice within the Constitution, Federalist Papers, state and colonial constitutions, etcetera. Also, a prospective researcher could look at the search for executive versus legislative foreign policy power as components in the history of ideas emanating out of the philosophical works of Locke, Montesquieu, Blackstone and others. In both the prospective analyzer would want to employ an issue areas perspective to find which issue areas of foreign policy differentiate themselves as historical entities and are "captured" within either the executive or legislative sphere as points of activity.

As to the issue of the historical construction of politics, Orren and Skowronek (2004) have claimed recently that this is the great nexus point for all past, current and future inquiries into American political development. They make this claim suggesting that history should be viewed as a systematic matrix wherein events and processes intersect across, within and between historical periods (Orren and Skowronek 2004). At both the structural and unit levels the multiple presidencies offers an empirical and theoretical application of such a matrix in action. The intersecting flows of history are captured at the nexus points of executive-legislative foreign issue area interaction conditioned by the dynamism of the larger political environment itself. Therefore both the vectors of intersection and the matrix of the structure itself are wedded together in a systematic flow that carries the executive-legislative foreign policy divide across a political template of time. And, now to conclude the conclusion!

The movie is almost finished, people are starting to file out of the theater but as you leave you may be thinking, so what have I learned. Hopefully, you have developed an appreciation for both the multiple presidencies thesis and the opportunities inherent in viewing foreign policy as a "sum of parts" rather than just this "one thing." Analytically, the multiple presidencies thesis provides both a unit and structural level explanation for executive-legislative relations within the foreign policy domain. This is something not often done in either foreign policy studies and especially not in presidential-congressional analysis. Methodologically, the issue areas approach offers a kind of synthesis relative to state-centrist versus domestic variables conceptions of US foreign policy construction. This kind of mixing is not done much in an academic world defined by vested paradigmatic interests and should be seen as the "Aristotelian Mean between the Extremes" that it is. Finally, I hope that someone somewhere gets something worthwhile out of this effort!

Table 8-1. Mixed Issue Areas of Foreign Policy Success correlation analysis with Partisan Determinants Extra Systemic Dilemma Order (2001-present)

	Mean	Std. Deviation	N
Extra-Systemic Dilemma Order annual mixed issue area success score	1.000	.000	60
House Partisan Roll Calls	.420	.015	60
Senate Partisan Roll Calls	.495	.048	60
House Party Unity (D)	.847	.014	60
House Party Unity (R)	.904	.004	60
Senate Party Unity (D)	.855	.029	60
Senate Party Unity (R)	.856	.019	60
Presidential Party Seat % in Senate	.490	.000	60
Presidential Party Seat % in House of Representatives	.510	.000	60
Presidential Election Year	.00	.000	60
Mid-Term Election Year	.58	.497	60
Unified Government	1.03	.181	60

Table 8-2. Foreign Policy Success Regression Analysis of Partisan Determinants Extra Systemic Dilemma Order (2001-present)

	Un-standardized Coefficients			Sig.
	B	Std. Error		
(Constant)	1.216		.000	.000
Senate Party Unity (D)	.269		.000	.000
Senate Party Unity (R)	-.654		.000	.000
Presidential Election Year	-.101		.000	.000
Unified Government	-4.227		.000	1.000

R Square	Adjusted R Square	Std. Error of the Estimate	Durbin-Watson
1.000	1.000	.000	.008

Predictors: (Constant), Unified Government, Senate Party Unity (D), Presidential Election Year, Senate Party Unity (R)
Dependent Variable: Extra-Systemic Dilemma Order annual foreign policy success score
N=110

Table 8-3. National Security Policy Success Regression Analysis of Partisan Determinants Extra Systemic Dilemma Order (2001-present)

	Un-standardized Coefficients			Sig.
	B	Std. Error		
(Constant)	-1.812	.000	.000	
Senate Party Unity (D)	3.692	.000	.000	
Senate Party Unity (R)	-.538	.000	.000	
Presidential Election Year	.062	.000	.000	
Unified Government	-1.351	.000	1.000	

R Square	Adjusted R Square	Std. Error of the Estimate	Durbin-Watson
1.000	1.000	.000	.005

Predictors: (Constant), Unified Government, Senate Party Unity (D), Presidential Election Year, Senate Party Unity (R)

Dependent Variable: Extra-Systemic Dilemma Order annual national security success score

N=110

Table 8-4. Trade Policy Success Regression Analysis of Partisan Determinants Extra Systemic Dilemma Order (2001-present)

	Un-standardized Coefficients		Sig.	
	B	Std. Error		
(Constant)	4.518	.000	.	
Senate Party Unity (D)	-6.308	.000	.	
Senate Party Unity (R)	1.962	.000	.	
Presidential Election Year	-.338	.000	.	
Unified Government	1.709	.000	.	

R Square	Adjusted R Square	Std. Error of the Estimate	Durbin-Watson
1.000	1.000	.000	.005

Predictors: (Constant), Unified Government, Senate Party Unity (D), Presidential Election Year, Senate Party Unity (R)

Dependent Variable: Extra-Systemic Order Annual Trade Policy Success Score

N=110

Table 8-5. Foreign Aid Policy Success Regression Analysis of Partisan Determinants Extra
Systemic Dilemma Order (2001-present)

| | Un-standardized Coefficients | | Sig. | |
	B	Std. Error		
(Constant)	-6.548		.000	.000
Senate Partisan Roll Calls	1.219		.000	.000
Senate Party Unity (D)	7.724		.000	.000
Unified Government	-1.803		.000	1.000

R Square	Adjusted R Square	Std. Error of the Estimate	Durbin-Watson
1.000	1.000	.000	.025

Predictors: (Constant), Unified Government, Senate Partisan Roll Calls, Senate Party Unity (D)
Dependent Variable: Extra-Systemic Dilemma Order Annual Foreign Aid Policy Success Score
N=110

Table 8-6. Annual Presidential Success Scores across Issue Areas of Foreign Policy. W. Bush Administration (2001-present) 107th-108th Congresses*+#

Year	Foreign Policy	Security	Domestic Security	Diplomacy	Trade	Foreign Aid	Immigration	Totals
2001	C=88% (22:3)	C=100% (8:0)	C=100% (6:0)	C=100% (1:0)	C=63% (5:3)	C=100% (1:0)	C=n/a (0:0)	N=25
	H=82% (14:3)	H=100% (4:0)	H=100% (4:0)	H=n/a (0:0)	H=57% (4:3)	H=100% (1:0)	H=n/a (0:0)	N=17
	S=100% (8:0)	S=100% (4:0)	S=100% (2:0)	S=100% (1:0)	S=100% (1:0)	S=n/a (0:0)	S=n/a (0:0)	N=8
2002	C=89% (31:4)	C=80% (8:2)	C=88% (7:1)	C=n/a (0:0)	C=93% (14:1)	C=n/a (0:0)	C=n/a (0:0)	N=35
	H=89% (16:2)	H=83% (5:1)	H=83% (5:1)	H=n/a (0:0)	H=100% (4:0)	H=n/a (0:0)	H=n/a (0:0)	N=18
	S=88% (15:2)	S=75% (3:1)	S=100% (2:0)	S=n/a (0:0)	S=91% (10:1)	S=n/a (0:0)	S=n/a (0:0)	N=17
2003	C=83% (25:5)	C=82% (9:2)	C=n/a (0:0)	C=n/a (0:0)	C=100% (6:0)	C=83% (10:2)	C=0% (0:1)	N=30
	H=93% (14:1)	H=75% (3:1)	H=n/a (0:0)	H=n/a (0:0)	H=100% (4:0)	H=100% (7:0)	H=n/a (0:0)	N=15
	S=73% (11:4)	S=86% (6:1)	S=n/a (0:0)	S=n/a (0:0)	S=100% (2:0)	S=60% (3:2)	S=0% (0:1)	N=15
2004	C=75% (15:5)	C=83% (5:1)	C=100% (3:0)	C=n/a (0:0)	C=71% (5:2)	C=50% (1:1)	C=50% (1:1)	N=20
	H=67% (10:5)	H=75% (3:1)	H=100% (2:0)	H=n/a (0:0)	H=60% (3:2)	H=50% (1:1)	H=50% (1:1)	N=15
	S=100% (5:0)	S=100% (2:0)	S=100% (1:0)	S=n/a (0:0)	S=100% (2:0)	S=n/a (0:0)	S=n/a (0:0)	N=5

* 1st term only.

+Some votes contain mixed categories (these are on a separate table) they are included in the aggregate annual foreign policy success scores but excluded from the individuated issue area success scores.

#Win-Loss Ratios are in parentheses.

244

Table 8-7. Issue Areas of Foreign Policy Mixed Categories, 1953-1968 Eisenhower-Johnson

Year	Issue Area of Foreign Policy	Total Votes	Win-Loss Ratio	Annual Presidential Success Score
1953	none	n/a	n/a	n/a
1954	none	n/a	n/a	n/a
1955	none	n/a	n/a	n/a
1956	D-T	5	3:2	60%
1957	D-S	1	1:0	100%
1958	none	n/a	n/a	n/a
1959	FA-T	3	1:2	33%
	D-T	6	3:3	50%
	D-DS	1	1:0	100%
1960	none	n/a	n/a	n/a
1961	none	n/a	n/a	n/a
1962	none	n/a	n/a	n/a
1963a	FA-T	1	1:0	100%
1963b	none	n/a	n/a	n/a
1964	FA-T	2	1:1	50%
	D-S	1	1:0	100%
	FA-D	1	1:0	100%
1965	T-I	2	2:0	100%
	FA-T	3	3:0	100%
	D-T	1	1:0	100%
1966	FA-T	7	5:2	71%
	D-T	5	4:1	80%
	FA-D	1	1:0	100%
	D-S	1	1:0	100%
1967	FA-T	12	8:4	67%
	D-T	6	6:0	100%
	FA-D	2	2:0	100%
	S-D	1	1:0	100%
	S-T	1	1:0	100%
1968	S-D	5	2:3	40%
	FA-T	10	8:2	80%
	D-T	6	6:0	100%
	FA-D	2	2:0	100%

Table 8-8. Issue Areas of Foreign Policy Mixed Categories, 1969-1980 Nixon-Carter

Year	Issue Area	Total	Win-Loss Ratio	% Success
1969	T-D	1	1:0	100%
1970	D-DS	1	1:0	100%
1971	FA-D	1	1:0	100%
1972	S-D	4	4:0	100%
	FA-T	3	3:0	100%
1973	S-D	1	0:1	0%
	T-D	10	10:0	100%
	FA-S	3	3:0	100%
	D-DS	3	3:0	100%
1974a	DS-T	1	0:1	0%
	FA-T	1	1:0	100%
	FA-D	1	1:0	100%
1974b	FA-T	16	5:11	31%
	I-T	3	3:0	100%
1975	FA-T	2	1:1	50%
	FA-S	4	3:1	75%
	T-DS	1	1:0	100%
	T-D	1	1:0	100%
1976	T-D	1	1:0	100%
	FA-T	4	0:4	0%
1977	FA-T	2	0:2	0%
	DS-D	1	1:0	100%
	S-D	1	1:0	100%
	T-D	1	1:0	100%
1978	T-D	3	3:0	100%
1979	FA-T	2	2:0	100%
	T-D	1	0:1	0%
	D-I	1	1:0	100%
	FA-I	1	1:0	100%
	D-DS	1	1:0	100%
1980	FA-T	6	3:3	50%

Table 8-9. Issue Areas of Foreign Policy Mixed Categories, 1981-1992 Reagan- Bush

Year	Issue Area of Foreign Policy	Total	Win-Loss Ratio	% Annual Presidential Success Rate
1981	FA-T	1	0:1	0%
1982	DS-I	1	1:0	100%
1983	T-D	1	1:0	100%
1984	D-FA	7	7:0	100%
1985	FA-T	1	0:1	0%
	FA-D	4	3:1	75%
1986	FA-D	5	5:0	100%
	D-DS	2	1:1	50%
	FA-T	1	1:0	100%
1987	T-D	1	1:0	100%
	D-S	1	0:1	0%
	S-T	5	2:3	40%
1988	FA-D	2	1:1	50%
	S-D	18	16:2	89%
	FA-T	3	2:1	67%
	DS-D	5	5:0	100%
1989	D-S	3	2:1	67%
	FA-T	1	0:1	0%
	FA-D	3	3:0	100%
1990	S-D	2	1:1	50%
	T-D	1	0:1	0%
	T-S	1	0:1	0%
	I-T	1	0:1	0%
1991	T-D	1	1:0	100%
	FA-T	3	0:3	0%
1992	FA-D	1	1:0	100%
	T-D	1	1:0	100%

Table 8-10. Issue Areas of Foreign Policy Mixed Categories, 1993-2004. Clinton-W. Bush

Year	Issue Area	Total	Win-Loss Ratio	% Success
1993	FA-T	2	2:0	100%
1994	T-S	6	3:3	50%
	S-FA	3	3:0	100%
1995	S-D	1	0:1	0%
	FA-T	1	1:0	100%
	T-S	1	0:1	0%
1996	FA-T	3	2:1	67%
	T-S	3	3:0	100%
	D-S	1	1:0	100%
	D-FA	1	0:1	0%
1997	S-T	1	1:0	100%
	DS-D	3	0:3	0%
	S-D	1	0:1	0%
	DS-T	1	0:1	0%
1998	D-FA	2	1:1	50%
	D-T	1	1:0	100%
	S-D	7	7:0	100%
	S-T	1	1:0	100%
	DS-D	1	0:1	0%
	S-FA	1	1:0	100%
1999	S-D	1	0:1	0%
	S-FA	1	1:0	100%
2000	S-D	1	1:0	100%
2001	DS-D	1	1:0	100%
2002	DS-T	1	1:0	100%
	FA-S	1	1:0	100%
2003	none	n/a	n/a	n/a
2004	none	n/a	n/a	n/a

Supporting Table for Figures 4-1 & 4-2   Issue Area of Foreign Policy

		Frequency	Percent	Valid Percent	Cumulative Percent
Valid	Deleted Cases	29	.9	.9	.9
	diplomacy	257	7.7	7.7	8.6
	diplomacy/domestic security	1	.0	.0	8.6
	diplomacy/foreign aid	34	1.0	1.0	9.6
	diplomacy/immigration	1	.0	.0	9.6
	diplomacy/trade	57	1.7	1.7	11.3
	domestic security	196	5.9	5.9	17.2
	domestic security/diplomacy	18	.5	.5	17.7
	domestic security/immigration	1	.0	.0	17.8
	domestic security/trade	4	.1	.1	17.9
	foreign aid	679	20.3	20.3	38.2
	foreign aid/immigration	1	.0	.0	38.2
	immigration	82	2.5	2.5	40.7
	security	1036	31.0	31.0	71.7
	security/diplomacy	50	1.5	1.5	73.1
	security/foreign aid	14	.4	.4	73.6
	security/trade	19	.6	.6	74.1
	trade	768	23.0	23.0	97.1
	trade/diplomacy	1	.0	.0	97.1
	trade/foreign aid	89	2.7	2.7	99.8
	trade/immigration	7	.2	.2	100.0
	Total	3344	100.0	100.0	

Supporting data for Table 4-1, Model 1

Autocorrelations: Annual Presidential Success Score in Foreign Policy
Transformations: difference (1)
    Auto- Stand.
Lag Corr. Err. -1 -.75 -.5 -.25 0 .25 .5 .75 1 Box-Ljung Prob.

Lag	Corr.	Err.	plot	Box-Ljung	Prob.
1	.000	.017	.*.	.000	1.000
2	.000	.017	.*.	.000	1.000
3	.000	.017	.*.	.000	1.000
4	.000	.017	.*.	.000	1.000
5	.000	.017	.*.	.000	1.000
6	.000	.017	.*.	.000	1.000
7	.000	.017	.*.	.000	1.000
8	.000	.017	.*.	.000	1.000
9	.000	.017	.*.	.000	1.000
10	.000	.017	.*.	.000	1.000
11	.000	.017	.*.	.000	1.000
12	.000	.017	.*.	.000	1.000
13	.000	.017	.*.	.000	1.000
14	.000	.017	.*.	.000	1.000
15	.000	.017	.*.	.000	1.000
16	.000	.017	.*.	.000	1.000
17	.000	.017	.*.	.000	1.000
18	.000	.017	.*.	.000	1.000
19	.000	.017	.*.	.000	1.000
20	.024	.017	.*.	1.924	1.000
21	.000	.017	.*.	1.924	1.000
22	.000	.017	.*.	1.924	1.000
23	.000	.017	.*.	1.924	1.000
24	.000	.017	.*.	1.924	1.000
25	.002	.017	.*.	1.938	1.000
26	.000	.017	.*.	1.938	1.000
27	.000	.017	.*.	1.938	1.000
28	-.004	.017	.*.	1.991	1.000
29	.000	.017	.*.	1.991	1.000
30	.005	.017	.*.	2.087	1.000
31	.000	.017	.*.	2.087	1.000
32	.000	.017	.*.	2.087	1.000
33	.000	.017	.*.	2.087	1.000
34	.000	.017	.*.	2.087	1.000
35	-.004	.017	.*.	2.146	1.000
36	-.027	.017	* .	4.674	1.000
37	.016	.017	.*.	5.487	1.000
38	.000	.017	.*.	5.487	1.000
39	.000	.017	.*.	5.487	1.000

40	.000	.017	.*.	5.487	1.000
41	.005	.017	.*.	5.583	1.000
42	-.009	.017	.*.	5.875	1.000
43	.000	.017	.*.	5.875	1.000
44	.000	.017	.*.	5.875	1.000
45	.001	.017	.*.	5.881	1.000
46	-.043	.017	* .	12.203	1.000

–

Autocorrelations: Annual Presidential Success Score in Foreign Policy

Auto- Stand.
Lag Corr. Err. -1 -.75 -.5 -.25 0 .25 .5 .75 1 Box-Ljung Prob.

47	-.016	.017	.*.	13.065	1.000
48	-.006	.017	.*.	13.186	1.000
49	.000	.017	.*.	13.186	1.000
50	.000	.017	.*.	13.186	1.000

Plot Symbols: Autocorrelations *   Two Standard Error Limits

Total cases: 3344   Computable first lags after differencing: 3342

1 case(s) will be lost due to differencing.

Listwise deletion.   Missing cases: 146   Valid cases: 3198
Some of the missing cases are imbedded within the series.

–

1 case(s) will be lost due to differencing.

Variable: NATSEC   Missing cases: 201   Valid cases: 3143
Some of the missing cases are imbedded within the series.

Supporting data for Table 4-1, Model 2

Autocorrelations: Annual Presidential Success Score in National Security

Transformations: difference (1)

Lag	Auto-Corr.	Stand. Error.	-1 -.75 -.5 -.25 0 .25 .5 .75 1	Box-Ljung	Prob.
1	.000	.018	.*.	.000	.997
2	.000	.018	.*.	.000	1.000
3	.000	.018	.*.	.000	1.000
4	.000	.018	.*.	.000	1.000
5	.000	.018	.*.	.000	1.000
6	.000	.018	.*.	.000	1.000
7	.000	.018	.*.	.000	1.000
8	.000	.018	.*.	.000	1.000
9	.000	.018	.*.	.000	1.000
10	.000	.018	.*.	.000	1.000
11	.000	.018	.*.	.000	1.000
12	.000	.018	.*.	.000	1.000
13	.000	.018	.*.	.000	1.000
14	.000	.018	.*.	.000	1.000
15	.000	.018	.*.	.000	1.000
16	.000	.018	.*.	.000	1.000
17	.000	.018	.*.	.000	1.000
18	.000	.018	.*.	.000	1.000
19	.000	.018	.*.	.000	1.000
20	-.061	.018	* .	11.996	.916
21	.000	.018	.*.	11.996	.940
22	.000	.018	.*.	11.996	.957
23	.000	.018	.*.	11.996	.971
24	.000	.018	.*.	11.996	.980
25	-.053	.018	* .	21.125	.686
26	.000	.018	.*.	21.125	.735
27	.000	.018	.*.	21.125	.780
28	-.022	.018	.*.	22.698	.748
29	-.010	.018	.*.	23.039	.775
30	.000	.018	.*.	23.039	.814
31	.005	.018	.*.	23.122	.845
32	.000	.017	.*.	23.122	.874
33	.000	.017	.*.	23.122	.900
34	.000	.017	.*.	23.122	.921
35	-.003	.017	.*.	23.147	.938
36	.000	.017	.*.	23.148	.952
37	.021	.017	.*.	24.587	.941

38	.000	.017	.*.	24.587	.955
39	.000	.017	.*.	24.587	.965
40	.000	.017	.*.	24.587	.974
41	.000	.017	.*.	24.587	.980
42	.000	.017	.*.	24.587	.985
43	.004	.017	.*.	24.646	.989
44	.000	.017	.*.	24.646	.992
45	.024	.017	.*.	26.612	.987
46	-.024	.017	.*.	28.578	.979

–

Autocorrelations: Annual Presidential Success Score in National Security
(continued)

```
      Auto- Stand.
Lag Corr. Err. -1 -.75 -.5 -.25  0  .25 .5 .75  1  Box-Ljung  Prob.
```

47	-.033	.017	* .	32.198	.951
48	.048	.017	. *	39.736	.796
49	.000	.017	.*.	39.736	.825
50	.000	.017	.*.	39.736	.850

Plot Symbols: Autocorrelations *   Two Standard Error Limits

Total cases: 3344   Computable first lags after differencing: 3135

1 case(s) will be lost due to differencing.

Variable: DOMSEC   Missing cases: 813   Valid cases: 2531
Some of the missing cases are imbedded within the series.

–

Supporting data for Table 4-1, Model 3

Autocorrelations: Annual Presidential Success Score in Domestic
Security
Transformations: difference (1)

```
      Auto-  Stand.
Lag  Corr.  Err. -1 -.75 -.5 -.25  0  .25  .5  .75  1  Box-Ljung  Prob.

 1  .000  .020              .*.              .000  1.000
 2  .000  .020              .*.              .000  1.000
 3  .000  .020              .*.              .000  1.000
 4  .000  .020              .*.              .000  1.000
 5  .000  .020              .*.              .000  1.000
 6  .000  .020              .*.              .000  1.000
 7  .000  .020              .*.              .000  1.000
 8  .000  .020              .*.              .000  1.000
 9  .000  .020              .*.              .000  1.000
10  .000  .019              .*.              .000  1.000
11  .000  .019              .*.              .000  1.000
12  .000  .019              .*.              .000  1.000
13  .000  .019              .*.              .000  1.000
14  .000  .019              .*.              .000  1.000
15  .000  .019              .*.              .000  1.000
16  .000  .019              .*.              .000  1.000
17  .000  .019              .*.              .000  1.000
18  .000  .019              .*.              .000  1.000
19  .000  .019              .*.              .000  1.000
20  .000  .019              .*.              .000  1.000
21  .000  .019              .*.              .000  1.000
22  .000  .019              .*.              .000  1.000
23  .000  .019              .*.              .000  1.000
24  .000  .019              .*.              .000  1.000
25  .000  .019              .*.              .000  1.000
26  .000  .019              .*.              .000  1.000
27  .000  .019              .*.              .000  1.000
28  .000  .019              .*.              .000  1.000
29  .000  .019              .*.              .000  1.000
30  .000  .019              .*.              .000  1.000
31  .000  .019              .*.              .000  1.000
32  .000  .019              .*.              .000  1.000
33  .000  .019              .*.              .000  1.000
34  .000  .018              .*.              .000  1.000
35  .000  .018              .*.              .000  1.000
36  .000  .018              .*.              .000  1.000
37  .000  .018              .*.              .000  1.000
```

38	.000	.018	.*.	.000	1.000
39	.000	.018	.*.	.000	1.000
40	.000	.018	.*.	.000	1.000
41	.000	.018	.*.	.000	1.000
42	.000	.018	.*.	.000	1.000
43	.000	.018	.*.	.000	1.000
44	.000	.018	.*.	.000	1.000
45	.000	.018	.*.	.000	1.000
46	.000	.018	.*.	.000	1.000

–

Autocorrelations: Annual Presidential Success Score in Domestic Security
(continued)

Auto- Stand.
Lag Corr. Err. -1 -.75 -.5 -.25 0 .25 .5 .75 1 Box-Ljung Prob.

47	.000	.018	.*.	.000	1.000
48	.000	.018	.*.	.000	1.000
49	.000	.018	.*.	.000	1.000
50	.000	.018	.*.	.000	1.000

Plot Symbols: Autocorrelations *   Two Standard Error Limits

Total cases: 3344   Computable first lags after differencing: 2509

1 case(s) will be lost due to differencing.

Variable: DIP   Missing cases: 140   Valid cases: 3204
Some of the missing cases are imbedded within the series.

–

Supporting data for Table 4-1, Model 4

Autocorrelations: Annual Presidential Success Score in Diplomacy

Transformations: difference (1)

	Auto-	Stand.											
Lag	Corr.	Err.	-1	-.75	-.5	-.25	0	.25	.5	.75	1	Box-Ljung	Prob.
1	.000	.018					.*.					.000	.999
2	.000	.018					.*.					.000	1.000
3	.000	.018					.*.					.000	1.000
4	.000	.018					.*.					.000	1.000
5	.000	.018					.*.					.000	1.000
6	.000	.018					.*.					.000	1.000
7	.000	.018					.*.					.000	1.000
8	.000	.018					.*.					.000	1.000
9	.000	.018					.*.					.000	1.000
10	.000	.018					.*.					.000	1.000
11	.000	.018					.*.					.000	1.000
12	.000	.018					.*.					.000	1.000
13	.000	.018					.*.					.000	1.000
14	.000	.018					.*.					.000	1.000
15	.000	.018					.*.					.000	1.000
16	.000	.018					.*.					.000	1.000
17	.000	.018					.*.					.000	1.000
18	.000	.018					.*.					.000	1.000
19	.000	.018					.*.					.000	1.000
20	.000	.018					.*.					.000	1.000
21	.000	.017					.*.					.000	1.000
22	.000	.017					.*.					.000	1.000
23	.000	.017					.*.					.000	1.000
24	.000	.017					.*.					.000	1.000
25	.000	.017					.*.					.000	1.000
26	.000	.017					.*.					.000	1.000
27	.000	.017					.*.					.000	1.000
28	.000	.017					.*.					.000	1.000
29	.000	.017					.*.					.000	1.000
30	.000	.017					.*.					.000	1.000
31	.000	.017					.*.					.000	1.000
32	.000	.017					.*.					.000	1.000
33	.000	.017					.*.					.000	1.000
34	.000	.017					.*.					.000	1.000
35	.000	.017					.*.					.000	1.000
36	.000	.017					.*.					.000	1.000
37	-.033	.017					*					3.493	1.000

```
38  .000  .017           .*.              3.493  1.000
39  .000  .017           .*.              3.493  1.000
40  .000  .017           .*.              3.493  1.000
41 -.004  .017           .*.              3.535  1.000
42 -.007  .017           .*.              3.676  1.000
43  .000  .017           .*.              3.676  1.000
44  .000  .017           .*.              3.676  1.000
45  .000  .017           .*.              3.676  1.000
46 -.007  .017           .*.              3.841  1.000
```

–

Autocorrelations: Annual Presidential Success Score in Diplomacy (continued)

```
        Auto- Stand.
Lag  Corr. Err. -1 -.75 -.5 -.25  0  .25  .5  .75  1  Box-Ljung  Prob.

47  .008  .017           .*.              4.058  1.000
48  .000  .017           .*.              4.058  1.000
49  .000  .017           .*.              4.058  1.000
50  .000  .017           .*.              4.059  1.000
```

Plot Symbols: Autocorrelations *   Two Standard Error Limits

Total cases: 3344   Computable first lags after differencing: 3198

1 case(s) will be lost due to differencing.

–

Supporting data for Table4-1, Model 5

Autocorrelations: Annual Presidential Success Score in Trade

Transformations: difference (1)

```
       Auto- Stand.
Lag Corr.  Err. -1 -.75 -.5 -.25  0  .25  .5  .75  1  Box-Ljung  Prob.
```

Lag	Auto- Corr.	Stand. Err.	Plot	Box-Ljung	Prob.
1	.000	.017	.*.	.000	1.000
2	.000	.017	.*.	.000	1.000
3	.000	.017	.*.	.000	1.000
4	.000	.017	.*.	.000	1.000
5	.000	.017	.*.	.000	1.000
6	.000	.017	.*.	.000	1.000
7	.000	.017	.*.	.000	1.000
8	.000	.017	.*.	.000	1.000
9	.000	.017	.*.	.000	1.000
10	.000	.017	.*.	.000	1.000
11	-.017	.017	.*.	1.013	1.000
12	.000	.017	.*.	1.013	1.000
13	.000	.017	.*.	1.013	1.000
14	.000	.017	.*.	1.013	1.000
15	.000	.017	.*.	1.013	1.000
16	.000	.017	.*.	1.013	1.000
17	.000	.017	.*.	1.013	1.000
18	.000	.017	.*.	1.013	1.000
19	.000	.017	.*.	1.013	1.000
20	-.031	.017	* .	4.167	1.000
21	.000	.017	.*.	4.167	1.000
22	.000	.017	.*.	4.167	1.000
23	.000	.017	.*.	4.167	1.000
24	.000	.017	.*.	4.167	1.000
25	-.037	.017	* .	8.714	.999
26	.000	.017	.*.	8.714	.999
27	.000	.017	.*.	8.714	1.000
28	.031	.017	. *	11.876	.997
29	.000	.017	.*.	11.876	.998
30	-.007	.017	.*.	12.028	.999
31	-.004	.017	.*.	12.076	.999
32	.000	.017	.*.	12.076	.999
33	.000	.017	.*.	12.076	1.000
34	.000	.017	.*.	12.076	1.000
35	.020	.017	.*.	13.486	1.000
36	.000	.017	.*.	13.486	1.000
37	-.003	.017	.*.	13.516	1.000

38	.000	.017	.*.	13.516	1.000
39	.000	.017	.*.	13.516	1.000
40	.000	.017	.*.	13.516	1.000
41	.005	.017	.*.	13.600	1.000
42	.000	.017	.*.	13.600	1.000
43	.000	.017	.*.	13.600	1.000
44	.000	.017	.*.	13.600	1.000
45	.025	.017	.*.	15.689	1.000
46	-.071	.017	* .	32.860	.927

–

Autocorrelations: Annual Presidential Success Score in Trade (continued)

```
      Auto- Stand.
Lag  Corr.  Err. -1 -.75 -.5 -.25  0  .25 .5 .75  1  Box-Ljung Prob.
```

47	.000	.017	.*.	32.860	.941
48	-.045	.017	* .	39.826	.793
49	.000	.017	.*.	39.826	.822
50	.000	.017	.*.	39.826	.848

Plot Symbols: Autocorrelations *   Two Standard Error Limits

Total cases: 3344   Computable first lags after differencing: 3342

1 case(s) will be lost due to differencing.

Variable: FORAID   Missing cases: 146   Valid cases: 3198
Some of the missing cases are imbedded within the series.

–

Supporting data for Table4-1, Model 6

Autocorrelations: Annual Presidential Success Score in Foreign Aid

Transformations: difference (1)

```
        Auto- Stand.
Lag  Corr.  Err. -1 -.75 -.5 -.25  0  .25  .5  .75  1   Box-Ljung  Prob.

 1   .000   .018              .*.               .000   .999
 2   .000   .018              .*.               .000  1.000
 3   .000   .018              .*.               .000  1.000
 4   .000   .018              .*.               .000  1.000
 5   .000   .018              .*.               .000  1.000
 6   .000   .018              .*.               .000  1.000
 7   .000   .018              .*.               .000  1.000
 8   .000   .018              .*.               .000  1.000
 9   .000   .018              .*.               .000  1.000
10   .000   .018              .*.               .000  1.000
11   .000   .018              .*.               .000  1.000
12   .000   .018              .*.               .000  1.000
13   .000   .018              .*.               .000  1.000
14   .000   .018              .*.               .000  1.000
15   .000   .018              .*.               .000  1.000
16   .000   .018              .*.               .000  1.000
17   .000   .017              .*.               .000  1.000
18   .000   .017              .*.               .000  1.000
19   .000   .017              .*.               .000  1.000
20   .031   .017              .  *             3.070  1.000
21   .000   .017              .*.              3.070  1.000
22   .000   .017              .*.              3.070  1.000
23   .000   .017              .*.              3.070  1.000
24   .000   .017              .*.              3.070  1.000
25   .000   .017              .*.              3.070  1.000
26   .000   .017              .*.              3.070  1.000
27   .000   .017              .*.              3.070  1.000
28   .000   .017              .*.              3.070  1.000
29  -.005   .017              .*.              3.142  1.000
30   .000   .017              .*.              3.142  1.000
31  -.002   .017              .*.              3.159  1.000
32   .000   .017              .*.              3.159  1.000
33   .000   .017              .*.              3.159  1.000
34   .000   .017              .*.              3.159  1.000
35  -.012   .017              .*.              3.663  1.000
36  -.002   .017              .*.              3.678  1.000
37  -.034   .017              *  .             7.628  1.000
```

38	.000	.017	.*.	7.628	1.000
39	.000	.017	.*.	7.628	1.000
40	.000	.017	.*.	7.628	1.000
41	-.002	.017	.*.	7.641	1.000
42	.001	.017	.*.	7.642	1.000
43	.010	.017	.*.	7.986	1.000
44	.000	.017	.*.	7.986	1.000
45	.000	.017	.*.	7.986	1.000
46	.004	.017	.*.	8.052	1.000

–

Autocorrelations: Annual Presidential Success Score in Foreign Aid (continued)

Auto- Stand.
Lag Corr. Err. -1 -.75 -.5 -.25 0 .25 .5 .75 1 Box-Ljung Prob.

47	-.003	.017	.*.	8.074	1.000
48	.000	.017	.*.	8.074	1.000
49	.000	.017	.*.	8.074	1.000
50	.000	.017	.*.	8.074	1.000

Plot Symbols: Autocorrelations *   Two Standard Error Limits

Total cases: 3344   Computable first lags after differencing: 3190

1 case(s) will be lost due to differencing.

Variable: IMM   Missing cases: 1797   Valid cases: 1547
Some of the missing cases are imbedded within the series.

–

Supporting data for Table 4-1, Model 7

Autocorrelations: Annual Presidential Success Score in Immigration

Transformations: difference (1)

```
      Auto- Stand.
Lag  Corr.  Err. -1 -.75 -.5 -.25  0  .25  .5  .75  1   Box-Ljung  Prob.
```

Lag	Auto-Corr.	Stand. Err.	Plot	Box-Ljung	Prob.
1	.000	.025	.*.	.000	.997
2	.000	.025	.*.	.000	1.000
3	.000	.025	.*.	.000	1.000
4	.000	.025	.*.	.000	1.000
5	.000	.025	.*.	.000	1.000
6	.000	.025	.*.	.000	1.000
7	.000	.025	.*.	.000	1.000
8	.000	.025	.*.	.000	1.000
9	.000	.025	.*.	.000	1.000
10	.000	.024	.*.	.000	1.000
11	.000	.024	.*.	.000	1.000
12	.000	.024	.*.	.000	1.000
13	.000	.024	.*.	.000	1.000
14	.000	.024	.*.	.000	1.000
15	.000	.024	.*.	.000	1.000
16	.000	.024	.*.	.000	1.000
17	.000	.024	.*.	.000	1.000
18	.000	.024	.*.	.000	1.000
19	.000	.024	.*.	.000	1.000
20	.000	.023	.*.	.000	1.000
21	.000	.023	.*.	.000	1.000
22	.000	.023	.*.	.000	1.000
23	.000	.023	.*.	.000	1.000
24	.000	.023	.*.	.000	1.000
25	.000	.023	.*.	.000	1.000
26	.000	.023	.*.	.000	1.000
27	.000	.023	.*.	.000	1.000
28	-.208	.023	***. .	84.675	.000
29	.000	.022	.*.	84.675	.000
30	.000	.022	.*.	84.675	.000
31	.000	.022	.*.	84.675	.000
32	.000	.022	.*.	84.675	.000
33	.000	.022	.*.	84.675	.000
34	.000	.022	.*.	84.675	.000
35	.000	.022	.*.	84.675	.000
36	.000	.022	.*.	84.675	.000
37	.000	.022	.*.	84.675	.000

38	.000	.022	.*.	84.675	.000
39	.000	.021	.*.	84.675	.000
40	.000	.021	.*.	84.675	.000
41	.000	.021	.*.	84.675	.000
42	.000	.021	.*.	84.675	.000
43	.000	.021	.*.	84.675	.000
44	.000	.021	.*.	84.675	.000
45	.000	.021	.*.	84.675	.000
46	.000	.021	.*.	84.675	.000

–

Autocorrelations: Annual Presidential Success Score in Immigration (continued)

Auto- Stand.
Lag Corr. Err. -1 -.75 -.5 -.25 0 .25 .5 .75 1 Box-Ljung Prob.

47	.000	.021	.*.	84.675	.001
48	.000	.021	.*.	84.676	.001
49	.000	.021	.*.	84.676	.001
50	.000	.020	.*.	84.676	.002

Plot Symbols: Autocorrelations *   Two Standard Error Limits

Total cases: 3344   Computable first lags after differencing: 1523

1 case(s) will be lost due to differencing.

Supporting data for Table 4-2, Model A

Cross Correlations: Annual Presidential Success Score in Foreign Policy
Annual Presidential Success Score in National Security

Transformations: difference (1)

```
       Cross  Stand.
Lag    Corr.  Err. -1  -.75  -.5 -.25   0   .25  .5  .75   1

-50    .000   .018                  .*.
-49    .000   .018                  .*.
-48    .026   .018                  .  *
-47   -.046   .018                *  .
-46   -.035   .018                *  .
-45   -.002   .018                  .*.
-44    .000   .018                  .*.
-43    .000   .018                  .*.
-42    .000   .018                  .*.
-41    .000   .018                  .*.
-40    .000   .018                  .*.
-39    .000   .018                  .*.
-38    .000   .018                  .*.
-37    .018   .018                  .*.
-36    .000   .018                  .*.
-35    .013   .018                  .*.
-34    .000   .018                  .*.
-33    .000   .018                  .*.
-32    .000   .018                  .*.
-31   -.002   .018                  .*.
-30   -.001   .018                  .*.
-29    .011   .018                  .*.
-28    .017   .018                  .*.
-27    .000   .018                  .*.
-26    .000   .018                  .*.
-25    .004   .018                  .*.
-24    .000   .018                  .*.
-23    .000   .018                  .*.
-22    .000   .018                  .*.
-21    .000   .018                  .*.
-20   -.033   .018                *  .
-19    .000   .018                  .*.
-18    .000   .018                  .*.
-17    .000   .018                  .*.
-16    .000   .018                  .*.
-15    .000   .018                  .*.
```

```
-14  .000  .018              .*.
-13  .000  .018              .*.
-12  .000  .018              .*.
-11  .000  .018              .*.
-10  .000  .018              .*.
 -9  .000  .018             .*.
 -8  .000  .018             .*.
 -7  .000  .018             .*.
 -6  .000  .018             .*.
```

–

Cross Correlations: Annual Presidential Success Score in Foreign Policy
                    Annual Presidential Success Score in National Security
                    (continued)

```
      Cross Stand.
Lag  Corr.  Err. -1 -.75 -.5 -.25  0  .25  .5  .75  1

 -5  .000  .018              .*.
 -4  .000  .018              .*.
 -3  .000  .018              .*.
 -2  .000  .018              .*.
 -1  .000  .018              .*.
  0  .564  .018              .  **********
  1  .000  .018              .*.
  2  .000  .018              .*.
  3  .000  .018              .*.
  4  .000  .018              .*.
  5  .000  .018              .*.
  6  .000  .018              .*.
  7  .000  .018              .*.
  8  .000  .018              .*.
  9  .000  .018              .*.
 10  .000  .018              .*.
 11  .000  .018              .*.
 12  .000  .018              .*.
 13  .000  .018              .*.
 14  .000  .018              .*.
 15  .000  .018              .*.
 16  .000  .018              .*.
 17  .000  .018              .*.
 18  .000  .018              .*.
 19  .000  .018              .*.
 20  .048  .018              .  *
 21  .000  .018              .*.
```

```
22  .000  .018           .*.
23  .000  .018           .*.
24  .000  .018       ‿   .*.
25 -.029  .018           *  .
26  .000  .018           .*.
27  .000  .018           .*.
28  .005  .018           .*.
29  .000  .018           .*.
30  .000  .018           .*.
31  .000  .018           .*.
32  .000  .018           .*.
33  .000  .018           .*.
34  .000  .018           .*.
35  .001  .018           .*.
36  .000  .018           .*.
37  .020  .018           .*.
38  .000  .018           .*.
39  .000  .018           .*.
40  .000  .018           .*.
41  .000  .018           .*.
‒
```

Cross Correlations: Annual Presidential Success Score in Foreign Policy
                    Annual Presidential Success Score in National Security
                    (continued)

      Cross Stand.
Lag Corr. Err. -1 -.75 -.5 -.25 0 .25 .5 .75 1

```
42  .000  .018           .*.
43 -.014  .018           .*.
44  .000  .018           .*.
45 -.019  .018           .*.
46 -.033  .018          *  .
47 -.012  .018           .*.
48 -.012  .018           .*.
49  .000  .018           .*.
50  .000  .018           .*.
```

Plot Symbols: Autocorrelations *   Two Standard Error Limits

Total cases: 3344   Computable 0-order correlations after differencing: 3139

1 case(s) will be lost due to differencing

Supporting data for Table 4-2, Model B

Cross Correlations: Annual Presidential Success Score in Foreign Policy
Annual Presidential Success Score in Trade

Transformations: difference (1)

```
      Cross Stand.
Lag  Corr.  Err. -1 -.75 -.5 -.25  0  .25  .5  .75  1

-50  .000  .017              .*.
-49  .000  .017              .*.
-48  .040  .017              . *
-47  .000  .017              .*.
-46 -.047  .017             *  .
-45  .002  .017              .*.
-44  .000  .017              .*.
-43  .000  .017              .*.
-42  .007  .017              .*.
-41  .009  .017              .*.
-40  .000  .017              .*.
-39  .000  .017              .*.
-38  .000  .017              .*.
-37 -.004  .017              .*.
-36  .010  .017              .*.
-35  .000  .017              .*.
-34  .000  .017              .*.
-33  .000  .017              .*.
-32  .000  .017              .*.
-31  .000  .017              .*.
-30 -.003  .017              .*.
-29  .000  .017              .*.
-28  .027  .017              . *
-27  .000  .017              .*.
-26  .000  .017              .*.
-25 -.002  .017              .*.
-24  .000  .017              .*.
-23  .000  .017              .*.
-22  .000  .017              .*.
-21  .000  .017              .*.
-20  .027  .017              . *
-19  .000  .017              .*.
-18  .000  .017              .*.
-17  .000  .017              .*.
-16  .000  .017              .*.
-15  .000  .017              .*.
```

```
-14  .000  .017           .*.
-13  .000  .017           .*.
-12  .000  .017           .*.
-11  .000  .017           .*.
-10  .000  .017           .*.
 -9  .000  .017           .*.
 -8  .000  .017           .*.
 -7  .000  .017           .*.
 -6  .000  .017           .*.
```

—

Cross Correlations: Annual Presidential Success Score in Foreign Policy
                    Annual Presidential Success Score in Trade (continued)

```
       Cross Stand.
Lag  Corr.  Err. -1 -.75 -.5 -.25  0  .25 .5 .75  1

 -5  .000  .017           .*.
 -4  .000  .017           .*.
 -3  .000  .017           .*.
 -2  .000  .017           .*.
 -1  .000  .017           .*.
  0  .525  .017           .  .**********
  1  .000  .017           .*.
  2  .000  .017           .*.
  3  .000  .017           .*.
  4  .000  .017           .*.
  5  .000  .017           .*.
  6  .000  .017           .*.
  7  .000  .017           .*.
  8  .000  .017           .*.
  9  .000  .017           .*.
 10  .000  .017           .*.
 11 -.009  .017           .*.
 12  .000  .017           .*.
 13  .000  .017           .*.
 14  .000  .017           .*.
 15  .000  .017           .*.
 16  .000  .017           .*.
 17  .000  .017           .*.
 18  .000  .017           .*.
 19  .000  .017           .*.
 20 -.027  .017           *  .
 21  .000  .017           .*.
 22  .000  .017           .*.
 23  .000  .017           .*.
 24  .000  .017           .*.
```

```
25  .033  .017              .  *
26  .000  .017              .*.
27  .000  .017              .*.
28 -.005  .017              .*.
29  .000  .017              .*.
30  .011  .017              .*.
31 -.002  .017              .*.
32  .000  .017              .*.
33  .000  .017              .*.
34  .000  .017              .*.
35 -.004  .017              .*.
36  .001  .017              .*.
37  .013  .017              .*.
38  .000  .017              .*.
39  .000  .017              .*.
40  .000  .017              .*.
41  .003  .017              .*.
```

–

Cross Correlations: Annual Presidential Success Score in Foreign Policy
                 Annual Presidential Success Score in Trade (continued)

```
        Cross Stand.
Lag Corr. Err. -1 -.75 -.5 -.25  0  .25  .5  .75  1

42  .000  .017              .*.
43  .000  .017              .*.
44  .000  .017              .*.
45  .022  .017              .*.
46 -.061  .017            *  .
47 -.004  .017              .*.
48  .007  .017              .*.
49  .000  .017              .*.
50  .000  .017              .*.
```

Plot Symbols: Autocorrelations *   Two Standard Error Limits

Total cases: 3344   Computable 0-order correlations after differencing: 3343

1 case(s) will be lost due to differencing.

–

1 case(s) will be lost due to differencing.

Listwise deletion.   Missing cases: 146   Valid cases: 3198
Some of the missing cases are imbedded within the series.

–

Supporting data for Table 4-2, Model C

Cross Correlations: Annual Presidential Success Score in Foreign Policy
Annual Presidential Success Score in Foreign Aid

Transformations: difference (1)

```
       Cross Stand.
Lag   Corr.  Err. -1 -.75 -.5 -.25  0  .25 .5  .75  1
-50   .000   .018              .*.
-49   .000   .018              .*.
-48   .000   .018              .*.
-47  -.008   .018              .*.
-46  -.020   .018              .*.
-45   .000   .018              .*.
-44   .000   .018              .*.
-43   .000   .018              .*.
-42   .002   .018              .*.
-41  -.003   .018              .*.
-40   .000   .018              .*.
-39   .000   .018              .*.
-38   .000   .018              .*.
-37   .028   .018              .  *
-36  -.028   .018              *  .
-35   .014   .018              .*.
-34   .000   .018              .*.
-33   .000   .018              .*.
-32   .000   .018              .*.
-31   .001   .018              .*.
-30   .000   .018              .*.
-29  -.008   .018              .*.
-28   .000   .018              .*.
-27   .000   .018              .*.
-26   .000   .018              .*.
-25   .000   .018              .*.
-24   .000   .018              .*.
-23   .000   .018              .*.
-22   .000   .018              .*.
-21   .000   .018              .*.
-20   .017   .018              .*.
-19   .000   .018              .*.
-18   .000   .018              .*.
-17   .000   .018              .*.
-16   .000   .018              .*.
-15   .000   .018              .*.
```

```
-14  .000  .018            .*.
-13  .000  .018            .*.
-12  .000  .018            .*.
-11  .000  .018            .*.
-10  .000  .018            .*.
 -9  .000  .018           .*.
 -8  .000  .018           .*.
 -7  .000  .018           .*.
 -6  .000  .018           .*.

 —
```

Cross Correlations: Annual Presidential Success Score in Foreign Policy
Annual Presidential Success Score in Foreign Aid (continued)

```
       Cross  Stand.
Lag    Corr.  Err. -1 -.75 -.5 -.25  0  .25  .5  .75  1
 -5   .000   .018             .*.
 -4   .000   .018             .*.
 -3   .000   .018             .*.
 -2   .000   .018             .*.
 -1   .000   .018             .*.
  0   .240   .018             .  .****
  1   .000   .018            .*.
  2   .000   .018            .*.
  3   .000   .018            .*.
  4   .000   .018            .*.
  5   .000   .018            .*.
  6   .000   .018            .*.
  7   .000   .018            .*.
  8   .000   .018            .*.
  9   .000   .018            .*.
 10   .000   .018           .*.
 11   .000   .018           .*.
 12   .000   .018           .*.
 13   .000   .018           .*.
 14   .000   .018           .*.
 15   .000   .018           .*.
 16   .000   .018           .*.
 17   .000   .018           .*.
 18   .000   .018           .*.
 19   .000   .018           .*.
 20   .058   .018           .  *
 21   .000   .018           .*.
 22   .000   .018           .*.
 23   .000   .018           .*.
```

```
24   .000   .018              .*.
25   .000   .018              .*.
26   .000   .018              .*.
27   .000   .018              .*.
28   .000   .018              .*.
29   .000   .018              .*.
30   .000   .018              .*.
31  -.001   .018              .*.
32   .000   .018              .*.
33   .000   .018              .*.
34   .000   .018              .*.
35   .004   .018              .*.
36  -.003   .018              .*.
37  -.026   .018             *  .
38   .000   .018              .*.
39   .000   .018              .*.
40   .000   .018              .*.
41   .005   .018              .*.
 _
```

Cross Correlations: Annual Presidential Success Score in Foreign Policy
　　　　　　　　　　Annual Presidential Success Score in Foreign Aid (continued)

```
        Cross Stand.
Lag  Corr.  Err. -1 -.75 -.5 -.25  0  .25  .5  .75  1

42  -.005   .018              .*.
43   .010   .018              .*.
44   .000   .018              .*.
45   .000   .018              .*.
46   .010   .018              .*.
47  -.007   .018              .*.
48   .000   .018              .*.
49   .000   .018              .*.
50   .000   .018              .*.
```

Plot Symbols: Autocorrelations *   Two Standard Error Limits

Total cases: 3344   Computable 0-order correlations after differencing: 3194

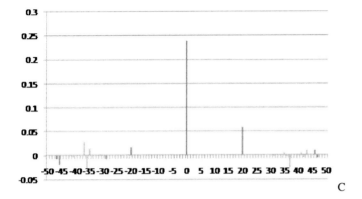

C

LIST OF REFERENCES

Aldrich, J. and Rohde, D. (2005) "Congressional Committees in a Partisan Era," in Dodd and Oppenheimer (eds.) *Congress Reconsidered*, 8th ed. Washington, D.C.: CQ Press.

Alison, G. & Zelikow, P. (1999) *The Essence of Decision: Explaining the Cuban Missile Crisis*, Boston, MA & NY, NY: Longman.

Alison, G. (1971) *The Essence of Decision: Explaining the Cuban Missile Crisis*, Boston, MA: Longman

Almond, G. (1950) *The American People and Foreign Policy* New York: Harcourt, Brace and World.

Anderson, P (1987) "What do Decision Makers do when they Make Foreign Policy? The Implications for the Comparative Study of Foreign Policy," in Hermann, Kegley & Rosenau (eds.) *New Directions in the Study of Foreign Policy* Boston, MA: Allen & Unwin.

Axelrod, A (2007) *Political History of America's Wars*, Washington, D.C.: CQ Press.

Bernstein, R. & Munro, R. (1999) "The New China Lobby," in Wittkopf & McCormick *The Domestic Sources of American foreign Policy: Insights and Evidence* Lanham, MD: Rowman and Littlefield.

Best, S. & Kelner, M. (1991) *Post Modern Theory: Critical Interrogations* NY, NY: Guilford Press.

Black, E. & Black, M. (2002) *The Rise of Southern Republicans*. Cambridge, MA & London, England: The Belknap Press of Harvard University Press.

Braybroke, D. & Lindbolm, C. (1969) "Types of Decision Making," in Rosenau (ed.) *International Politics and Foreign Policy* revised edition NY, NY: Free Press.

Bond, J & Fleisher, R. (2000) *Polarized Politics: Congress and the President in a Partisan Era* Washington, D.C.: CQ Press.

Bond, J. & Fleisher, R. (1990) *The President in the Legislative Arena*. Chicago, IL &London, England: University of Chicago Press.

Bond, J. & Fleisher (1988) "Are There Two Presidencies? Yes, but only for Republicans," *Journal of Politics* 50(3): 747-67.

Bond, J., Copeland, G., LeLoup, L., Renka, R. & Shull, S. (1991) "Implications for Research in Studying Presidential-Congressional Relations: Conclusion," in Shull (ed.) *The Two Presidencies: A Quarter Century Assessment* Chicago, IL: Nelson Hall.

Box, G. & Lijung, (1978) "Modified Q Statistics in Time Series Analysis," *Behavioral Science*,

Brady, D. & Volden C. (1998) *Revolving Gridlock* Boulder, CO: Westview Press.

Bueno De Mesquito, B (1981) *The War Trap* New Haven, CT: Yale University Press.

Burns, J. M. (1963) *The Deadlock of Democracy: Four Party Politics in America*, Englewood Cliffs, NJ: Prentice Hall.

Cameron, C. (2000) *Veto Bargaining: Presidents and the Politics of Negative Power*, New York: Cambridge University Press.

Campbell, A. Converse, P. Miller, W. & Stokes, D. (1960) *The American Voter*, NY, NY: John Wiley.

Carter, J. (1982) *Keeping Faith: Memoirs of a President*, New York: Bantam Books.

Caverly, M (2006) "The Two Presidencies an Unfinished Project: A Theoretical, Methodological, Empirical and Normative Meta-Analysis," paper presented at the Southwestern Social Science Association 2006 Annual Meeting at San Antonio, TX April 11-15, 2006.

Chamberlain, L.H. (1946) "President, Congress and Legislation," *Political Science Quarterly* 61: 42-60.

Cheney, R. (2002) "The Unitary Executive Theory," interview with Timothy Russert on March 30, 2002 at NBC's *Meet the Press* in NY, NY.

Cigler, A. & Loomis, B. (1997) *Interest Group Politics*, 6th edition, Washington, D.C.: CQ Press.

Cohen, J. (1982) "A Historical Reassessment of Wildavsky's Two Presidencies Thesis," *Social Science Quarterly*, 63/3 (September 1982): 549-555.

Congressional Quarterly *1953 CQ Almanac* Washington D.C.: CQ Press.

Congressional Quarterly (1954) "Election Report," *1954 CQ Almanac* Washington, D.C.: CQ Press.

Congressional Quarterly *1955 CQ Almanac*, Washington D.C.: CQ Press.

Congressional Quarterly *1957 CQ Almanac*, Washington, D.C.: CQ Press.

Congressional Quarterly (1958) "Election Report," *1958 CQ Almanac* Washington, D.C.: CQ Press.

Congressional Quarterly (1959) "Economic Report," *1959 CQ Almanac* Washington, D.C.: CQ Press.

Congressional Quarterly *1961 CQ Almanac*, Washington, D.C.: CQ Press

Congressional Quarterly (1962) "Report on Cuban Missile Crisis," *1962 CQ Almanac*, Washington, D.C.: CQ Press.

Congressional Quarterly (1963) "Nuclear Test Ban Treaty Report," *1963 CQ Almanac*, Washington, D.C.: CQ Press.

Congressional Quarterly (1964) "Gulf of Tonkin Incident Report," *1964 CQ Almanac*, Washington D.C.: CQ Press.

Congressional Quarterly (1966) "Election Report," *1966 CQ Almanac*, Washington, D.C.: CQ Press.

Congressional Quarterly *1966 CQ Almanac*, Washington D.C.: CQ Press.

Congressional Quarterly *1967 CQ Almanac*, Washington, D.C.: CQ Press.

Congressional Quarterly (1967) "Senate Foreign Relations Committee Reports on Vietnam War, excerpts;" *1967 CQ Almanac*, Washington, D.C.: CQ Press.

Congressional Quarterly (1968) "Senate Foreign Relations Chairman J. William Fulbright's public remarks on Johnson Vietnam War Policy," *1968 CQ Almanac*, Washington, D.C.: CQ Press.

Congressional Quarterly (1971) "Report on Nixon Global Currency Policy," *1971 CQ Almanac*, Washington, D.C.: CQ Press.

Congressional Quarterly *1971 CQ Almanac*, Washington, D.C.: CQ Press.

Congressional Quarterly *1972 CQ Almanac*, Washington D.C.: CQ Press.

Congressional Quarterly (1973) "Report on War Powers Resolution," *1973 CQ Almanac*, Washington, D.C.: CQ Press.

Congressional Quarterly *1975 CQ Almanac* Washington D.C.: CQ Press.

Congressional Quarterly Almanac 1975 "Foreword" Washington, D.C.: CQ Press

Congressional Quarterly (1975) "Report on War in Southeast Asia," *1975 CQ Almanac*, Washington, D.C.: CQ Press.

Congressional Quarterly (1975) "Report on Operations and Intelligence Activities, excerpts from Church Committee Hearings;" *1975 CQ Almanac*, Washington, D.C.: CQ Press.

Congressional Quarterly (1976) "Report on Foreign Aid Restrictions leveled at the Executive Branch," *1976 CQ Almanac*, Washington, D.C.: CQ Press.

Congressional Quarterly (1977) "Report on Executive-Legislative Relations with Carter Administration," *1977 CQ Almanac*, Washington, D.C.: CQ Press.

Congressional Quarterly *1978 CQ Almanac*, Washington, D.C.: CQ Press.

Congressional Quarterly (1979) "Report in Panama Canal Treaties and Enforcement Legislation," *1979 CQ Almanac*, Washington, D.C.: CQ Press.

Congressional Quarterly (1979) "Report on Camp David Accords between Israel and Egypt," *1979 CQ Almanac*, Washington, D.C.: CQ Press.

Congressional Quarterly (1979) "Report on Carter Energy Policy and the Oil Shocks," *1979 CQ Almanac*, Washington, D.C.: CQ Press.

Congressional Quarterly (1980) "Report on Iranian Hostage Crisis," *1980 CQ Almanac*, Washington, D.C.: CQ Press.

Congressional Quarterly (1980) "Elections Report," *1980 CQ Almanac*, Washington, D.C.: CQ Press.

Congressional Quarterly *1981 CQ Almanac*, Washington D.C.: CQ Press.

Congressional Quarterly (1981) "Report on 1982 Budget," *1981 CQ Almanac*, Washington, D.C.: CQ Press.

Congressional Quarterly (1985-89) "Legislative Histories," *1985-89 CQ Almanac*, Washington, D.C.: CQ Press.

Congressional Quarterly (1986) "Report on South African Sanctions Policy," *1986 CQ Almanac*, Washington, D.C.: CQ Press.

Congressional Quarterly (1986) "Elections Report," *1986 CQ Almanac*, Washington, D.C.: CQ Press.

Congressional Quarterly (1990) "Base Closure Commission Report, excerpts" *1990 CQ Almanac*, Washington, D.C.: CQ Press.

Congressional Quarterly (1991) "Persian Gulf War Report," *1991 CQ Almanac*, Washington, D.C.: CQ Press.

Congressional Quarterly *1991 CQ Almanac*, Washington, D.C.: CQ Press.

Congressional Quarterly (1992) "Election Report," *1992 CQ Almanac*, Washington, D.C.: CQ Press.

Congressional Quarterly *1993 CQ Almanac*, Washington, D.C.: CQ Press.

Congressional Quarterly (1995) "Report on Balkans," *1995 CQ Almanac*, Washington, D.C.: CQ Press.

Congressional Quarterly (1999) "Report on Kosovo," *1999 CQ Almanac*, Washington, D.C.: CQ Press.

Congressional Quarterly (2001) "Presidential Address on 9/11 Attacks," given September 12, 2001 to joint session of Congress at Capitol Hill, Washington, D.C. reprinted in *2001 CQ Almanac*, Washington, D.C.: CQ Press.

Congressional Quarterly (2001) "Report on War in Afghanistan," Washington, D.C.: CQ Press.

Congressional Quarterly *2001 CQ Almanac*, Washington, D.C.: CQ Press.

Congressional Quarterly *2002 CQ Almanac*, Washington, D.C.: CQ Press.

Congressional Quarterly (2002) "State of the Union Address," reprinted in *2002 CQ Almanac*, Washington, D.C.: CQ Press.

Congressional Quarterly (2002) "Election Report," *CQ Almanac*, Washington D.C.: CQPress.

Congressional Quarterly, (2003) "Report on War in Iraq," Washington, D.C.: CQ Press.

Congressional Quarterly *2003 CQ Almanac*, Washington, D.C.: CQ Press.

Conley, R. (2005) "Presidential and Congressional Struggles over the Formation of the Department of Homeland Security," in Conley (ed.) *Transforming the American Polity*, Upper Saddle River, NJ: Pearson-Prentice Hall.

Conley, R. (2003) "Comparing the Legislative Presidencies of Eisenhower and Reagan: The Lessons of Political Time," in *Reassessing the Reagan Presidency* Conley (ed.) Lanham, MD: University Press of America.

Conley, R. (2002) *The Presidency Congress and Divided Government: A Postwar Assessment*, College Station, TX: Texas A&M University Press.

Conley, R. (1997) "Unified Government, the Two Presidencies Thesis, and Presidential Support in the Senate: An Analysis of President Clinton's First Two Years," *Presidential Studies Quarterly* 27/2: 229-251.

Cox, G. & McCubbins, M. (1993) *Legislative Leviathan: Party Government in the House* Berkeley, CA: University of California Press.

Davidson, R. (1996) "The Presidency in Congressional Time," in *Rivals for Power: Presidential-Congressional Relations* (ed.) Thurber Washington D.C.: CQ Press.

Deering, C. and Smith, S. (1997) *Committees in Congress*, 3rd ed. Washington, D.C.: CQ Press.

Department of Commerce (2006) "Archive Reports on Economic Business Cycles," Washington, D.C.: Government Printing Office www.whitehouse.gov/DoC accessed on April 1, 2006.

Dierks, R. (2001) *Introduction to Globalization*, NY, NY: Burnham.

278

Dodd, L (2005) "Entrapped in the Narrative of War: Reflections, Questions and Commentary," in *Transforming the American Polity: The Presidency of George W. Bush and the War on Terrorism* Conley (ed.) Upper Saddle River, NJ: Pearson-Prentice Hall.

Dodd, L (1986) "The Cycles of Legislative Change," in Weisberg (ed.) *Political Science: The Science of Politics*, New York: Agathon Press.

Dodd, L. (1977) "Congress and the Quest for Power," in Dodd and Oppenheimer (eds.) *Congress Reconsidered*. Washington, D.C.: CQ Press.

Edwards, G. (2000) "Neustadt's Power Approach to the Presidency," in Shapiro, Kumar & Jacobs *Presidential* (eds.) *Power: Forging the Presidency for the 21st Century* NY, NY: Columbia University Press.

Edwards, G. (1989) *At the Margins: Presidential Leadership of Congress*. New Haven, CT: Yale University Press.

Edwards, G. (1986a) "Presidential Legislative Skills: At the Core or at the Margin?" Paper presented at the 1986 Annual meeting of the Midwest Political Science Association Chicago, IL April 10-12, 1986.

Edwards, G. (1986b) "The Two Presidencies: A Reevaluation," *American Politics Quarterly* 14 (July): 247-263.

Edwards, G. (1980) *Presidential Influence in Congress* San Francisco, CA: WH Freeman.

Ellsberg, D. (1971) "The Quagmire Myth and the Stalemate Machine," *Public Policy*16 (spring 1971):217-274.

Enders, W. (2004) *Applied Econometric Time Series*, 2nd edition, Hoboken, NJ: John Wiley & Sons.

Evans, C. & Lipinski, D. "Obstruction and Leadership in the US Senate," in Dodd and Oppenheimer (eds.) *Congress Reconsidered*, 8th ed. Washington D.C.: CQ Press.

Fearon, J. (1994) "Domestic Political Audiences and the Escalation of International Disputes," *American Political Science Review* 88(1994): 577-592.

Fenno, R. (1973) *Congressmen in Committees*. Boston, MA: Little Brown Publishing.

Fisher, L (2000) *Congressional Abdication on War & Spending* College Station, TX: Texas A&M University Press.

Fisher, L. (2004) *Presidential War Power* 2nd edition, revised Lawrence KS: University Press of Kansas.

Fisher, L. (1972) *President and Congress Power and Policy*, New York: Free Press.

Fleisher, R. Bond, J. Krutz, G. & Hanna, S. (2000) "The Demise of the Two Presidencies," *American Politics Quarterly* 28/1: 3-25.

Freedman, L & Karsh, E. (1993) *The Gulf Conflict 1990-1991: Diplomacy and War in the New World Order*, Princeton, NJ: Princeton University Press.

Ford, G. (1980) "Two Ex-Presidents Assess the Job: The Imperiled Presidency," *Time Magazine*, (November 10, 1980) 116/19: 1-9.

Gallagher, H.G. (1977) "The President, Congress and Legislation," in Cronin and Tugwell (eds.) *The Presidency Reappraised* 2nd ed. New York: Praeger Publishing.

Gimple, J. & Edwards, J (1998) *The Congressional Politics of Immigration Reform*, NY, NY: Pearson-Longman.

Gourevitch, P. (1996) "Squaring the Circle: The Domestic Sources of International Relations," *International Organizations* 50 (1996): 349-373.

Gourevitch, P. (1978) "The Second Image reversed: The International Sources of Domestic Politics," *International Organization* 32 (1978): 881-911.

Greenstein, F. (1988) "Introduction: Toward a Modern Presidency," in Greenstein (ed.) *Leadership in the Modern Presidency*, Cambridge, MA: Harvard University Press.

Hamilton, A. (1960 [1789]) "Federalist Paper Number Seventy," Hamilton, Madison & Jay in *The Federalist Papers* edited by Rossiter, NY, NY: Basic Books

Hastedt, G. & Eksterowicz, A. (1999) "Presidential Leadership and American Foreign Policy: Implications for a New Era," in Wittkopf & McCormick (eds.) *The Domestic Sources of American Foreign Policy: Insights & Evidence* Lanham, MD: Rowman & Littlefield.

Holbrooke, R. (1998) *To End a War*, New York: Random House.

Huntington, S. (1996) *The Clash of Civilizations*, New York: Simon & Schuster.

Huntington, S. (1965) "Congressional Responses to the Twentieth Century," in Truman (ed.) *Congress and America's Future*, Englewood Cliffs, NJ: Prentice Hall.

Huntington, S. (1961) *The Common Defense: Strategic Programs in National Politics* NY: Columbia University Press.

Ikenberry, J., Krasner, S. & Mastanduno, M. (1988) "Introduction: Approaches to Explaining American foreign Economic Policy," *International Organization* 42/1 (Winter 1988): 1-14.

Janis, I. (1982) *Groupthink*, Boston, MA: Houghton-Mifflin.

Jones, C (1988) "Ronald Reagan and the US Congress," in Jones (ed.) *The Reagan Legacy*, Chatham, NJ: Chatham House.

Kaine, T (2004) "Democratic Rebuttal to State of the Union Address," aired on CNN January 20, 2004 from Virginia Governor's Mansion located at Jefferson, VA.

Kegley, C. & Wittkopf, E. (2001) *Introduction to World Politics*, 7th edition NY, NY: Pearson-Longman.

Kennan, G. (1979) *American Diplomacy*. Chicago, IL: University of Chicago Press.

Kennedy, P. (1986) *The Rise and Fall of the Great Powers* New York: Vintage-Random House.

Keohane, R. & Nye, J. (1977) *Power and Interdependence*. Boston, MA: Little Brown.

Kerouac, J (1957) *On the Road*, New York: Viking Press.

Key. V.O. (1955) "A Theory of Critical Elections," *Journal of Politics* 17: 3-18.

Key, V.O. (1949) *Southern Politics in State and Nation*. New York: Knopf.

Kissinger, H. (1994) *Diplomacy*. NY, NY: Touchstone Book/Simon & Schuster.

Kissinger, H. (1956) *Nuclear Weapons and Foreign Policy* Cambridge, MA: Harvard University Press.

King, G. and Ragsdale, L. (1988) *The Elusive Executive: Discovering Statistical Patterns In the Presidency*. Washington, D.C.: CQ Press.

Krasner, S. (1978) *Defending the National Interest: Raw Materials Investments and US Foreign Policy* Princeton, NJ: Princeton University Press.

Lee, S & Ditko, S (1962) "Amazing Fantasy No. 15," NY, NY: Marvel Comics Group.

LeLoup, L. & Shull, S. (2003) *The President and Congress: Collaboration and Conflict*, NY, NY: Longman-Pearson.

Leloup, L. & Shull, S. (1979) "Congress versus the Executive: The Two Presidencies Reconsidered," *Social Science Quarterly* 59 (March 1979): 704-719.

Lewis, D. (1997) "The Two Rhetorical Presidencies: An Analysis of Televised Speeches 1947-1991," *American Politics Quarterly* 25/3: 380-395.

Lindsay, J. (1999) "End of an Era: Congress & Foreign Policy after the Cold War," In Wittkopf & McCormick *The Domestic Sources of American Foreign Policy:*

Insights and Evidence, Lanham, MD: Rowman & Littlefield.

Lindsay, J (1994) *Congress and Foreign Policy* Ann Arbor, MI: University of Michigan Press.

Lindsay, J. & Steger, W. (1993) "The 'Two Presidencies' in Future Research: Moving Beyond Roll-Call Analysis," *Congress and the Presidency*, 20/2.

Lowi, T. (1964) "American Business, Public policy, Case Studies and Political Theory," *World Politics* Lanham, MD: Rowman and Littlefield.

Lowi, T. (1972) "Four Systems of Policy, Politics and Choice," *Public Administration Review* (July/August 1972).

Low, T. (1985) *The Personal President: Power Invested Promise Unfulfilled*, Ithaca, NY:

Cornell University Press.

Malbin, M. & Brookshire, R. (2000) "'Two Presidencies?' Assessing the First Two Hundred Years," *Legislative Studies Quarterly*, 25/1: 156-157.

Mandelbaum, M. (1996) "Foreign Policy as Social Work," *Foreign Affairs* 75/1 (January/February 1996).

Mannheim and Rich (1995) *Empirical Political Analysis: Research Methods in Political Science*, 4th edition, New York: Longman Publishers.

Manning, B. (1977) "The Congress, the Executive and Intermestic Affairs: Three Proposals," *Foreign Affairs* (1977) 55/2: 306-320.

Mathews, J. (1989) "Redefining Security," *Foreign Affairs*, 68/2 (spring 1989).

May, E. (1973) *"Lessons" of the Past: The Use and Misuse of History in American Foreign Policy* NY, NY: Oxford University Press of New York

Mayhew, D. (2002) *Electoral Realignments*, New Haven, CT: Yale University Press.

McAdam, D. (1982) *Political Process and the Development of Black Insurgency, 1930-1970.* Chicago, IL: University of Chicago Press.

McCleary, R. & Hay, R. (1975) *Applied Time Series for the Social Sciences*, Beverly Hills, CA: Sage Publications.

McCubbins & Scwartz (1984) "Congressional Oversight Overlooked: Police Patrol versus Fire Alarm," *American Journal of Political Science* 1:165-177. Association, University of Indiana, IN: Blackstone Publishing.

Mearsheimer, J. (2001) *The Tragedy of the Great Powers*, NY, NY: Norton & Company.

Mezey, M. (1989) *Congress, the President and Public Policy*. Boulder, CO: Westview.

Mills, C. Wright (1956) *The Power Elite* Cambridge, MA: Harvard University Press.

Milkis, S. & Nelson M. (2003) *The American Presidency: Origins and Development* Washington D.C.: CQ Press.

Moe, R.C. and Teel, S. (1970) "Congress as Policymaker a Necessary Reappraisal," *Political Science Quarterly* 85: 443-470.

Morgenthau, H. (1993) *Politics among Nations: The Struggle for Power &Peace*, revised by Thompson, Boston, MA: McGraw-Hill.

Morrison, W. (1990) *The Elephant and the Tiger: The Full Story of the Vietnam War*, NY, NY: Hippcrene Books.

Neustadt, R. (1990) *Presidential Power and the Modern Presidents: The Politics of Leadership from Roosevelt to Reagan.* NY, NY: The Free Press.

Neustadt, R. (1960) *Presidential Power: The Politics of Leadership.* New York: John Wiley.

Niemi, R & Stanley, H (2006) *Vital Statistics on American Politics*, 6th edition, Washington, D.C.: CQ Press.

Niemi, R. & Weisberg, H. (2001) "Part IV Introduction," Niemi and Weisberg (eds.) *Controversies in Voting Behavior.* Washington, D.C.: CQ Press.

Oldfield, D. & Wildavsky, A. (1989) "Reconsidering the Two Presidencies," *Society* 26 (July 1989): 54-59.

Oppenheimer, B. (2005) "Deep Red and Blue Congressional Districts: The Causes and Consequences of Declining Party Competitiveness," in Dodd and Oppenheimer (eds.) *Congress Reconsidered*, 8th ed. Washington, D.C.: CQ Press.

Orfield, G. (1975) *Congressional Power: Congress and Social Change.* New York: Harcourt Brace-Jovanovich.

Oren, I. (2003) *Our Enemies & US: America's Rivalries and the Making of Political Science*, Ithaca, NY: Cornell University Press.

Orren, K. & Skowronek, S. (2004) *In Search of American Political Development*, NY, NY: Oxford University Press of New York.

Orren, K. and Skowronek, S. (1994) "Beyond the Iconography of Order: Notes for a New 'Institutionalism'" in Dodd and Jillson (eds.) *The Dynamics of American Politics: Approaches & Interpretations.* Boulder, CO: Westview Press.

Page, B. & Jordan, D (1992) "Shaping Foreign Policy Opinions: The Role of TV News," *Journal of Conflict Resolution* 36/2: 227-241.

Papp, D. Johnson, L. & Endicott, J. (2006) *American Foreign Policy, History, Politics and Policy*, NY, NY: Pearson-Longman.

Parkin, M. (1993) *MacroEconomics*, 2nd edition, Reading, MA: Addison-Wesley.

Peppers, D. (1975) "Two Presidencies Thesis: Eight Years Later," Wildavsky (ed.) *Perspectives on the Presidency*. Boston, MA: Little and Brown.

PBS (2000) *Kosovo*, documentary aired June 1, 2000 narrated by Bill Moyer.

Peterson, M. (1990) *Legislating Together: The White House and Capitol Hill from Eisenhower to Reagan*, Cambridge, MA: Harvard University Press.

Peterson, P.E. (ed.) (1994) *The President, the Congress and the Making of Foreign Policy*. Norman, OK: University of Oklahoma Press.

Pierson, P. & Skocpol, T. (2002) "Historical Institutionalism in Contemporary Political Science," Katznelson & Milner (eds.) *Political Science: the State of the Discipline*. NY: WW Norton.

Pika, J. A. & Maltese, J. A. (2006) *The Politics of the Presidency*, 7th edition, Washington, D.C.: CQ Press.

Putnam, R. (1988) "Diplomacy and Domestic Politics: The Logic of Two-Level Games," *International Organization* 42: 427-460.

Ragsdale, L. (1998) *Vital Statistics on the Presidency: Washington to Clinton* 2nd edition, Washington, D.C.: CQ Press.

Renka, R. & Jones, B. (1991) "The Two Presidencies in the Reagan and Bush Administrations," *Congress and the Presidency* 18/1 USA.

Renka, R. & Jones, B. (1989) "The 'Two Presidencies' in the Reagan and Bush Administrations" paper presented at the *Southern Political Science Association Annual Conference* held at Memphis, TN on November 2-4, 1989.

Ripley, R.B. & Lindsay, J.M. (1993) "Introduction," in Ripley and Lindsay (eds.) *Congressional Resurgence in Foreign Policy*, Ann Arbor, MI: University of Michigan Press.

Robkopf, B. (2005) *International Politics*, New York: Pearson-Longman.

Robinson, J. (1967) *Congress and Foreign Policymaking: a Study in Legislative Influence and Initiative*, revised edition, Homeword, IL: Dorsey Press.

Rogowski, R. (1987) "Political Cleavages and Changing Exposure to Trade," *American Political Science Review*, 81 (1994): 1121-1138.

Rohde, D. (1991) *Parties and Leaders in the Post-Reform Congress*, Chicago, IL: University of Chicago Press.

Rosati, J. (2006) *US Foreign Policy*, Belmont, CA: Thomson-Wadsworth.

Rossiter, C. (1956) *The American Presidency* New York: Harcourt Brace.

Schelling, T. (1978) *Micromotives for Macrobehavior* Cambridge, MA: Harvard University Press.

Schelling, T. (1960) *The Strategy of Conflict* Cambridge, MA: Harvard University Press.

Schickler, E. and Pearson, K. (2005) "The House Leadership in an Era of Partisan Warfare," in Dodd and Oppenheimer, (eds.) *Congress Reconsidered*, 8th edition, Washington, D.C.: CQ Press.

Schlesinger, A. M. Jr. (2005) *War and the American Presidency* NY, NY: WW Norton

Schlesinger, A.M. Jr. (1989) *The Imperial Presidency* 2nd edition, Boston, MA: Houghton-Mifflin.

Schlesinger, A. M. Jr. (1973) *The Imperial Presidency* Boston, MA: Houghton-Mifflin.

Shubick, M (1964) "Game Theory and the Study of Social Behavior: An Introductory Exposition," in Shubick (ed.) *Game Theory and Related Approaches to Social Behavior* NY, NY: Wiley.

Shull, S. (1997) *Presidential-Congressional Relations: A Policy and Political Time Perspective*, Ann Arbor, MI: University of Michigan Press.

Shull, S. (1991) "Introduction," Shull (ed.) *Two Presidencies: A Quarter Century Assessment* Chicago, IL: Nelson-Hall.

Shull, S & Leloup, L. (1979) "Introduction," in Shull and Leloup (eds.) *The Presidency: Studies in Policy Making*. Brunswick, OH: King's Court Communications.

Shull, S. & LeLoup, L. (1981) "Reassessing the Reassessment: Comment on Sigelman's Note on the Two Presidencies Thesis," *Journal of Politics* 43 (May 1981): 563-564.

Shull, S. & Shaw, T. (1999) *Explaining Congressional-Presidential Relations: A Multiple Perspectives Approach* Albany, NY: SUNY Press.

Sigelman, L. (1979) "A Reassessment of the Two Presidencies Thesis," *Journal of Politics* 41:1195-1205.

Sigelman, L. (1981) "Response to Critics," *Journal of Politics* 43 (May 1981):565.

Sinclair, B (2005) "Patriotism, Partisanship, and Institutional Protection: The Congressional Response to 9/11," in Conley (ed.) Transforming the American Polity: The Presidency of George W. Bush and the War on Terrorism," Upper Saddle River, NJ: Pearson-Prentice Hall.

Skowronek, S. (1997) *The Politics Presidents Make: Leadership from John Adams To Bill Clinton*. Cambridge, MA & London, England: The Belknap Press of Harvard University Press.

Smith, H. (1982) "The President as Coalition Builder: Reagan's First Year," in Cronin (ed.) *Rethinking the Presidency*, Boston, MA: Little Brown.

Smith, S. and Gamm, G. (2005) "The Dynamics of Party Government in Congress," in Dodd and Oppenheimer, (eds.) *Congress Reconsidered*, 8th ed. Washington, D.C.: CQ Press.

Snow, D. & Brown, E. (1997) *Beyond the Water's Edge* NY, NY: St. Martin's Press.

Snyder, J. (1991) *Myths of Empire: Domestic Politics and International Ambition* Ithaca, NY: Cornell University Press.

Snyder, J & Diesing, P. (1977) *Conflict among Nations: Bargaining, Decision Making and System Structuring in International Crisis* Princeton, NJ: Princeton University Press.

Sorensen, T.(1965) *Kennedy*, New York: Harper & Row.

Spanier, J. (1975) *Games that Nations Play*, 2nd edition, New York: Praeger.

Spitzer, R. (1993) *The President and Congress*. New York: McGraw Hill Publishing

Spitzer, R. (1983) *The Presidency and Public Policy: A Preliminary Inquiry*, Birmingham, AL: University of Alabama Press.

Stewart, C. (2001) *Analyzing Congress: The New Institutionalism in American Politics*. NY, NY & London, England: WW Norton and Company.

Sullivan, T. (1991) "A Matter of Fact: The Two Presidencies Thesis Revisited," in Shull (ed.) *The Two Presidencies Thesis: A Quarter Century Assessment*. Chicago, IL: Nelson Hall.

Sundquist, J. (1981) *The Decline and Resurgence of Congress* Washington, D.C.: Brookings Institution.

Sundquist, J. (1968) *Politics and Power: The Eisenhower, Kennedy and Johnson Years*. Washington, D.C.: Brookings Institution.

Thiele, L. (2003) *Thinking Politics: Perspectives in Ancient, Modern and Postmodern Political Theory*, 3rd edition, New York: Chatham House.

Thurber, J. (1996) "Introduction," in Thurber (ed.) *Rivals for Power: Presidential-Congressional Relations*, Washington, D.C.: CQ Press.

Tullis, J. (1987) *The Rhetorical Presidency*, Princeton, NJ: Princeton University Press.

Tsebelis, G. (2002) *Veto Players: How Political Institutions Work*, Princeton, NJ: Princeton University Press.

Vessey, J. (1984) "To Provide for the Common Defense," paper presented at 1984 Conference on the Presidency at the Center for the Study of the Presidency at American University in Washington D.C. March 12-15, 1984.

Von Nuemann, J. & Morgenstern, O. (1943) *Game Theory*, Princeton, NJ: Princeton University Press.

Waltz, K. (1979) *Theory of International Politics* NY, NY: Random House.

Weaver, B. & Rockman, R.K. (1993) *Do Institutions Matter? Government Capabilities in the United States and Abroad* Washington, D.C.: Brookings Institute.

Wildavsky, A. (1966) "The Two Presidencies," *Trans-Action* 4 (December): 7-14, Philadelphia, PA: Transaction Publishing, Inc.

Wilson, W. {1963(1885)} *Congressional Government*, Boston, MA: Houghton-Mifflin Company.

Wittkopf, E. & McCormick, J. (1999) "Introduction," in Wittkopf and McCormack (eds.) *The Domestic Sources of American Foreign Policy: Insights & Evidence* 3rd ed. Lanham, MD: Rowman & Littlefield.

Wolfsenberger, D. (2005) "Congress and Policymaking in an Age of Terrorism," in Dodd and Oppenheimer (eds.) *Congress Reconsidered*, Washington, D.C.: CQ Press.

Zakaria, F. (1999) *From Wealth to Power: The Unusual Origins of America's World Role*, Princeton, NJ: Princeton University Press.

Zeidenstein, H. (1981) "The Two Presidencies Thesis is Alive and Well and Has Been Living in the US Senate since 1973," *Presidential Studies Quarterly* 11: 511-525.

Wissenschaftlicher Buchverlag bietet

kostenfreie

Publikation

von

wissenschaftlichen Arbeiten

Diplomarbeiten, Magisterarbeiten, Master und Bachelor Theses
sowie Dissertationen, Habilitationen und wissenschaftliche Monographien

Sie verfügen über eine wissenschaftliche Abschlußarbeit zu aktuellen oder zeitlosen
Fragestellungen, die hohen inhaltlichen und formalen Ansprüchen genügt,
und haben **Interesse an einer honorarvergüteten Publikation**?

Dann senden Sie bitte erste Informationen über Ihre Arbeit per Email
an info@vdm-verlag.de. Unser Außenlektorat meldet sich umgehend bei Ihnen.

VDM Verlag Dr. Müller Aktiengesellschaft & Co. KG
Dudweiler Landstraße 125a
D - 66123 Saarbrücken

www.vdm-verlag.de

CPSIA information can be obtained at www.ICGtesting.com
Printed in the USA
LVOW081514090412

276825LV00010B/90/P